John Bowlby – From Psychoanalysis to Ethology

Frank van der Horst applies his background in both History and Psychology to unravel the origins of a major developmental theory. What is obvious now is how attachment theory continues to grow and provide a framework for both research and practice. Less obvious now is that John Bowlby's theory of the development of a child's tie to mother was revolutionary. This well-written volume focuses on those crucial years when Bowlby discovered Ethology. He wove its concepts into extensive clinical observations to provide an explanation for long-lasting effects of maternal care, including separation. This volume sets the development of Bowlby's thinking within the context of his whole life, to provide a coherent account of how a dedicated clinician came to develop an influential theory of human emotional development, from the cradle to the grave.

Dr. Joan Stevenson-Hinde,
Senior Research Fellow, Sub-Department of Animal Behaviour, Department of Zoology, University of Cambridge, UK

John Bowlby – From Psychoanalysis to Ethology

Unraveling the Roots of Attachment Theory

Frank C. P. van der Horst

WILEY-BLACKWELL
A John Wiley & Sons, Ltd., Publication

This edition first published 2011

Wiley-Blackwell is an imprint of John Wiley & Sons, formed by the merger of Wiley's global Scientific, Technical, and Medical business with Blackwell Publishing.

Registered Office
John Wiley & Sons Ltd, The Atrium, Southern Gate, Chichester, West Sussex, PO19 8SQ, UK

Editorial Offices
The Atrium, Southern Gate, Chichester, West Sussex, PO19 8SQ, UK
9600 Garsington Road, Oxford, OX4 2DQ, UK
350 Main Street, Malden, MA 02148-5020, USA

For details of our global editorial offices, for customer services, and for information about how to apply for permission to reuse the copyright material in this book please see our website at www.wiley.com/wiley-blackwell.

Library of Congress Cataloging-in-Publication Data

Van der Horst, Frank C.P.
John Bowlby : from psychoanalysis to ethology : unravelling the roots of attachment theory / Frank C.P. van der Horst.
p. cm.
Includes bibliographical references and index.
ISBN 978-0-470-68364-4 (cloth)
1. Bowlby, John. 2. Attachment behavior. 3. Attachment behavior in children. 4. Psychoanalysis. 5. Human behavior. I. Title.
BF575.A86V36 2011
155.4′18–dc22

2010046385

A catalogue record for this book is available from the British Library.

This book is published in the following electronic formats: ePDF 9781119993117; Wiley Online Library 9781119993100

Set in 11.5/13.5pt Minion by SPi Publisher Services, Pondicherry, India
Printed and bound in Singapore by Markono Print Media Pte Ltd

1 2011

To Francisca

Contents

About the Author

Frank C.P. van der Horst was born on August 5, 1977 in Delft, the Netherlands. He obtained a Master's in History and one in Education and Child Studies from Leiden University and was offered the chance to do research on a crossroads of both disciplines. Under the supervision of Professors Van der Veer and Van IJzendoorn – both notable experts in the field – he expanded on the historical and theoretical work at the Centre for Child and Family Studies at Leiden University and focused on the cross-fertilization of ethology and attachment theory, resulting in his Ph.D. thesis *John Bowlby and ethology: A study of cross-fertilization*. During this project, he discovered many hitherto unknown data in private and public archives and used oral histories to relate the historical development of John Bowlby's ideas.

Currently, Van der Horst works as a psychologist at De Waag Rotterdam, an outpatient clinic for forensic psychiatry, and as a researcher at the Centre for Child and Family Studies, Leiden University. His research aims at describing the history of ideas in the behavioral sciences, such as the ideas and work of John Bowlby, René Spitz, William Goldfarb, Jean Piaget, and Harry Harlow. His aim is also to further unravel the roots of attachment theory in, for example, the work of James Robertson and that of developmental psychologist Mary Ainsworth. These studies are necessary to complete our picture of the historical embeddedness of theoretical innovations in developmental psychology.

Foreword

by Professor Jerome Kagan

A question guaranteed to pique the interest of scientists and non-scientists asks, for each phenomenon, to what degree was this event constrained by its past and, therefore, potentially predictable? That is why millions of viewers will watch documentaries describing the origin of our universe or the evolution of life forms. The imprint of the past on the present assumes a special significance when we ask why some adults believe they are less happy than their friends. Economists and political scientists who gather questionnaire evidence from adults in varied societies report that extreme poverty and serious illness are a major cause of unhappiness. Philosophers, on the other hand, argue that a failure to honor one's ethical standards is the enemy of continued serenity or joy. A reasonable proportion of biologists and psychologists share the belief held by Alice James, the younger sister of William and Henry James, that a sanguine or melancholic mood is due, in part, to one's genes.

The strong claim that the experiences of early childhood make a major contribution to adult moods, and by inference quality of adaptation, is relatively recent in the history of ideas. This notion began to gain credence in Europe during the eighteenth century after the size of the middle class had grown and many mothers could stay at home rather than work in the field or at a loom. As a result, society needed to find a critical function for these women and influential commentators nominated a mother's love for her child as the elixir necessary for healthy psychological development. A large proportion of contemporary psychiatrists and psychologists are certain that the quality of the infant's emotional relationship with its primary caretaker, preferably the biological mother, affected the probability that the adult will or will not be vulnerable to frequent bouts of anxiety or depression.

John Bowlby tweaked consensual opinion when he replaced the infant's need for the sensory pleasures accompanying feeding, which Freud had nominated as formative, with the more psychological need for a feeling of security that a loving mother provides. Bowlby's childhood may have prepared him for this hypothesis. As the fourth child in an upper-middle-class, English family whose care was entrusted to nursemaids who tended the young Bowlby and his siblings in rooms on the top floor of the family's spacious home, Bowlby recalled seeing his mother for about an hour a day and his father once a week. In addition, his favorite nurse left the household when Bowlby was only four years old. Bowlby spent a long, productive career trying to prove that the quality of the interaction between the mother and infant constrained the child's future in a serious way.

Frank van der Horst's beautifully crafted, even-handed history of the 50-year interval between Bowlby's intuition that infants deprived of maternal love were at risk for an unhappy life and Mary Ainsworth's 1978 volume, *Patterns of Attachment*, provides readers with a trail of facts so rich in detail each can decide on the validity of Bowlby's bold idea.

The Bowlby narrative can be divided into four relatively discrete stages. The first centers around Bowlby's brief employment at one of the many progressive schools established in the 1920s as an educational application of Freud's ideas. Most of the children attending this school were emotionally disturbed and some had experienced early separation from parents or obvious neglect. Bowlby regarded these facts as supporting the writings of Ian Suttie, with whom Bowlby was familiar, arguing that a mother's love for the child was as vital for its psychological development as good nutrition was for its physical growth.

The second stage began in 1946 when Bowlby joined the staff of the Tavistock Clinic where he met James Robertson, a social worker, who shared Bowlby's distress over the policy of hospitals forbidding mothers from visiting their young children hospitalized for surgery because the staff wanted to prevent the mothers from bringing infections into the ward. Robertson's 1952 film, *A Two-Year-Old Goes to Hospital*, had an emotional impact on audiences far greater than either Bowlby or Robertson had anticipated. I showed this film for several years to large undergraduate classes at Harvard and always noted tears flowing down the faces of the stunned audiences when the film ended.

Van der Horst documents the significance of Bowlby's reading of the ethological research of Lorenz, Tinbergen, and Hinde and the fruitful collaboration with the American psychologist Harry Harlow. Harlow's experiments on rhesus monkeys, which implied that the opportunity to cling to something soft was more critical than food in establishing a bond to a surrogate object, and the ethological investigations allowed Bowlby to detect the relevance of the concept of a releaser and the reactions it evoked. He applied these ideas to the mother–infant relationship by arguing that the face, hair, and hands of the mother acted as releasers for the infant's grasping, clinging, smiling, and babbling which, through their implementation, established an attachment bond between infant and caretaker. Bowlby regarded the attachment process as analogous to the imprinting of newly hatched goslings which follow the first moving object they see.

Mary Ainsworth's research in Uganda and her invention of the Strange Situation at Johns Hopkins University represent the final stage in Van der Horst's reconstruction. Ainsworth joined Bowlby's staff at the Tavistock because her husband decided to work in London for a short period and she needed a job. Ainsworth had been mentored by William Blatz at the University of Toronto and the latter shared Bowlby's conviction that the infant's security was critical for healthy development. Hence, Ainsworth came to Bowlby prepared to share his fundamental premises. She began to develop her ideas systematically after spending 1954–55 in Uganda observing 28 Ganda infants. This experience led her to posit the three categories of secure attachment, insecure attachment, and non-attachment. Ainsworth acknowledged in the 1967 book *Infancy in Uganda* that the infant's temperament can influence the mother–child relationship and she wrote, "We must concede that there are genetically based individual differences between babies … It is quite impossible to differentiate genetic, prenatal, and perinatal influences from environmental influences" (p. 387).

Ainsworth described one infant she had classified as non-attached because the girl did not cry or attempt to follow the mother when she left the room, even though this child struck her as happy and comfortable. I suspect this girl belonged to the temperamental group my colleagues and I call low-reactive. Ainsworth also described a small group of infants classified as insecurely attached because they cried frequently – this is category she would later call type C, insecure-resistant. Ainsworth had noticed that these children were chronically fussy babies who cried not only when their mother left them, but also when they were held by the mother. Always a careful observer, Ainsworth informs readers that two of these infants were chronically malnourished. Crying because of hunger should not be equated with crying because of an insecure attachment. In a telling sentence toward the end of the book Ainsworth suggested, "Therefore, the warmth of the mother and her observed affectionate contact behavior do not explain the differences between groups" (p. 394), and she later adds, "There is no evidence that care by several people necessarily interferes with the development of healthy attachment" (p. 395).

However, Ainsworth and her three colleagues failed to mention the role of temperament when they summarized the results of the study of Baltimore infants in *Patterns of Attachment*. This investigation, based on extensive observations of a small group of infants at home over the course of the first year and their reactions in the Strange Situation at one year, was the origin of the currently popular attachment categories called type B, securely attached, and types A and C, insecurely attached.

The events of these four stages came together like a perfect storm in the Bowlby and Ainsworth volumes to raise the consciousness of Americans and Europeans to the possibly dangerous consequences of an infant's insecure attachment to its parents. Historians will praise Van der Horst for a critically neutral narrative, free of the author's prejudices, that allows each reader to judge the validity of the Bowlby–Ainsworth inferences.

Nonetheless, it is possible to discern beneath the surface of the seamless prose the possible effects of the historical context in which Bowlby formed his ideas. Wise commentators on human nature have been brooding on the causes of human unhappiness for a long time. Because assigning significance to a mother who failed to be sensitive to her infant's need for security did not emerge as an explanation until the twentieth century, it is appropriate to speculate that the unique pattern of conditions during the last century that made quality of attachment an attractive explanatory concept. The changes in the family during the twentieth century were discontinuous with the form that dominated Europe and North America during the prior two centuries. Young mothers began to enter the work force in large numbers after 1945 and needed surrogate care for their young children. This disruption in the usual form of infant care worried many citizens who automatically assumed that this novel arrangement probably had malevolent consequences. Richard Kearsley, Philip Zelazo, and I shared that belief in the late 1970s when we studied the effect of day care on Boston infants during their first 29 months.

It is also relevant that the first half of the last century was marked by two destructive wars, the horrors of the Holocaust, an undisguised challenge to the concept of God (a *Time* magazine cover during this period declared, "God is Dead"), increased geographic mobility, and erosion in the moral authority of traditional elites. It is reasonable to assume that this blizzard of events provoked bouts of uncertainty in many adults who naturally searched for an explanation of their cognitive dissonance. Because Americans and Europeans regard the results of scientific research as providing the most reliable access to correct explanations, and Western scientists typically look to distant origins to account for the present, it was easy to be persuaded by statements from respected scientists that the causes of the contemporary angst lay in the events of early childhood. I suspect, however, that this explanation had its roots in the insecurity of the adults who projected their mood on to the young child. Some nineteenth-century scholars were convinced that the origin of adult greed could be seen in the newborn's reflex grasping of a pencil placed in the palm. If middle-class adults from the majority ethnic and religious groups in their society, who suffered neither extreme poverty nor bigotry, believe that their current tensions and anxieties are due, in part, to their infant experiences, most will be able to retrieve enough evidence to construct an explanation that places some of the blame on their parents. Equally unhappy African-American and Hispanic-American adults who were raised in poverty in urban ghettoes usually blame their mood on their society not their mothers.

The evidence does indicate that serious neglect or abuse of infants can have undesirable effects on their future psychological development. No one quarrels with that opinion. But the vast majority of infants escape these real threats to psychological growth. It is less obvious that the normal variation in maternal sensitivity to infants has the power to constrain the future indefinitely, unless adults, reflecting on their childhoods, decide that they should have had more loving care than they believe they received. Millions of Chinese infants born during Mao Zedong's reign rarely saw their parents and spent most of their days in day care centers with many infants and few caretakers. But I know of no evidence suggesting that the 50- to 70-year-olds currently living in the People's Republic of China, who spent their early years in these centers, are significantly more anxious, depressed, addicted, or incarcerated than the generations born 30 years earlier or later. Indeed, today's headlines imply that feelings of insecurity may be more salient today in a capitalist China with a one child policy and fewer day care centers than in the China of the 1960s.

This foreword is not the place to review the extensive evidence bearing on the validity of Bowlby's hypothesis and the child's behavior in the Strange Situation. However, it is fair to suggest that the available evidence neither proves nor refutes Bowlby's creative synthesis with certainty. The existing data are simply inadequate for a consensus on these questions and, therefore, impossible to decide whether we should reject or accept these ideas. But no matter what future research reveals, scientists, parents, and other citizens will profit from Van der Horst's coherent, gracefully written, even-handed, and richly detailed description of how these important ideas rose to a position of prominence.

Acknowledgments

The present book is the fruit of my work at the Centre for Child and Family Studies, Leiden University, the Netherlands, between 2004 and 2010. During these years, I was guided by Professor René van der Veer, whom I consider my scientific mentor. His warm-hearted, enthusiastic, and humane support was of immeasurable importance to the outcome of my scientific work. I am grateful to him for keeping up with my ignorance.

The many discussions with René – back and forth from our offices to the coffee machine – have contributed much to the result that lies in front of you. On the basis of a rough estimation of the distance we covered, I calculated that during these discussions, we walked from Leiden to Paris, and back. During this trip to the City of Light we consumed several thousands cups of coffee. I am very thankful that we were spared from both blisters and ulcers.

Over the years, many people have contributed to my research on the roots of attachment theory. I am particularly indebted to Inge Bretherton for reading and extensively commenting on earlier drafts of this book. Her knowledgeability with respect to the history of attachment theory is unprecedented. Several people were willing to be interviewed on the cross-fertilization of attachment theory and ethology: Inge Bretherton, Robert Hinde, Joan Stevenson-Hinde, Helen LeRoy, Howard Steele, Stephen Suomi, and Everett Waters. I thank Marinus van IJzendoorn for his suggestions and comments to several chapters in this book. René van der Veer was of immense help and corrected many errors and inconsistencies in the text. For those flaws that remain, I am fully and solely responsible.

For permission to use photographs in this book, I thank Mary Gatling, Helen LeRoy, Hillary Wakefield, and Mirrorpix. Parts of this book have been published in journal articles in the past few years. I am grateful for the publishers of these journals (American Psychological Association, John Wiley & Sons Ltd., Routledge, and Springer) for their permission to use parts of the articles in this book. As the saying goes 'the whole is greater than the sum of its parts': by compiling the insights from these different papers, a better and richer picture of Bowlby's move from psychoanalysis to ethology will be painted.

Frank van der Horst
Leiden, April 2010

Introduction

In the late 1950s and early 1960s, British child psychiatrist John Bowlby in a series of six papers (Bowlby, 1958d, 1960a, 1960b, 1961a, 1961b, 1963a), basically formulated what is now known as "attachment theory." He later elaborated his ideas in his trilogy *Attachment and Loss* (Bowlby, 1969/1982b, 1973, 1980a). Attachment theory, in which Bowlby tried to explain how and why children form bonds with their parents and caregivers, has been influential ever since its initial formulation.

Bowlby's theorizing on the mother–child relationship was the ultimate result of his interest in issues of separation. In her description of Bowlby's early life, Van Dijken (1998) has shown that the roots of this interest lie in his own early childhood, in experiences while working as a volunteer in several progressive schools, and in clinical observations when he was training as a psychoanalyst shortly before World War II. Bowlby was shaped by the psychoanalytic training he received from his supervisors Joan Riviere and Melanie Klein, but he differed with them about the influence of internal and external factors on child development and clinical problems. Bowlby's focus was more on observation of real-life events and

John Bowlby – From Psychoanalysis to Ethology: Unraveling the Roots of Attachment Theory, First Edition. Frank C. P. van der Horst.

experimentation, while Klein emphasized "research limited to analytic sessions" (Bowlby, 1940a, p. 154) and unconscious fantasies as the origin of psychopathology. As a result of this theoretical disagreement, Bowlby's position within the British Psycho-Analytical Society was at a certain point in time rather precarious (Van der Horst, Van der Veer and Van IJzendoorn, 2007; Van Dijken *et al.*, 1998). But by ignoring what he considered to be the limited views of some of his psychoanalytic colleagues and taking an eclectic approach instead, Bowlby arrived at new and revolutionary insights. In Van Dijken's study (1998), she concluded that "by combining and synthesizing the various viewpoints he accepted, Bowlby gradually developed his own view," a view that "was enriched by ethological insights and by Ainsworth's contribution" (p. 161).

In this study, I will build on Van Dijken's findings and describe both the "ethological insights" that enriched Bowlby's view on the mother–child relationship, i.e., how Bowlby turned from psychoanalysis to ethology as a frame of reference, and Mary Ainsworth's contribution to attachment theory. The focus of this book, therefore, is the historical development of attachment theory between 1951 and 1969. The year 1951 marks the publication of Bowlby's (1951, 1952) WHO report on *Maternal Care and Mental Health*, a study which was of immense importance to Bowlby's thinking. Also, 1951 is the year Bowlby got acquainted with ethology, which I will argue is an Archimedean point in the history of attachment theory. Finally, 1951 is the year Ainsworth applied for a job at the Tavistock Clinic. In 1969, of course, the first part of Bowlby's trilogy was published. If we consider the pre-1951 period as the psychoanalytic phase of John Bowlby's career, then the period between 1951 and 1969 can perhaps best be defined as the "ethological era of attachment theory."

Although the historiography on Bowlby's ideas has grown rapidly in the last two decades – alongside the ever-growing interest in the clinical applications of attachment theory – so far this episode in the history of attachment theory has received little attention. In the available historical accounts, Bowlby's life and work have been described from different angles. For example, Bretherton (1991, 1992) mentions some of the highpoints of the ethological period, but her article is an account of Bowlby's and Ainsworth's joint contributions to attachment theory, with emphasis on its roots and growing points. Newcombe and Lerner (1982) paid attention to the historical and societal context in which Bowlby developed his ideas. Mayhew (2006) described Bowlby's political activities in relation to his theoretical ideas. Holmes (1993) contributed to the historiography of attachment theory by describing the implications of Bowlby's ideas for clinical practice, while Karen (1994) added new biographical information. Van Dijken (1998) has traced the core of attachment theory to Bowlby's early childhood and advanced the thesis that early separation experiences influenced his further development and thinking. However, until now, no systematic and detailed analysis of Bowlby's (and Ainsworth's) use of the new science of ethology has been made.

Because this crucial period cannot be dealt with as an isolated story, I will start with a comprehensive description of Bowlby's early life and career (see Chapter 1). I will try to show that Bowlby's intellectual development and his turning toward ethological methods were not coincidental. His focus on separation as a subject of research, his valuing of children's real-life experiences for further personality development, his emphasis on observation, and his interest in nature and the emerging science of ethology, were certainly part of a historical development, as will become clear from his biography.

In Chapter 2, I will discuss the different issues of separation of young children that Bowlby encountered during the late 1930s, the 1940s, and the early 1950s. These issues include separation due to wartime evacuations, observations made in residential nurseries, the debate concerning visiting of children in hospital, results of clinical studies, and studies on the so-called "hospitalization" effect. The results of these studies and observations were the core of Bowlby's WHO publication and convinced him of the importance of early-life experiences for child development.

This description of the issues of separations and the observations reported in the WHO report is followed by an account of the post-World War II years at the Tavistock Clinic and Bowlby's cooperation with James Robertson. It will become clear that Robertson's work was highly influential for Bowlby's thinking on attachment. Robertson's observations of young children in hospital – the so-called sanatorium study – confirmed the early retrospective work that Bowlby had summarized in his WHO report.

In Chapter 4, I will focus on the cross-fertilization of Bowlby's ideas and those of various leading European scientists in the field of ethology. From the 1950s, Bowlby was in close personal and scientific contact with the likes of Niko Tinbergen, Konrad Lorenz, and Robert

Hinde and he used their new viewpoints and theoretical framework to explain his earlier observations and to develop his new theory on attachment. These ethologists in their turn were influenced and inspired by Bowlby's thinking. Attention will be paid to Bowlby's influence on ethological studies in general and on Hinde's work more specifically.

Subsequently, I will show how Bowlby made the move from theoretical and observational claims to experimental evidence through his interactions with American animal psychologist Harry Harlow, with whom he was in contact from 1957 through the mid-1970s. Bowlby profited highly from Harlow's experimental work on the effects of separation in infant rhesus monkeys. Here again, an attempt is made to delineate the cross-fertilizing aspect of the interaction by showing that Harlow in his turn was influenced and inspired by Bowlby as well.

Chapter 6 deals with the contributions of Mary Ainsworth to Bowlby's theory, as I consider her a co-founder of the attachment paradigm. I will relate Ainsworth's development as an experimental researcher by describing her work in Uganda and in Baltimore. I will trace the origin of the concept of a secure base, a notion Bowlby later incorporated into attachment theory, to the work of Ainsworth's mentor William Blatz. Also, I will describe the early development of the Strange Situation Procedure and the crucial role of maternal sensitivity for the development of attachment.

Finally, I will integrate and discuss the evidence presented in this book. How did Bowlby make his move from psychoanalysis to ethology during the most eventful years of his career in the 1950s and 1960s? What influences on his thinking and ideas can be exposed? How can the impact of people like Robertson, Ainsworth, Hinde, Harlow, and others best be described? What is the result of the interaction with ethology in Bowlby's *Attachment and Loss*? And what about Bowlby's scientific descent: was it Freudian or Darwinian?

1
Biographical Notes and Early Career

Childhood, Upbringing, and Schooling

Edward John Mostyn Bowlby was born in a Victorian upper-middle-class family in London in 1907. He was the fourth of six children to May Bridget Mostyn and Anthony Alfred Bowlby. His parents belonged neither to the old land-owning class nor to the new rising class of merchants and entrepreneurs, but to the top group of higher professionals (Van Dijken, 1998). John's father Anthony was a high-ranked officer in the British army. He was appointed surgeon to the household of King Edward VII and later surgeon-in-ordinary to King George V. He was knighted in 1923 and the Bowlby baronetcy is in existence to this day.[1] Father Bowlby had a successful career and is typified as a "strong personality who stuck to his ideas when he believed they were right" (Van Dijken, 1998, p. 18). As a father, though, Anthony Bowlby was not much available to his children – owing partly to his work as a military surgeon in wartime. This pattern was repeated by his son John. Also, as we shall see, John Bowlby would in his professional career stick to his ideas. He would almost stubbornly look for evidence to support

John Bowlby – From Psychoanalysis to Ethology: Unraveling the Roots of Attachment Theory, First Edition. Frank C. P. van der Horst.

them and for ways of convincing other people, just because "he knew he was right" (Van der Horst, Van de Veer, and Van IJzendoorn, 2007, p. 324). Also, just like his father, John was not much involved in the day-to-day matters of the Bowlby family (see later in the chapter).

Less is known about John's mother May Mostyn, who was from a comfortable – though not wealthy – family. She had no formal education, but was taught by her parents. She seems to have had a very good relationship with her father, but a rather ambivalent one with her mother (Van Dijken, 1998). It is difficult to say in what way this influenced her as a parent, but as a mother she is sometimes typified as "remote and self-centered" (Holmes, 1993, p. 36) and "cold" (Parkes, 1995, p. 248). What we do know is that she passed on to the children her unequivocal passion for nature. During stays in the English countryside and during long summer holidays in Scotland, where John's maternal grandparents lived, John's mother "tried to pass on her love for nature to her children" (Van Dijken, 1998, p. 24) and the children learned "to identify flowers, birds and butterflies, to fish, ride and shoot" (Holmes, 1993, p. 17). This is of interest, as this 'inherited' passion for nature probably made John more receptive to ethological ideas later on in life (see Chapter 4).

The six Bowlby children were often grouped into couples by their parents: John's older sisters Winnie and Marion – 'the girls' – his 13-months-older brother Tony and John – 'the boys' (see Figure 1.1), and 'the babies' Jim and Evelyn. John had a very close relationship with his only-slightly-older brother Tony, but they were rivals too: John did not accept his brother's seniority and Tony would "fight like a little tiger" (Van Dijken, 1998, p. 19) whenever he was challenged. So apart from close friendship, there was some rivalry and jealousy between the brothers (Holmes, 1993).

Typical of their social class, the Bowlby children were raised in a distant, reserved manner. The children spent most of the day in the nursery on the top floor of the Bowlby residence, isolated from the rest of the house and from their parents. A nanny and several nursemaids took over the care and most of the education of the children from father and mother Bowlby, and the children saw their parents only occasionally – their mother for an hour a day, and their father typically only on Sundays. Nanny Friend was in charge of the Bowlby children, but in practice John's favorite nursemaid Minnie took care of him on a daily basis. So when Minnie left when John was four years old, he was conceivably hurt by the event. When Bowlby (1958a) later stated that "for a child to be looked after entirely by a loving nanny

Figure 1.1 From left to right: John and Tony (the 'boys'), May Mostyn, and Anthony Bowlby. Courtesy of the Wellcome Library, London (AMWL: PP/BOW/L.29).

and then for her to leave when he is two or three, or even four or five, can be almost as tragic as the loss of a mother" (p. 7), could he possibly have had in mind his own separation from Minnie?

The education of the children began at home where a governess instructed them from age six onward. Subsequently, 'the boys' attended day school in London, but the outbreak of the Great War changed all that. As a consequence of the air raids on London in 1917, John underwent another separation experience (Hunter, 1991). In 1918, at age 11, he was sent to preparatory boarding school together with Tony (see Figure 1.2). He did not have good memories of his time at Lindisfarne, as the school was called, and later stated that "he would not send a dog to boarding school at that age" (Van Dijken, 1998, p. 34). After leaving Lindisfarne, in 1921, Bowlby started training as a naval cadet at the Royal Naval College in Dartmouth. Interestingly, it was here that he was first introduced to the writings of Freud (Newcombe and Lerner, 1982). What influence reading Freud had on him at that point is unclear, but soon Bowlby decided that he wanted to pursue a career that "would improve the community as a whole" (Van Dijken, 1998, p. 46). In order to legally leave the Royal Naval College, John's father had to buy him out first (he was not free to leave, having committed himself to a military career).

Figure 1.2 School picture of John Bowlby (2nd row, 5th from right) and Tony Bowlby (2nd from top, 4th from left). Courtesy of the Wellcome Library, London (AMWL: PP/BOW/L.29).

Encouraged by father Anthony to follow in his footsteps, John decided to "go up to university" (Van Dijken, 1998, p. 38), and he started his pre-medical studies, a so-called Natural Sciences Tripos, in Cambridge in 1925.

Although in public Bowlby referred to his childhood as perfectly conventional (Hunter, 1991; see also Karen, 1994), in private he stated that it had a great effect on him and that he had been "sufficiently hurt but not sufficiently damaged" (Van Dijken, 1998, p. 11). These early experiences in Bowlby's personal life arguably influenced his subsequent thinking and research. The distant, upper-middle class upbringing by his parents, the frequent absence of his father, the departure of his favorite nanny, and the attendance at a boarding school, taught him that young children can be hurt by separation experiences.

Studying Medicine at Cambridge

Bowlby began studying medicine at Trinity College in Cambridge in 1925, but more and more he became "interested in psychology, especially what would now be called developmental psychology" (Senn,

1977a, p. 1). It eventually, after two years, led him "to read psychology and to give up medicine" (Senn, 1977a, p. 1). Bowlby was exposed to the more experimental Cambridge variant of psychology (see Smuts, 1977b) which emphasized careful observation and experimentation in real-life settings (Van Dijken, 1998). Of course, Bowlby was to make this approach to the study of human behavior his own in later years, although, as we shall see, he had to climb a mountain to gainsay the ideas of Melanie Klein and others in the psychoanalytic world.

Since we know that Bowlby later on would turn to psychoanalytic thinking and since attachment theory is rooted in Freudian theory, it is of interest to look at possible psychoanalytic influences at university. These seem to have been scarce, at least they were not evident in the official curriculum, and in later years Bowlby would claim that he had not been completely satisfied with his psychological training at Cambridge. In his opinion there was too much fuss "about IQ and animals in cages" (Van Dijken, 1998, p. 43). However, at Cambridge, Bowlby's tutor in the natural sciences was Lord Edgar D. Adrian, the expert in the field of nerve conduction (Boring, 1950), who displayed a vivid interest in Freudian theory from its very beginning. In a paper published in the *International Journal of Psycho-Analysis*, Adrian (1946) would claim that psychoanalysis "went far beyond a single range of facts: it showed or tried to show quite unexpected relations between different fields" (p. 1). This leaves open the possibility that Bowlby discussed matters of Freudian theory with his tutor. What we know for sure (Van Dijken *et al.*, 1998) is that two years later, in 1927, Bowlby purchased W. H. R. Rivers' *Instinct and the Unconscious* (1920), a book that was widely used in medical circles and that contained a moderate (or watered-down, according to some) version of psychoanalysis, i.e., psychoanalytic considerations which de-emphasized the dynamic role of the sexual instinct. Shortly thereafter, in 1928, Bowlby bought and read Freud's *Introductory Lectures on Psycho-analysis* (1917), a book which he would later rank among the 11 most important books he ever read.[2] Bowlby's interest in Freudian theory would be further stimulated when he volunteered at two progressive schools – schools that were heavily influenced by Freud's ideas. It was at these schools that Freud's work "came alive" for Bowlby and it would remain "a major influence on all his later work" (AMWL: PP/BOW/A.1/7; dated October 24, 1979).[3]

Bowlby and Progressive Schooling

Freud's psychoanalytic ideas slowly began to infiltrate the British educational system in the 1920s. Various books on how teaching could benefit from psychoanalytic insights were published around this time (e.g., Green, 1921; MacMunn, 1921; Miller, 1927; Revel, 1928) and different psychoanalytically oriented 'progressive' schools were founded in Britain, following the international examples (e.g., Bernfeld's *Kinderheim Baumgarten* in Vienna and Vera Schmidt's *International Solidarity* in Moscow; see Van der Veer and Valsiner, 1991). Among them were Malting House School, founded by Susan Isaacs, and Summerhill, founded by A.S. Neill (Van Dijken, 1998). Experts in the field of education claimed that even teachers at ordinary schools could benefit from an acquaintance with psychoanalytic theory as the teacher would be "in a better position to study his pupils with advantage than was his forerunner of the pre-psycho-analytical times" (Adams, 1924, p. 269).

It was at two of such 'progressive' schools, in the second half of 1928 and the first half of 1929, that Bowlby spent a year as a teacher. Both schools – called Bedales and Priory Gate – espoused a philosophy which combined a belief in G. Stanley Hall's recapitulation theory (i.e., the children were believed to go through the stages that mankind had gone through) with 'progressive' ideas about the need for children's 'free expression' and strict reservations about adult intervention. In the second school, called Priory Gate School, these ideas were mixed with clearly psychoanalytic ones (Van Dijken *et al.*, 1998). Here, it was head master Theodore Faithfull who was responsible for the grafting of Freud's insights onto those of Hall (Van Dijken, 1998). Faithfull also found inspiration in the Order of Woodcraft Chivalry – an anti-industrialistic, Scouting-like movement in England that propagated a frugal life and an emphasis on nature and craftsmanship (Van Dijken, 1998). Another source of inspiration was Homer Lane, an American psychotherapist who was among the first to use psychoanalytical ideas in the education of children. Lane (1928) claimed that deprivation of love in childhood is the source of later delinquency and mental disturbance, a claim that Bowlby would make his own.[4] The psychological problems of the children at Priory

Gate School – it was a school for 'difficult children' – were as a rule attributed to adverse experiences in the children's families, notably to inadequate parent–child relationships.

The period spent at these two progressive schools made an unforgettable impression on Bowlby, as did his acquaintance with staff member John Alford (Holmes, 1993; Senn, 1977a; Smuts, 1977b; Van Dijken, 1998). Bowlby would later say about this experience:

> I spent twelve months in ... [two] of the progressive and free schools [i.e. Bedales and Priory Gate School], which was very valuable experience, because I saw a number of disturbed children at first hand, I lived with them, indeed I had to look after them, and I met there the first 'affectionless character' of my career. (Tanner and Inhelder, 1971, p. 26)

So, not only did Bowlby have the opportunity to witness the behavior of these "difficult" children on a daily basis, he was also presented with an explanatory model for their problems: they were pilfering, lying, and so on, *because* they had grown up in a family that did not provide the security and love that normal parents supposedly do (see Lane, 1928). The cause of mental disturbances and deviant behavior at large is deprivation of love in childhood. More than 50 years later, Bowlby (1981a) remembered that "apart from a medical background and an interest in psychology, my choice of career had been determined by what I had seen and heard during the six months that I had spent in a school for disturbed children [i.e. Priory Gate School]" (p. 2).

It is clear that Bowlby was now definitely won for the psychoanalytic viewpoint. Psychoanalysis seemed to provide a satisfactory model in which adult mental problems are explained by reference to adverse emotional experiences in childhood. In 1929 – at the age of only 22 – Bowlby, at the suggestion of Alford, began his psychoanalytical training at the Institute of Psycho-Analysis, the training center of the British Psycho-Analytical Society – and not with the Tavistock group, it being "a bit amateur" (Smuts, 1977b, p. 3; see also Hunter, 1991). His training analyst was Joan Riviere, a friend and follower of Melanie Klein, who by that time had already gained a prominent position in the British Psycho-Analytical Society.

Different Schools of Psychoanalysis in Interbellum Britain[5]

Now that Bowlby had decided to engross himself in psychoanalytic theory, he became more and more familiar with the different schools within British psychoanalysis. At the turn of the previous century, Freud had postulated revolutionary ideas about human mental life. Ever since the formulation of his theory debates about its value and applicability in clinical practice have been commonplace. In this respect, it is of interest to pay some more attention to the reception of Freudian theory by both scientists and laymen in British society of the time. As we have seen above, Freud's ideas were applied to teaching in British schools, but there are other striking examples.

For instance, the authors of baby manuals (e.g., Bennett and Isaacs, 1931; Brereton, 1927; Hartley, 1923; Isaacs, 1929; Thom, 1927), i.e., books that advised parents how to take care of infants and young children, now began to picture the infant and young child as little savages who were torn apart by violent emotions, who showed marked preference for the parent of the opposite sex, and might be strongly jealous of their (newly-born) brothers and sisters. The sinister chapter headings of Thom's (1927) manual, for example – e.g., Anger, Fear, Jealousy, Destructiveness, Inferiority, Delinquency, Sex – spelled misery for the unprepared parent. Thom's (1927) statement that "children who have vivid sex phantasies often find a certain relief in the excitement associated with stealing" (p. 243) was typical for that period during which common sense notions about education became mixed with the "scientific" ideas of Freud, Adler, and Jung (Beekman, 1977; Hardyment, 1995).

Meanwhile, the British public press was paying increasing attention to psychoanalytic ideas (Rapp, 1988). In the period from 1920 to 1925, the number of publications in newspapers and journals grew considerably. According to the *New Statesman*, it was "as difficult for an educated person to neglect the theories of Freud and his rivals as it would have been for his father to ignore the equally disconcerting discoveries of Darwin" (Hynes, 1990, p. 366). The chances were quite high, then, that 'educated persons' were at least partially acquainted with – although not necessarily receptive to – psychoanalytic or semi-psychoanalytic ideas.

As for the reception of Freud's work in scientific circles, there are many ways to subdivide psychoanalysts of that time – and probably none of them does justice to reality. One possible division into groups is to make a distinction between Kleinian and Freudian psychoanalysts in the British Psycho-Analytical Society. Whereas Melanie Klein and her followers emphasized Sigmund Freud's clinical practice and paid much attention to the child's hostile fantasy life – based on Freud's (1905) *Beyond the Pleasure Principle* – Anna Freud and her followers focused on his theoretical ideas on child development and emphasized ego functioning, referring to Freud's (1923) *The Ego and the Id* (see Donaldson, 1996). But there is more. Bowlby, Donald Winnicott, Ronald Fairbairn, Michael Balint, and others were neither Kleinians nor Freudians and were reckoned to be members of the Independents or the so-called Middle Group (see Van Dijken, 1998, pp. 121–127) and adhered to an object relations version of psychoanalysis (see later in the chapter). Despite his independent ideas, Bowlby was respected in the British Psycho-Analytical Society and played a conciliatory role in the conflict between followers of Anna Freud and Melanie Klein. At that time, he was Training Secretary of the society and credited with keeping the Freudian and Kleinian factions from splitting up by instituting two separate, concurrent training programs (Van Dijken, 1998).

Another way of depicting different schools of psychoanalysis is to distinguish between the so-called "eclectic" psychiatrists (mainly at the Tavistock Clinic), on the one hand, and "orthodox Freudian" psychiatrists, on the other (see Newcombe and Lerner, 1982). The "eclectics" used Freudian concepts such as unconscious motivation and repression – albeit sometimes in modified forms – but rejected the search for infantile sexual trauma. This "eclectic" movement ultimately evolved into a school centered around the Tavistock Clinic (with Ian Suttie as the central figure; see Gerson, 2009; see later in this chapter).

The eclectic and orthodox Freudian opponents essentially differed in opinion on one major point: the role of infantile sexual trauma in personality development as put forward by Freud (1905) in his *Three Essays on the Theory of Sexuality*. During World War I, this debate was fueled by descriptions of the many cases of "shell shock" – soldiers who had developed neurotic disorders in combat. At first, medical doctors thought these symptoms to be of a purely physical nature, others dispatched them as mere evidence of cowardice. But during the war medical opinion gradually changed: increasingly, experts became convinced of the psychological origin of war neuroses. Unfortunately, prevailing theories of development could not explain the etiology of war neurosis. For example, it seemed impossible to retrace these traumata to unresolved sexual conflicts in childhood or infancy, as Freud had suggested. To come to terms with this felt lacuna in Freud's theory, both the eclectic and orthodox schools of psychoanalysis therefore had to come up with new explanations.

As a result of the discussion on "shell shock," Freud revised parts of his theory in his monograph *Beyond the Pleasure Principle* (Freud, 1920; see also Lomax, Kagan, and Rosenkrantz, 1978). He used concepts such as "repetition compulsion," the "death instinct" (*Thanatos*), and "life instinct" (*Eros*) in a complicated attempt to explain the symptoms of "shell shock." Not everybody was convinced of the clinical relevance of this hypothetical construction, though. Melanie Klein, Bowlby's later supervisor in psychoanalytic training, developed the position that adult mourning (one of the factors supposedly causing "shell shock") is conditioned by the way infants and young children manage separation experiences (e.g., in weaning). These issues and the ones mentioned above led to differences between Melanie Klein and Anna Freud shortly before World War II – when Anna Freud arrived in London from Austria in 1938. However, despite the fact that Klein was very much influence by the Budapest or Hungarian school of Sándor Ferenczi (who placed emphasis on object relations as opposed to drives), both Klein and Anna Freud can be considered as orthodox Freudians in their own ways (Donaldson, 1996; Van Dijken, 1998). At least "opposition to [Bowlby's] views provided one small area of common ground for the followers of Anna Freud and Melanie Klein, and for the next decades Bowlby was a relatively isolated figure in psychoanalysis" (Fonagy, 2001, p. 1). In all, the orthodox Freudian reaction to the issue differed from that of the eclectic school, to which I will now turn.

In the 1930s, the eclectic movement formed into a school centered around the Tavistock Clinic. But the clinic was initially founded in 1920 by doctors – led by Hugh Crichton-Miller – who had been concerned with neurosis during World War I (Trist and Murray, 1990). One example of the eclectic approach was that of the before mentioned W. H. R. Rivers, who was one of the first to explain how soldiers who had been in psychologically grievous war experiences could become ill by repression or "the active or voluntary process by which it is attempted to remove some part of the mental content out of the field of attention with the aim of making it inaccessible to memory" (Rivers, 1918, p. 173). His therapy consisted in encouraging the soldiers to remember their war experiences and to reinterpret them. Rivers further posited that there is an instinct for self-preservation side by side with the sexual instinct (Rivers, 1920). This led Bernard Hart, another "eclectic," to explain what was later to be called "shell shock" as an unconscious conflict in which the instinct for self-preservation clashed with the conscious sense of duty to be a brave soldier (Southborough, 1922, p. 77; see also Hart, 1910, 1912).[6]

Another characterization of the eclectic approach is by Harry Edelston, who stated that "without necessarily accepting the *whole* doctrine of Freud (or Jung or Adler), it is possible to take advantage of the psychological techniques introduced and elaborated by these and other pioneers which have created a revolution in extramural psychiatry and allied fields" (Edelston, 1960, p. 744; original italics). He added that "there are many like myself who, having been trained at the old (pre-war) Tavistock Clinic, practice an eclectic brand of analytic psycho-therapy. One should almost call it the 'English school', based as it is on the teaching of Hadfield and Suttie, etc." (Edelston, 1960, p. 744). I will now turn to the ideas of Ian Suttie, who is regarded by Edelston as a central figure of the "English school."

Suttie was the most prolific in finding eclectic alternatives for orthodox Freudian theory (Newcombe and Lerner, 1982). Although the two men never met (Bowlby in Suttie, 1935/1988, p. xxiii), Suttie and Bowlby developed ideas that were quite similar in a number of respects. First of all, they – together with Melanie Klein, Ronald Fairbairn, and Donald Winnicott for that matter – can be seen as adherents to the object relations version of psychoanalysis (Greenberg and Mitchell, 1983). This current in psychoanalysis emphasized the development of the self in relation to real people. In the Foreword to Suttie's *The Origins of Love and Hate,* Bowlby stated that:

> [w]ith the notable exception of Melanie Klein, all those named [i.e., Bowlby, Fairbairn, Klein, Suttie, and Winnicott] have held explicitly that most differences in individual development that are of consequence to mental health are to be traced either to differences in the way children are treated by their parents or else to separations from or losses of parent-figures to whom the children had become attached. (Bowlby in Suttie, 1935/1988, p. xvi)

According to object relations theory, not all motivation is sexual, real-life interpersonal relationships have an independent and autonomous status, and experiences of children mattered for their subsequent development. In the early 1930s, Suttie (1935/1988) regarded as a major shortcoming of classical Freudian theory "the Freudians' obstinate determination to leave out of account social situations" (pp. 39–40). Historically, Suttie's position owed much to the Hungarian school of Ferenczi, Imre Hermann, and Michael and Alice Balint. Ferenczi's (1931) statement that real-life experiences matter was clearly in accordance with Suttie's views. Through Suttie, but also independently, Bowlby was familiar with the ideas of Ferenczi and his colleagues as well (Bacciagaluppi, 1994; Bowlby, 1958d).

This eclectic line of thought concerning the value of real-life experiences evolved in the Middle Group of the British Psycho-Analytical Society and in object relations theory. Many independent thinkers were considered members of either or even both groups. As shown by Edelston, Suttie and other psychoanalytically oriented psychiatrists at the Tavistock Clinic were often referred to as the so-called "English school" of British psychiatry. This school emphasized the importance of a primitive need for security and thought "that a child begins life completely helpless and dependent, and that it responds with every expression of terror to … loss of mother" (Dicks, 1939, p. 20) and therefore has "a tendency to seek love and security as such" (Dicks, 1939, p. 90). For example, Fairbairn (1941) – a member of the Middle Group of the British Psycho-Analytical Society and an object relations theorist – advanced that the libido is object-seeking (i.e., directed toward a person) not pleasure-seeking. According to Edelston (1943), "even the strict psycho-analytical school" had at that time "been compelled … to recognize the importance of this earliest of human needs" (p. 74). Bowlby certainly picked up the idea of a primary need for mother in this context (Newcombe and Lerner, 1982).

In his work on *The Origins of Love and Hate,* Suttie (1935/1988) wondered whether the "attachment-to-mother is merely the sum of the infantile bodily needs and satisfactions which refer to her [i.e. a secondary drive], or whether the *need for a mother is primarily presented to the child mind as a need for company and as a discomfort in isolation*" (p. 16; original italics). He explicitly stated that "love of mother is primal in so far as it is the *first formed and directed* emotional relationship" (p. 31; original italics). These statements about the primary need for the mother were, of course, all very much similar to Bowlby's ideas – although for

Bowlby it was the need for protection, not the need for company that was focal. Also in line with Bowlby's later theorizing on attachment, Suttie related that in the "ideal state anxiety is at a minimum and resentments are only transient. There is no abiding sense of insecurity or of grievance." Unfortunately, "the exigencies of life itself... interrupt [the] happy symbiotic relationship" between mother and child, which leads "the infant [to] feel insecure." Now that "the 'separation anxiety' is in full force ... all effort is devoted to ... remove the *cause* of the anxiety and hate by restoring harmonious social relationships" (pp. 39–40; original italics). Of course, it is impossible to exactly equate Suttie's and Bowlby's ideas, but the above statements make clear that they both emphasized the relationship to the mother.

Remarkably, Suttie (1935/1988) also highlighted the survival value of the interaction with the caregiver when he introduced "the innate need-for-companionship which is the infant's only way of self-preservation" (p. 6). Suttie went on by stating that "instead of an armament of instincts – latent or otherwise – the child is born with a simple attachment-to-mother who is the sole source of food and protection" (p. 15). Of course, the evolutionary view of the mother–infant relationship was to become Bowlby's favorite topic in later years when he made an attempt to rewrite psychoanalysis in the light of ethological principles (see Van der Horst, 2008; see also Chapter 4). Thus, we can see that Suttie's terminology and conceptual framework was similar to Bowlby's (e.g., attachment-to-mother, insecurity, separation anxiety, innate need-for-companionship) and that Bowlby was neither the first nor the only one to emphasize the potential importance of such real-life events as mother–child separations for child development. It is important to note, however, that Bowlby did not claim that he was the first to think of the importance of the quality of early mother–infant relationships. In "The nature of the child's tie to his mother," for example, Bowlby (1958d) made a very careful review of which other psychoanalysists held views that were acceptable to him.

Medical and Psychoanalytic Training

Although Bowlby turned to psychoanalysis and entered a training analysis, he – again at the advice of Alford – also started his normal medical career (Bretherton, 1991). He worked as a clinical assistant at the Maudsley Hospital under Aubrey Lewis, a critic of the psychoanalytic movement. After obtaining his M.D. degree in 1933, and encouraged by his close friend Evan Durbin, Bowlby registered as a Ph.D. student at University College London under the formal supervision of Sir Cyril Burt. This experience as a doctoral student was something Bowlby never talked about in interviews. Maybe this was because he never finished his project "Examination of guilt and anxiety on the basis of case-studies" (see Van Dijken, 1998, p. 73); but more likely he wished not to be associated with Burt, who was later accused of gross scientific fraud. In practice, his supervisor was Susan Isaacs, the psychoanalytic psychologist and writer of baby manuals mentioned above.

Although Bowlby never finished his Ph.D., his formal involvement with Burt is still of interest. By that time Burt was investigating the psychological causes of delinquency (e.g., Burt, 1925). He professed as his belief that "nearly every tragedy of crime is in its origin a drama of domestic life," (as cited in Wooldridge, 1994, p. 99) argued that it is frequently parents rather than children who require treatment, and warned that removing children from their home should only be undertaken as a last resort (Hearnshaw, 1979; Wooldridge, 1994). By the end of the 1930s and in the 1940s Bowlby would express the same views. Moreover, Burt had been one of the founding members of the London Psycho-Analytical Society and became a member of the British Psycho-Analytical Society. He also was a member of the Council of the Tavistock Clinic and thus might be reckoned to be a member of the "eclectic" group mentioned above.

From 1934 to 1938 Bowlby worked part-time at the Institute for the Scientific Treatment of Delinquency (ISTD). Staff members of the ISTD carried out scientific research into the causes and prevention of crime and gave therapy to young offenders. The basic philosophy of the ISTD was that juvenile crime was caused by mental problems. The ISTD recruited its members from both the 'orthodox' British Psycho-Analytical Society and the "eclectic" Tavistock Clinic.

In 1936 Bowlby began working part-time at the London Child Guidance Clinic. Child Guidance Clinics (see Figure 1.3) – an originally American phenomenon that had been imported in Britain by (again) Cyril Burt (Hearnshaw, 1979) – treated "difficult" children in multidisciplinary teams consisting of a psychiatrist, a psychologist, and a social worker. The general conviction at these clinics – and especially that of the social workers – was that the children's

Figure 1.3 Photograph of a child therapy session with Bowlby, titled "Just child's play." "The doctor and Joan discuss the drawing and after a time, Joan tells him all about it. From the drawing and the things she said, he realized that her trouble was loneliness. The father was in the army, a railway journey from home, and the mother missed her husband too acutely to pay enough attention to the child." Courtesy of the Wellcome Library, London (AMWL: PP/BOW/L.4, nr. 11).

problems might result from an inadequate relationship with their parents (e.g., unresolved conflicts from the parents' own childhood might cause or perpetuate the problems of their children). Bowlby would later state that he "learned a hell of a lot more from those … social workers than [he] learned from [his] psychiatric colleagues" (Senn, 1977a; see Smuts, 1977b). It was while working at this clinic that Bowlby first came across two cases of the so-called "psychopathic personality type," i.e., he identified two children who seemed unaffected by praise or blame and did whatever they wanted. Both children had suffered a major separation experience in their infancy (being sent to a hospital for many months without any visiting from the parents) and Bowlby hypothesized that it was the separation from their mother that had caused their characters to deviate (Van Dijken *et al.*, 1998).

Bowlby worked at these various institutions which all belonged largely to the "eclectic" current in British psychiatry, i.e., while psychoanalytic insights were being widely used they did not follow the 'orthodox' therapy model (of five therapy sessions per week) or accept all of Freud's ideas (e.g., his heavy emphasis on childhood sexuality). Simultaneously, he was exposed to the 'orthodox' and Kleinian tracks within the British Psycho-Analytical Society. His training analysis with Riviere lasted for more than seven years and was finally concluded in the summer of 1937, supposedly because his future wife Ursula disapproved of him continuing to spend money on it (Bretherton, personal communication, April 28, 2009). His training had been full of frictions, partly because Riviere (1927) espoused the Kleinian view that "analysis … is not concerned with the real world … It is concerned simply and solely with the imaginings of the childish mind" (pp. 376–377).

However, through his work at the Maudsley Hospital, at the ISTD, and at the London Child Guidance Clinic, Bowlby became convinced that "the real world" (in the form of mentally disturbed or neglective parents, etc.) does matter in causing problematic child behavior and that neglect, emotional and physical deprivation, etc., do not just exist in the "imaginings of the childish mind" – convictions that were formed during his time at Priory Gate School. Small wonder, then, that when Bowlby started his training in child analysis under the supervision of no less than Melanie Klein herself, that this led to immediate conflict (Van Dijken *et al.*, 1998).

From Kleinian Psychoanalysis to Real Life

In an interview with Robert Karen (1994), Bowlby described an influential experience in 1938, while training as a child psychiatrist under the supervision of Melanie Klein. Contrary to Klein, who believed all behavior was motivated by inner feelings or drives, Bowlby felt that external relationships, e.g., the way a parent treats a child, were important to consider in understanding the child's behavior. At the time, he was seeing an anxious, hyperactive child as a patient five days a week. The boy's mother would sit in the waiting room, and Bowlby noticed that she too seemed quite anxious and unhappy. When he told Klein he wanted to talk to the mother as well,

Klein refused adamantly, dismissing the mother as a possible causal or related factor in the child's behavior, and saying: "Dr. Bowlby, we are not concerned with reality, we are concerned only with the fantasy" (Kagan, 2006, p. 43). When the mother was subsequently taken to a mental hospital for treatment of anxiety and depression, Klein was unaffected and untouched and only replied that it was "a nuisance," because now they had "to find another case" (Karen, 1994, p. 46). Bowlby was thoroughly annoyed – even 50 years later, in a conversation with the well-known developmental psychologist Jerome Kagan, he still became angry when relating this case (Kagan, 2006) and distanced himself from the Melanie Klein school of thought. It is apparent his views conflicted with those of Klein. Many years later, Bowlby described as his own view that:

> most of what goes on in the internal world is a more or less accurate reflection of what an individual has experienced recently or long ago in the external world. Of course, in addition to all that, we imagine things … but most of the time we're concerned with ordinary events. If a child sees his mother as a very loving person, the chances are that his mother is a loving person. If he sees her as a rejecting person, she is a very rejecting person. (Bowlby, Figlio, and Young, 1986, p. 43)

Despite his theoretical differences with Klein, a leading member of the British Psycho-Analytical Society, Bowlby stuck to his views and when he had to submit a paper to qualify as a full member in 1939 he deliberately focused on the importance of real-life experiences in causing neurosis and neurotic character. Bowlby made clear, however, that he stuck to the psychoanalytical principles, i.e., that he at least disregarded most of the child's environment.

> My own approach to the role of environment in the causation of neurosis has of course been from the analytic angle. For this reason I have ignored many aspects of the child's environment such as economic conditions, the school situation, diet and religious teaching. (Bowlby, 1940a, p. 155)

In his paper, Bowlby subsequently explained that he was primarily interested in (1) the history of the mother–child relationship and the possible separations between them; (2) the mother's treatment of the child (her unconscious attitude included); and (3) illness and death in the family and how it affected the child. By far the most important in his view were the actual separations between mother and child.

Here, for the first time, Bowlby (1940a) explicitly stated (in print) that it was his "belief that the early environment is of vital importance" and that in his treatment of children he made "careful inquiries into the history of the child's relations to his mother and whether and in what circumstances there have been separations between mother and child" (Bowlby, 1940a, p. 156). He first acquired this idea at Priory Gate School and therefore resisted Kleinian notions which (presumably) came up in his training analysis with Riviere. Over the years, his view did not change "in any material way" (Bowlby, 1958b, p. 248). Even in the 1970s, after the publication of the first and second part of his trilogy, whenever "people preach[ed] to him" (Smuts, 1977b, p. 19) about the all importance of the way parents treat their children, Bowlby used to react: "I thought that forty years ago but wasn't allowed to say it" (Smuts, 1977b, pp. 19–20). That Bowlby knew he would have his hands full getting his ideas accepted in the psychoanalytic movement, becomes clear from a remark he once made to his wife Ursula when she asked him what he would pursue in his further career – after his research on separation would be completed: "Separation … will keep me busy for the rest of my life" (Dinnage, 1979, p. 323). In all, despite his wide-ranging mind, Bowlby "confess[ed] to a rather one-track, one-problem mind" (Tanner and Inhelder, 1971, p. 27).

We have seen that Bowlby, at the suggestion of Alford, pursued training in psychoanalysis with the British Psycho-Analytical Society, instead of with the Tavistock Clinic, which was supposedly a bit "amateur." But the fact of the matter is that the people who were at the pre-war Tavistock Clinic (e.g., Jack Rees, Henry Dicks, Wilfred Bion, Ronald Hargreaves, John Rickman, Jock Sutherland, and Eric Trist) would become Bowlby's colleagues in army psychiatry during World War II. Most of them were involved, with Bowlby, in evaluating the admission process to officer training. Because of this connection Bowlby was invited to the Tavistock Clinic after the war. Moreover, their "eclectic" ideas about children's needs were much more in accordance with Bowlby's. The "English school" emphasized the emergent object relations approach in psychoanalysis, emphasizing relationships rather than instinctual drives and psychic energy (Gerson, 2009; Trist and Murray, 1990; see also earlier in the chapter). This was, of course, all grist for the mill for Bowlby, who found support for his idea of a primary need for mother, ideas he expressed from very early on in his career (Van der Horst and Van der Veer, 2010).

It is interesting to note that Bowlby first became acquainted with Freud's views through Adrian and Alford, subsequently picking up Klein's idea of the connectedness of childhood separation experiences and adult reactions to loss, but in his search for an explanation of that phenomenon he came into contact with the eclectic group of the Tavistock Clinic whose ideas were more congenial to the views he already held (see Hinshelwood, 1991; Pines, 1991). But although the Tavistock was known to be "eclectic," the Kleinian approach to clinical practice was still very much around when Bowlby became head of the Children's Department of the Tavistock Clinic after the war – too much, according to Bowlby, which made him remark once: "So in certain respects I have been a stranger in my own department" (Senn, 1977a, p. 16). The fact that the therapists and analysts at the clinic held clearly different views was the reason why Bowlby later founded a separate research lab across the street, so he could pursue his own ideas there.

Bowlby's Forty-four Juvenile Thieves

After qualifying as an analyst in 1937 and becoming a full member of the British Psycho-Analytical Society in 1939, Bowlby "documented his position in much greater detail" (Bowlby, Figlio and Young, 1986, p. 39) than he had done in the paper he had read to the British Psycho-Analytical Society. In a study, published as *Forty-four Juvenile Thieves*, Bowlby (1944, 1946), tried to corroborate his view that separation from the caregiver is the source of later delinquency and mental disturbance – a view that he clearly adopted from people like Cyril Burt and Homer Lane, as we have seen earlier. According to Robert Hinde – Bowlby's later mentor in ethology (see Chapter 4) – "the real key [to the development of Bowlby's thinking] is the forty-four thieves paper," because Bowlby "noticed that many of the delinquent adolescents had disrupted childhoods and that put him on the trail" (Van der Horst *et al.*, 2007, p. 322).

In this classic study, Bowlby compared the case histories of 44 thieves treated at the London Child Guidance Clinic by Bowlby and his colleagues with a control group of 44 non-thieves. The goal of the paper was "a systematic investigation of possible adverse effects in the young child's environment ... and in particular that part of it comprised by the parents" (Bowlby, 1944, p. 125). Bowlby distinguished three different factors that might lead to maladjusted behavior: (1) genetic factors; (2) early home environment; and (3) contemporary environment. To no surprise, Bowlby particularly emphasized the adverse effects in the early environment when a child is "separated from his mother or mother-substitute for long periods or permanently during his first five years of life" (Bowlby, 1944, p. 109).

On the basis of an examination of his and his colleagues' files, Bowlby (1940a) predicted that a "broken mother-child relationship" in the first three years of life leads to emotionally withdrawn children who do not develop "libidinal ties" (p. 158) with others. Bowlby sample consisted of 31 boys and 13 girls aged 5 to 17. The average intelligence of the children was above the average of the population. Unfortunately, Bowlby (1944) was unable to provide the economic status of the children, but the "general impression of the cases suggests that there were relatively few who were dependent on support from public funds and many were comfortable" (p. 23). Of 16 cases of emotionally withdrawn children who were prone to stealing, the so-called 'affectionless thieves', 14 turned out to have experienced major separations from their mother in the critical age period. In 30 cases of other thieves, Bowlby found another five separations, whereas in 44 cases of non-thieves (his control group) there were only three separations to be found. He concluded "that the socially satisfactory behavior of most adults is dependent on their having been brought up in circumstances ... which have permitted ... satisfactory development of ... object-relationships" (Bowlby, 1944, p. 125) and that a certain clinical syndrome – the affectionless thief – is caused by major separation experiences. The statistical analysis in Bowlby's study was greatly ameliorated by advice from his army colleagues (e.g., Eric Trist, Jock Sutherland; see also Chapter 3).

The basic idea of the influence of early separation from the mother on later development again becomes clear (see Van der Horst and Van der Veer, 2010), although of course phrased in the psychoanalytic jargon of the time (i.e., 'emotionally withdrawn children do not develop libidinal ties or object-relationships'). Bowlby did not explain why exactly mother–child separations would lead to stealing whereas other pathogenic environments would lead to other forms of deviant behavior, but made clear that "a child separated from his mother comes o crave ... for her love," and "by stealing ... hopes for libidinal satisfaction" (Bowlby, 1944, p. 121). Also, he did find it necessary to warn that in his view the further conclusion followed that minor breaks too might have a damaging effect on the child's development.

The study of the 44 thieves ultimately led to Bowlby's assignment with the World Health Organization (WHO). Ronald Hargreaves, whom Bowlby had met during the war, had become Chief of the Mental Health Section at the WHO in Geneva. Hargreaves was impressed by Bowlby's earlier work and in 1949 asked him to do a report on mental health problems of homeless children, who had become a major problem after World War II (Van der Horst *et al.*, 2007). Bowlby accepted the offer and undertook a literature survey in order to test the hypothesis that "separation experiences are pathogenic" (Bowlby, Robertson, and Rosenbluth, 1952, p. 82). He read extensively into the early work on deprivation and travelled around to consult international experts in Europe and the US in an effort to "draw the strands together into one coherent argument" (Rutter, 1972a, p. 121). His efforts resulted in a monograph titled *Maternal Care and Mental Health* (Bowlby, 1951, 1952). The outcome of this research would greatly and decisively influence his further career and his research activities (Holmes, 1993). How Bowlby embarked on this new venture is the subject of the next chapter.

Personal Life During the Pre-war Years

It is of interest to pay some attention to Bowlby's personal life during the pre-war period. In the 1920s and 1930s, while pursuing a clinical and scientific career, Bowlby's private circumstances changed in several ways. While he was at Cambridge, his brother Tony studied chemistry in Oxford. Through him, Bowlby got acquainted – and roomed in – with Tony's group of "Oxford friends", amongst whom where his later brother-in-law Henry Phelps Brown, who married his sister Evelyn, and Evan Durbin, "an immensely impressive personality" (Ursula Bowlby, personal communication, April 29, 1996) and "a remarkable fellow" (Smuts, 1977b, p. 10). These two close friends, both academic economists, "were very powerful debaters and any position which [Bowlby] took up [he] had to justify up to the hilt by argument and evidence" (Senn, 1977a, p. 5). Phelps Brown and Durbin challenged Bowlby's newly acquired psychoanalytic views – views that Bowlby admitted were "still very controversial and needed a lot of academic justification" (Senn, 1977a,

p. 5). Often they had "long discussions" during which Bowlby learned that:

> it was necessary for [him] to give good reasons why psychoanalysis 'and all that' was about important things. The intellectual climate in which [he] was living was one where one had to think rigorously and give good reasons and good evidence for one's statements. (Smuts, 1977b, p. 10)

Soon Durbin became Bowlby's closest friend – they shared the same house in London from 1929 to 1939 (Smuts, 1977b) and "were each other's 'best men' at their weddings" (Ursula Bowlby, personal communication, April 29, 1996). Also, Durbin had a profound influence on Bowlby's scientific orientation and academic interest: instead of thinking of himself as a clinician, Durbin "encouraged [him] to think of [him]self as an academic, not to <u>become</u> an academic, but to think of [him]self as having an academic orientation" (Smuts, 1977b, p. 10; original underlining). As we have seen above, it was Durbin who encouraged Bowlby to register as a Ph.D. student under Burt. Their close personal friendship, as well as their analogous political ideas, led them to publish a book called *Personal Aggressiveness and War* (Durbin and Bowlby, 1939). According to Bowlby, it was "a strange book – Evan wrote ... a fifty page essay, and I wrote a hundred page appendix ... [which] reviewed the evidence" (Smuts, 1977b, p. 11). The basic theme of the book was that "war is due to the expression in and through group life of the transformed aggressiveness of individuals" (Durbin and Bowlby, 1939, p. 41). In the appendix, Bowlby explained war and aggression by connecting Freud's views with evolutionary and anthropological thinking. He put forward the view that aggressiveness in humans is caused by the same basic biological forces as in apes and stated that "men will fight ... like any monkey" (Durbin and Bowlby, 1939, p. 59). Bowlby thus saw a straight progression from the behaviours of apes via primitive men and modern-day children to adults in Western society. Of course, these views are highly relevant in light of Bowlby's move to ethological thinking in later years (see Chapter 4).

The joint project with Durbin was Bowlby's "first venture into a quasi academic sort of article" (Durbin and Bowlby, 1939, p. 59). So, we may conclude that Durbin was of great importance to Bowlby, not only at a personal level, but at a professional level as well. All the more dramatic, then, is the fact that Evan Durbin drowned in 1948, while trying to rescue two children; according to Ursula (personal communication, April 29, 1996) this "was the worst loss John suffered." She could not "see how [his] death ... could fail to affect John's feelings about loss and mourning" (Ursula Bowlby, personal communication, May 26, 1996).

Another important event in these years was Bowlby's introduction to his future wife Ursula, in 1937, and their subsequent marriage in 1938. In the preceding years, Bowlby had had difficulties in forming lasting relationships with women and several relationships were ended for rather dramatic reasons – such as Bowlby sleeping with the sister of one of his girlfriends (Holmes, 1993; Van Dijken, 1998). But when he met Ursula Longstaff during a shooting holiday in Ireland, he immediately fell in love with her. This time it would prove to be a long-lasting love – they were together until John died in 1990. Together they had four children: Mary (b. 1939), Richard (b. 1941), Pia (b. 1945), and Robert (b. 1948). Ursula almost entirely took care of the children by herself, and Bowlby is said to have been a far better grandfather than he was a father (Holmes, 1993). Apart from a "remote" (Holmes, 1993, p. 25) parenting style, Bowlby also followed his father's tradition of hard work – both were involved in the army in wartime, when several of the children were small – and long holidays. However, during long vacations on the Scottish Isle of Skye, where the Bowlbys had bought a second house, the family enjoyed walking, boating, bird-watching, shooting, and fishing – just as John had done in his childhood. So a family tradition was continued for better or for worse.

Concluding Remarks

In this chapter I have argued that the course of Bowlby's later career – his interest in the caregiver–child relationship and its importance for the child's well-being – ultimately had its roots in his formative years: in his personal life and in professional experiences in the 1920s and 1930s. For example, Bowlby's typical distant, upper-middle class upbringing was marked by separation experiences (e.g., the departure of his favourite nanny, the absence of his father, and the attendance at boarding school). This led him to remark that during his childhood he was "sufficiently hurt but not sufficiently damaged." In all, these moulding experiences taught him that young children can be hurt by separation experiences and this arguably influenced his subsequent thinking and research. In addition, in 1948, Bowlby experienced a traumatic loss through the death of his best friend, something that, according to his wife, clearly influenced his later ideas on grief and mourning.

Of specific interest for the purport of this book is the early interest Bowlby showed in nature. He "inherited," so to speak, his mother's passion for the outdoors. Also, as a naval cadet at Dartmouth, Bowlby was an enthusiastic bird-watcher and photographer (Van Dijken, 1998) – like many ethologists were (Burkhardt, 2005; Roëll, 2000). When he had a family of his own, Bowlby took his children to the countryside, just as his parents had done with him. Thus, Bowlby's later choice for ethology as a framework was preceded by an interest in nature combined with an emphasis on observation of behavior. In other words, "his love for the outdoors and his keen eye for observation made him naturally responsive to the basic tenets of classical ethological theory and methodology" (Suomi, 1995, p. 185).

In the late 1920s, Bowlby's attention was drawn to psychoanalysis as a new frame of reference – first at the Naval College, and later by his mentors Adrian and Alford. While following the usual track of training through training analysis – being exposed to "orthodox" Kleinian ideas but never fully accepting them – he simultaneously worked at several "eclectic" institutions and became familiar with the influential "English school" of psychiatry. The views that Suttie, Dicks, and others adhered to were much closer to Bowlby's own ideas regarding the all-importance of real-life events than were the views of his Kleinian colleagues who emphasized the fantasies of children. So the "early Bowlby" (for which, see Van Dijken, 1998) is best characterized as a rather independent thinker within the psychoanalytic movement – leaning towards the ideas of the eclectic "English school" of psychiatry – but a psychoanalyst nonetheless. Moreover, he was a psychoanalyst who arrived at the position that the early social and socio-economical environment of children had a strong influence on their later development – which was in sharp contrast with views of more orthodox members of the British Psycho-Analytical Society.

Notes

1 The baronetcy is currently held by John Bowlby's son Richard, who inherited the title from his uncle, and John's brother, Tony Bowlby when the latter died in 1993.

2 The full list of these 11 books reads: Ainsworth (1967), De Beer (1958), Erdelyi (1974), Freud (1917), Hinde (1956), Hinde (1966), Kuhn (1962), Lane (1928), Lorenz (1935), Marris (1958), Sommerhoff (1950).

3 AMWL stands for Archives and Manuscripts, Wellcome Library for the History and Understanding of Medicine, 183 Euston Road, London NW1 2BE. The letters PP/BOW stand for Personal Papers Bowlby.

4 During his time at Priory Gate School Bowlby read Lane's (1928) *Talks to Parents and Teachers*. This work was listed among the eleven most influential books – see footnote 2 (AMWL: PP/BOW/A.1/7; dated October 24, 1979).

5 The labels assigned in this chapter to different groups or schools within psychoanalysis are of limited value. Just like in politics one can take a 'liberal' viewpoint with respect to one issue and a 'conservative' one with respect to another, psychoanalysts could be both 'orthodox' and 'eclectic' or 'independent' at different times.

6 The phrase "shell shock" was coined by army psychologist C. S. Myers in a series of papers in *The Lancet* (Myers, 1915, 1916a, 1916b, 1916c; see also Jones, 2010).

2
Loneliness in Infancy: The WHO Report and Issues of Separation

Separation as a Theme

In the previous chapter we have seen that, from very early on in his career, Bowlby attributed potentially harmful effects to separation of a child from its mother or mother-substitute. In complete accordance with this early view, Bowlby later stated that "young children, who for any reason are deprived of the continuous care and attention of a mother or a substitute-mother, are not only temporarily disturbed by such deprivation, but may in some cases suffer long-term effects which persist" (Bowlby *et al.*, 1956, p. 211) and that a "rupture leads to separation anxiety and grief and sets in train processes of mourning" (Bowlby, 1961b, p. 317). Bowlby's career was largely focused around the theme of separation and its consequences and he was fairly single-minded in that sense or to phrase it in his own words, he had a rather "one-track, one-problem mind." On the other hand, Bowlby's main employment was as a top administrator in a large clinic, rather than as a theorist or researcher; yet he fitted in theorizing, reading, and writing.

Bowlby's single-mindedness with regard to issues of separation was, of course, very influential when working on the WHO report on

John Bowlby – From Psychoanalysis to Ethology: Unraveling the Roots of Attachment Theory, First Edition. Frank C. P. van der Horst.

mental health problems of homeless children. Although the importance of different observations of the consequences of separation for Bowlby's thinking and for the development of attachment theory is self-evident, so far little attempt has been made to give a complete overview of the different studies on the effect of separation and deprivation that drew the attention of many in the 1940s and 1950s and to which Bowlby was clearly exposed. This chapter is an attempt to do so. What exactly was known or believed about separation effects shortly before, during and after World War II, when Bowlby wrote his first letters to scientific journals and published his first articles? Here we may distinguish between findings from several different but interconnected areas. Attention will be paid to observations made during wartime evacuations and observations made in residential nurseries, to the discussion concerning visiting of children in hospital, and, finally, to results of studies on the "hospitalization" effect. I will show that Bowlby met with and was heavily influenced by leading researchers in the field of psychology and psychiatry while working on his report for the WHO. Finally, I will also take a closer look at the film *Grief: A peril in infancy* by Spitz (1947) that supported these new ideas on the effects of maternal deprivation. Spitz's film was quite similar to those of Robertson (1952, 1958c); these films greatly influenced public opinion – at least in Britain. Robertson's contributions to the debate on separation and on Bowlby's thinking are presented in Chapter 3.

Here, from a discussion of the different "issues of separation" it will become clear how, in the 1940s and 1950s, Bowlby gathered (retrospective) evidence for his views on the early mother-child relationship that would eventually refute classic psychoanalytic views. Shortly before he first came across ethology in 1951, Bowlby (1951, 1952) summarized his findings on separation and deprivation in his report to the WHO. He would eventually turn to the ethological perspective to explain his observations on the influence of early environment on the development of children (see Chapter 4).

Issues of Separation: Evacuation of Children

Sadly enough, World War II supplied psychologists and psychiatrists with many opportunities to observe the effects of parent–child separations. As early as 1924 a committee chaired by John Anderson started to lay out plans for the evacuation of children in case of aerial bombing by a "belligerent" force. These evacuations were part of the so-called Air Raid Precautions (ARP) and were necessary because at that time there was no efficient way of stopping air attacks. The official evacuations started on E-day, September 1, 1939 – the day of the German invasion of Poland and two days before the British declaration of war to the Third Reich. Within days, 734 883 unaccompanied children were evacuated from the London area to the countryside (Editorial, 1940). Immediately, details of this operation and its effects on the children started to fill the editorial and correspondence columns of the leading medical journals – the *British Medical Journal* and *The Lancet*. On September 9, an editorial in the BMJ (1939a) hailed the "successful exodus" of the evacuated children. On November 1, a discussion in the House of Lords led to the conclusion that "the evacuated children were happy and were gaining in health. Very often the hosts, too, were happy" (Editorial, 1939b, p. 977).

Not everyone was satisfied though. General practitioners warned against the dangers (spreading of vermin, uncleanliness) and undesirable social effects (Carling, 1939; Evans, 1939; Prance, 1939; Thursfield, 1939). In reception areas, people felt that "the scum of the town ha[d] been poured into the clean countryside" (Keir, 1939, p. 745). Also, it soon turned out that from a psychological viewpoint the evacuation of children was not a complete success. Frequent bed-wetting and other nervous symptoms were often observed in evacuated children. Feelings of concern about the emotional well-being of the children were expressed. Rickman (1939, p. 1192), in a letter to *The Lancet*, expressed his doubts about the plan to separate a child from two to five from its mother, because "at a time when his need for security, and the comforting assurance of familiar faces, is great, his removal from his parents will tax him severely ... [and] may show [itself] in unsatisfactory or unhappy social relationships later in life." In the *British Medical Journal* psychoanalysts Donald Winnicott, Emmanuel Miller, and John Bowlby protested against the evacuations for similar reasons:

> It is quite possible for a child of any age to feel sad or upset at having to leave home, but ... such an experience in the case of a little child can mean far more than the actual experience of sadness. It can in fact amount to an emotional 'black-out' and can easily lead to a severe disturbance of

> the development of the personality which may persist throughout life. [E]vacuation of small children without their mothers can lead to very serious and widespread psychological disorder. For instance, it can lead to a big increase in juvenile delinquency in the next decade. (Bowlby, Miller and Winnicott, 1939, pp. 1202–1203)

Clearly, here Bowlby and his colleagues referred to Bowlby's (1940a) early work on juvenile delinquency. They may have somewhat overstated their case, but for many children the sudden evacuation was indeed traumatic (see Wolf, 1945, for an attempt to summarize the findings). Many years later, Wicks (1988) gathered the often moving memories of persons who spent part of their childhood as an evacuee.[1]

Issues of Separation: Observations in Residential Nurseries

While many children during World War II were billeted with private persons, others ended up in residential nurseries, for example, because they lost their parents in an air raid. The great authority in this area became Anna Freud, who together with Dorothy Burlingham published various books on her experiences with young children in the Hampstead Nurseries (Burlingham and Freud, 1942, 1944; see Freud, A., 1973). Their often moving accounts "describe the wholly admirable administration of a group of three nurseries (two residential and one for day children)" and include " – with an endearing lack of technical terms – an account of child development and psychopathology so simple and yet so profound that the unlearned in psychology and the experienced psychiatrist alike may read it with enjoyment and profit" (Editorial, 1942b). An example of such a moving account is their description of Dell, a little girl of two-and-a-half years old:

> Dell was a beautiful little girl … sparkling with life and gaiety … Dell was taken to the nursery where she was deep in play after a few minutes. She said good-bye to her mother in a friendly way, but hardly noticed when her mother left her. Only half an hour [later] … Dell suddenly realized what had happened. She interrupted her play, rushed out of the nursery, and opened every single door … to look for her mother … This lasted a

> few minutes and then she rejoined the play group. These attacks of frantic search repeated themselves with ever greater frequency. Dell's expression changed, her brightness disappeared, her smile gave way to a ... frown which changed the whole aspect of the child. (Freud, A., 1973, pp. 36–37)

In their studies, Burlingham and Freud posited that it is of the utmost importance for the child's personality formation and the development of consciousness to develop attachments with (substitute) adult persons. The logical people to play this role in the life of residential children are the grown-ups of the nursery. If these grown-ups remain remote and impersonal figures, or if they change so often that no permanent attachment can be formed, there is great danger that the children will show defects in their character development and inadequate adaptation to society, Burlingham and Freud (1944, pp. 105–106) argued. They concluded:

> Residential Nurseries offer excellent opportunities for detailed and unbroken observation of child-development.[2] If these opportunities were made use of widely, much valuable material about emotional and educational response at these early ages might be collected and applied to the upbringing of other children who are lucky enough to live under more normal circumstances. (Burlingham and Freud, 1944, p. 108)

To the editors of the *British Medical Journal* it was clear "that these [Hampstead] nurseries are run with an efficiency, devotion, and human understanding that should serve as a model for others, whether in time of peace or of war" (Editorial, 1942b, p. 579). In subsequent years, Freud would repeatedly intervene in a debate concerning visits to children in hospital, warning against the psychological dangers of separations (see Editorial, 1944, 1949; Robertson, 1956). We will now turn to this debate.

Issues of Separation: Visits to Children in Hospital

In January 1940, *The Lancet* published an editorial in which it was announced that Ayr County Hospital – following the example of other hospitals (see Editorial, 1937) – had decided to no longer admit visitors to its children's wards. The editor argued that the danger of infection indeed made forbidding access logical and added the then very common argument that parental visits only upset the child. He was sure that children quickly settle in the hospital and "cheerfully adopt the … staff *in loco parentis*" (Editorial, 1940, p. 179). It was not the children who needed parental visits, the editor argued, but the "over-anxious mother" (Editorial, 1940, p. 179). However, parental stress could be alleviated by interviews with staff and an occasional peep when the child was asleep. The editor concluded his account by stating that in these matters sentiment was not a weighty enough argument. It was Bowlby (1940b) who first reacted to this editorial note. In a letter to the editor he argued that, although more research was needed, there was reason to assume that visiting was essential, especially for younger children. He suspected that non-visiting might lead to chronic delinquency in children and mentioned an antisocial boy of six and a pilfering girl of eight from his practice, both with a history of unvisited hospital stay. Referring to Rickman (1939), he suggested that the younger the child, the more visits are needed. Two weeks later, Harry Edelston (1940), one of Bowlby's colleagues at the London Child Guidance Clinic, supported his argument and stated that, he too, had seen children in the Child Guidance Clinic who suffered from prolonged hospital stays (see later in the chapter). Edelston added that children's quiet attitude may be deceptive, because they may repress their feelings until they come home. Edelston would several times intervene in debates in *The Lancet* about visiting times in children hospitals, stating the possible harmful effects of separation experiences but at the same time emphasizing that they are not inevitable (Edelston, 1941, 1946, 1953, 1955, 1958).

These letters by two child psychiatrists seem to have had no effect whatsoever on hospital practice. The majority of hospitals vehemently opposed (frequent) visiting by parents for a variety of reasons. (See Figure 2.1.) Parents brought filthy germs into the wards and only upset their children, who would be crying for hours after they left, causing the nursing staff much trouble. Parents only wished to visit their children for egocentric reasons; they were being over-anxious and neurotic. The children themselves certainly did not need the visits; they quickly felt at home in the hospital. Besides, even if a child was not happy – and some doctors and nurses admitted that these children existed – it was always better to have a sad child than a dead child. Taking the viewpoints of the parents, it was also suggested that many parents had no wish or time to visit their children, for

Hilary WELLS
THE GIRLS' HERITAGE HOSPITALS
CHAILEY, SUSSEX.
VISITING DAYS
Children in hospital may be Visited on the FIRST SUNDAY in each month
BY THEIR PARENTS OR TWO VISITORS ONLY
(NO CHILDREN WHATEVER, OF ANY AGE, ADMITTED)
Time: 3 to 4.30 p.m.
With the exception of Eggs, Fruit, Biscuits or Sweets NO FOOD may be brought.
PLEASE BRING THIS CARD WITH YOU

Figure 2.1 Hilary Wells' visiting card. Courtesy of Hillary Wakefield (née Wells).

example, because they had to travel a long time to the hospital, or there were other children to take care of. And who would make father's tea when he got home from work? (Herzog, 1958a, 1958b; Meadow, 1964; Schoo, 1954) Apparently, parents were seen as ignorant and noisy intruders who only criticized the staff and disturbed the quiet and disciplined course of events in the ward. Meanwhile, the parents themselves had few possibilities to change the existing situation. Even if they had been eloquent and knowledgeable enough and realized that something was awry, there was little that they could have done to oppose the medical doctors who had allegedly introduced all those rules to the benefit of their child. In sum, the emotional problems of isolated children in hospital were not appreciated or considered serious enough. And even if the problems were acknowledged there were always weighty grounds to oppose any change of the existing regulations.

What many British people did not know at the time was that both in Britain and abroad other models of child care in hospital were being practiced with considerable success. In 1945, the readers of the *British Medical Journal* first heard of an experiment that had been going on for quite some time in New Zealand. In that year, Henry and Cecile Pickerill, plastic surgeons in Wellington, first described their new method of dealing with the dangers of cross-infection, a method they had already introduced in 1927. Over the next decade, the Pickerills would repeatedly discuss their approach in both the *British Medical Journal* and *The Lancet*, claiming its unprecedented success, and actively participate in the debate about child care (e.g., visiting regulations) in hospital (Pickerill, 1955a, 1955b; Pickerill and Pickerill, 1945, 1946, 1947, 1954a, 1954b, 1954c, 1954d, 1954e). Other writers in these journals regularly referred to the Pickerills' approach and were obviously well acquainted with it. What was that approach? As the Pickerills (Pickerill and Pickerill, 1945) explained, they sought to create an environment where the child would be protected against the danger of cross-infection. To this goal, a separate surgical unit was built with accommodation for 12 mother–child pairs. For, contrary to other approaches, the Pickerills wished to isolate the infant or young child *with* its mother. The rationale of that idea was their belief that "a baby is born with a certain degree of passive immunity to its mother's organisms, and that it acquires further immunity in the next few months … [and that it should be exposed] to no other organisms whatever." After surgery, the contact between the medical staff and the baby was minimal and mothers took responsibility for the majority of the care of their children. Although the Pickerills stressed the importance of isolation (or rather insulation) for medical reasons, they did mention other factors relevant for our account. In 1946, they expressed their opinion that mothers should be happy when taking care of their babies and not "reduced to a nervous wreck by an autocratic ward sister" (Pickerill and Pickerill, 1946, p. 337). One year later, in their reaction to Spence's paper (see later in the chapter), they added that "babies want constant attention and 'mothering'; to break the bond between mother and baby is to introduce an unnecessary hurdle into treatment" (Pickerill and Pickerill, 1947, p. 826). From their articles and letters, it also transpires that they wished to create a healthy and happy environment for mothers and children with plenty of sunshine and good food. Later researchers, e.g. Mac Keith (1953), would dismiss the insulation idea as irrelevant and claim that it was the continuous presence of the mother that accounted for the success of the Pickerills' approach. However, it may have been exactly the "unsentimental" aspect of their approach that made it acceptable in medical circles.

In May 1945, the readers of *The Lancet* were able to take note of a letter that was unusual in two respects. First, it was written by a parent. Second, it addressed the issue of social class. The letter was written by Lady Patricia Russell, the third wife of the philosopher Bertrand

Russell. She related that she had just returned from America when her seven-year old son Conrad, the later historian and politician, suddenly developed a high fever and had to be admitted to the local hospital. Russell wished to stay with her son but was told to leave at once. This she refused to do. When the doctors arrived after 12 hours, they accused her of bringing "filthy germs" (Russell, 1945a, p. 642) from the United States. Russell left for the night but when she returned the next day her son told her that when he asked for his mother, the nurse "threatened to smack him and removed his teddy-bear" (Russell, 1945a, p. 642). What made Lady Russell's letter even more shocking was her observation that as soon as the medical staff realized who she was, she was immediately treated with the utmost courtesy. Apparently, she suggested, "the gross neglect, rudeness, and enforced separation" (Russell, 1945a, p. 642) were reserved for the members of the lower social classes. Russell opposed the existing visiting rules with the following words:

> I feel very strongly that when children are patients in hospitals some member of their family should be allowed to remain with them whenever this is possible ... to restrict parental visits to two days a week, as in this hospital, is inhuman. (Russell, 1945a, p. 642)

Russell's letter elicited rather vehement reactions. Nicholson (1945) and Foster (1945) claimed her story could not be true. Batten (1945) expressed as his opinion that "everybody would deplore the continual presence of a mother at the bedside of a sick child" (p. 834), and Bliss (1945) wondered whether she was a socialist. However, she also received support from correspondents (Cantab, 1945; Hardy, 1945; Nicholls, 1945) and, most importantly, from the editors of *The Lancet*, who claimed her account was not unique. According to the editors (Editorial, 1945), removing the teddy-bear was to deprive the boy of his last link with the security of home. Doctors should place themselves in the shoes of the child and its mother. The hospital should always be able to arrange for the mother to stay in comfort if she is needed, and the existing rule should become much more flexible. Kindness, comfort, and attention were the keywords, according to the editors. In her follow-up letter, Russell told she had received many letters with similar stories and once more argued that visiting rules should be relaxed. One of her arguments was that "studies of evacuated children have abundantly proved that young children may be gravely harmed by enforced separation from their parents" (Russell, 1945b, p. 771).

Russell's letter was important, because it pointed out a social evil – private patients and their relatives were treated much better and could arrange flexible visiting times – and because her plea for more humane regulations was supported by the editors of one of the most important medical journals of Britain. Of course, much of the problems in this period could be excused by saying that there was a war going on. The nursing staff was underpaid, overburdened, and often unqualified. No wonder they were rude to parents and did not wish to see hordes of parents rushing into the hospital. Such excuses were valid to a degree, but there was more to it. By training and tradition doctors and nurses had never learned to take the viewpoint of the child patients and their parents. It would need very forceful descriptions and eventually films to open their eyes to the feelings of bewildered and frightened young patients. A veritable milestone in this respect was Spence's (1946; see also Spence, 1947) famous lecture on the care of children in hospital. Bowlby (1952) used the title of Spence's "inspiring lecture" (p. 69) for one of the chapters in his WHO report: *The purpose of the family*. Spence's description of children's wards is worth quoting at some length.

> The room is vast … The roof is … terrifyingly remote to the eyes of a child who lies many hours gazing at it. Some of the beds are three feet from the ground … to the discomfort of the child who has not slept so far from the ground before … The beds stink just a little … [He conceals] his personal treasures under his pillow until they are again put out of his reach … A plaintive 2-year-old standing behind the bars of his cot clad in a shapeless night-gown with a loose napkin sunk to his ankles below … Night comes on, but there is no bedtime story, no last moment of intimacy, no friendly cuddle before sleep. The nurse is too busy for that … This daily rhythm of anxiety, wonder, apprehension, and sleep is better than it sounds, because it is made tolerable by the extraordinary resilience and gaiety of the children … But it is a deceptive cheerfulness. (Spence, 1947, pp. 127–128)

Spence followed up on his description with a number of practical recommendations. Among other things, he proposed that a number of rooms in each hospital should be special mother-child suites where the mother could live with, nurse, and care for her own child. Thus, he suggested "admit[ting] the mothers to the hospital to nurse their own children. This is no theoretical proposal. I have worked under this arrangement for many years ... the majority of all children under the age of 3 derive benefit from it. The mother lives in the same room with her child" (Spence, 1947, p. 128). Spence argued that having such suites would bring many advantages: the mothers would gain confidence, nurses would learn how to handle children, students would learn courtesy, nurses would have more time for other duties, and so on.

What Spence for some reason did not do in his lecture was to spell out his own experiences with mother–child suites. But the fact of the matter was that he had been practicing this arrangement since he founded the Babies' Hospital in Newcastle upon Tyne in 1925. Spence's masterly description of a children's ward and his recommendations for improvement would serve as a model for those who championed a more humane child care in hospitals in the decades to come. Judging by the many references to his work, he came to be seen as one of the principal figures in the debate about child care in hospital.

Meanwhile, the few immediate reactions to the published version of his lecture were not altogether positive. Crosbie (1947) suggested mothers were to busy to take care of their sick child in the hospital and Lorber (1947) claimed he tried Spence's suggestion only to find out that mothers had other children to take care of, or were ill themselves. The Pickerills came to Spence's rescue and suggested that in extreme cases a granny could replace the mother. And, of course, they could not help to note that Spence "approves what we did as much as possible for the last 20 years and exclusively for the past 6 years" (Pickerill and Pickerill, 1947, p. 826).

Spence's lecture was followed by an article in *The Lancet* by Maclennan (1949) two years later. In that article, she argued that discipline was too harsh in hospitals, that there was an undue emphasis on cleanliness that thwarted the child's natural instincts. Maclennan complained that nurses knew little about child psychology and that the child's emotional needs were ignored when he was "perhaps for the first time in his life, [separated] from the people he loves and from the familiar home atmosphere" (p. 209). Maclennan then proposed a number of very sensible measures: the children should not be left alone too much; ideally, one nurse should take care of one child; children should have the possibility to play; nurses should know something about developmental psychology; children's fears and worries about going home should be discussed with them; the staff should cooperate with parents. Finally, "the parents should be encouraged ... to visit their children as often as possible.

They should always be given the choice of remaining with their children when they are acutely ill" (p. 210). Maclennan's paper showed once again that there were many people in the 1940s who saw the shortcomings of the existing regulations and advocated radical changes.

The early writings of the Pickerills, Spence, Maclennan, and others were important and influential in the sense that they inspired others and showed that other arrangements of child care in hospital were possible. But massive practical changes in hospital conditions were very slow to come (see Monro Davies, 1949). Experiments with living in, such as practiced by Spence, were still the exception. Meanwhile, the editors of *The Lancet* were already convinced that visiting times should be more flexible and argued so repeatedly in no mean words, e.g. "no savage needs to be told that separation from the mother damages young children" (Editorial, 1953a, p. 531), and "advantages to the child in maintaining real contact with its parents outweigh any of the objections" (Editorial, 1953b, p. 539). They deplored the fact that so many hospitals had ignored repeated advices by the Ministry of Health to allow daily visiting. In 1952, of 1300 hospitals only 300 allowed daily visiting (Editorial, 1953b, 1953d). But considerable numbers of the readers of *The Lancet* and the *British Medical Journal* were still unimpressed by their arguments. For example, a certain prof. Moir, consulting surgeon to the United Leeds Hospitals, maintained there was

> a lot of sloppy sentiment talked about this. If children are left alone for a day or two they forget their parents. The hours in hospital after the visit of parents are chaotic. The children all cry and shriek and will not go to sleep. (Editorial, 1953c; see also Neville, 1953; Penfold, 1953)

Bowlby would in subsequent years continue to do the utmost to change hospital practices and "to influence policy" (Heinicke, personal communication, October 6, 2008). His colleague Christoph Heinicke "was asked to present [his own] findings in the House of Lords, did so, and joined various efforts to influence hospital administrators" (Heinicke, personal communication, October 6, 2008). Nevertheless, it would take decades before Britain had essentially reached the present system of open visiting of hospitalized children (see Van der Horst and Van der Veer, 2009a, 2009c; see also Lindsay, 2009; Robertson and McGilly, 2009).

Issues of Separation: Studies on the "Hospitalization Effect"

Shortly before and during World War II the first systematic indications that separations from the parents might be potentially harmful started to appear in studies concerning the ill-effects of hospitalization of children in hospitals as well as in children orphanages and other residential institutions (e.g., Bakwin, 1942; Bender and Yarnell, 1941; Beverly, 1936; Dennis, 1941; Edelston, 1943; Goldfarb, 1943b; Levy, 1937; Lowrey, 1940; Ribble, 1943; Skeels, 1936; Spitz, 1945). As we have seen, Bowlby (1944, 1946) himself was one of many who contributed to the weight of clinical evidence with his paper on juvenile thieves, who had been seen and treated at the London Child Guidance Clinic (see Chapter 1).

One of the first to address the issue of hospitalization in the 1930s was psychologist Harold Skeels, but rather surprisingly his work did not show up in Bowlby's WHO report. This probably was because Skeels' work was "scathingly attacked for lack of scientific rigor" (Karen, 1994, p. 21) and only later, after the publication of Bowlby's report, did Skeels receive recognition for his important work. The major controversy involved the issue of the invariability of IQ in young children. Skeels and his colleagues found evidence to suggest that the IQs of children could be improved, but key figures in child development research such as G. Stanley Hall's student Lewis Terman disagreed and argued that IQs remained stable in young children. For example, in one of his studies, Skeels (1936) examined 73 children "from rather low educational, occupational, and socio-economic levels of society" (p. 96) who were placed in foster care before six months old. He discovered that "the mean level of intelligence of these children is higher than would be expected" (p. 104) on the basis of "the educational, socio-economic, and occupational level … [of] the true parents" (p. 105). The suggestion was, of course, that the rich environment provided by the foster parents is more stimulating than that of the true parents' home or at an institution. At first Skeels' conclusions were rather cautious, but in his later work "with thirteen mentally retarded orphanage children from one to two years of age," he positively concluded that "an intimate and close relationship between the child and an interested adult seems to be a factor of importance in the mental development of young children" (Skeels and Dye, 1939/2002, p. 32). Skeels and Dye concluded that the warm and close relationship with the foster parents accounted for a "change from mental retardation to normal intelligence" (Skeels and Dye, 1939/2002, p. 32).

In another study, psychiatrist Lawson Lowrey (1940) observed "the development and integration of personality" (p. 576) of 28 children from institutions who were placed in foster homes and of whom nine were described in detail. The children showed very high percentages of "hostile aggressiveness, temper tantrums, enuresis [bedwetting], speech defects, attention demanding behavior, shyness and sensitiveness, difficulties about food, stubbornness and negativism, selfishness, finger sucking and excessive crying" (p. 579). According to Lowrey, "[t]he conclusion seems inescapable that infants reared in institutions undergo an isolation type of experience" and that children "should not be reared in institutions" (p. 585).

More influential than these studies by Skeels and Lowrey was the work of paediatrician Harry Bakwin (1942), who described the care of small children in New York's Bellevue Hospital. The high mortality rate in this hospital was first attributed to malnutrition and then to cross-infection. In an attempt to lessen the danger of cross-infections, "the open ward … ha[d] been replaced by small, cubicled rooms in which masked, hooded and scrubbed nurses and physicians move[d] about cautiously so as to not stir up bacteria" (Bakwin, 1942, p. 31). Visiting parents were strictly excluded and the infants received a minimum of handling by the staff. Surprisingly enough to people involved at the time, these measures had no effect whatsoever on mortality. Rather by accident, Bakwin noted that infants slowly withered away and, despite their high caloric diets, would only gain in weight after they had returned home. He presumed that the "psychologic neglect" (Bakwin, 1942, p. 32) they endured, the total lack of mothering, and the sterile environment in the wards were damaging the children. Following a change in hospital policy, nurses were encouraged to mother and cuddle the children, to pick them up and play with them, and parents were invited to visit. The results of this change in policy were dramatic: despite the increased possibility of infection, the mortality rate for infants under one year of age fell sharply from 30–35% to less than 10%. Bakwin's paper was noticed by experts all over the world, including Britain. The impact of Bakwin's paper in Britain was amplified by the editors of the *British Medical Journal*, who discussed and supported Bakwin's ideas, and stated that "in infancy the loneliness involved in separation may be not only undesirable but lethal" (Editorial, 1942a, p. 345). The editors also noted that Bakwin's descriptions of children's symptoms "correspond disturbingly with those of some observers in our wartime nurseries" (Editorial, 1942a, p. 345) and suggested that "the biological unity of mother and little child cannot be disregarded with impunity" (Editorial, 1942a, p. 345). Different correspondents (Hutton, 1942; Macdonald, 1942; Salaman, 1942) sided with the editors and enthusiastically welcomed Bakwin's contribution. Bowlby's psychoanalytic colleague Donald Winnicott (1942) considered the review of Bakwin's paper "the most important you have published over a long period" and warned that "we cannot take mothers from infants without seriously increasing the psychological burdens which the next generation will have to bear" (p. 465).

It is less known that at the time Bakwin made his observations in the US, Bowlby's colleague at the Child Guidance Clinic, Harry Edelston (1943), did a similar (though retrospective) study on separation anxiety in young children in Britain. Edelston suspected that children's feelings of insecurity and various forms of misbehavior might be partially caused by earlier hospital stays. In 1938 and 1939, he investigated 42 clinical cases of problem children who had experienced repeated admissions to hospital without the parents being allowed to visit. Edelston found that many of these children afterward suffered from feelings of being abandoned or unwanted and that they were very anxious, clung to their mother, and, in general, showed disturbed behavior. According to Edelston, the "separation from home (i.e., from the mother) form[ed] the essentially traumatic element in the experience" (p. 14) and "the younger and more helpless the child the greater the separation anxiety" (p. 83). In all, "the determining factor seem[ed] to be the degree of rejection or insecurity *felt by the child*" (p. 85, original italics). Clearly, Edelston's ideas were in line with those of people at the 'eclectic' Tavistock Clinic (see Chapter 1). Unfortunately, Edelston's findings seem to have escaped the attention of experts owing to the outbreak of the war in Britain (see also Edelston, 1940). Other such studies on hospitalized children – by Goldfarb and Spitz, for example – did not.

In nine publications on the care of (Jewish) children in foster homes in New York, psychologist William Goldfarb (1943a, 1943b, 1943c, 1943d, 1944, 1945a, 1945b, 1947, 1949) compared the prevalence of "aggressive behavior disorders" (Goldfarb, 1943a, p. 250) in foster children with experience in institutions in the first three years of life to the behavior of foster children without such experiences. Goldfarb hypothesized that in the "institution group" these behavior disorders were more likely to be found than in the "foster home group." The conditions in the institutions were similar to those described by Bakwin:

> The children … had … been cared for in an institution with … an outstanding programme of medical prevention. Babies … were each kept in their own little cubicles to prevent the spread of epidemic infection. Their only contacts with adults occurred during those few hurried moments when they were dressed, changed, or fed by the nurses. These nurses had neither training nor time and resources to offer love and attention to a large group of babies … [A]lmost complete social isolation during th[e] first year of life, … and [an] only slight enrichment of experiences that followed in the next two years. (Goldfarb, 1947, p. 456)

Goldfarb (1943b, p. 127) noted that the institutionalized children had "an exceedingly impoverished, meagre, undifferentiated personality with related deficiency in inhibition and control" and a "passivity or apathy of personality" (Goldfarb, 1943b, p. 127). In the explanation of his findings, Goldfarb laid special emphasis on three main features in the institutions: (1) absence of stimulation, (2) absence of psychological interaction and reciprocal relation with adults, and (3) absence of normal identifications. The sterile climate in which the children lived, apparently had major consequences for later social interaction and Goldfarb concluded that a healthy interaction between children and their caregivers was of the utmost importance.

Psychoanalyst René Spitz had worked on the issue of sterile children's wards with Katherine Wolf in Austria, before he fled the European continent to New York with hope of joining Bakwin and Goldfarb in their work on deprivation (Blum, 2002). Spitz's main interest was in the relationship between mother and child and he was the first to coin the terms of "hospitalism" and "anaclitic depression" in children (Spitz, 1945, 1946, 1951; Spitz and Wolf, 1946, 1949). "The term hospitalism designates a vitiated condition of the body to long confinement in a hospital, or the morbid condition of the atmosphere of a hospital" (Spitz, 1945, p. 53). With the term hospitalism, Spitz gave a name to phenomena that Goldfarb had described earlier. Spitz defined an anaclitic depression as a "psychiatric syndrome of a depressive nature ... related to a loss of the love object, combined with a total inhibition of attempts at restitution through help of the body ego acting on anaclitic lines" (Spitz and Wolf, 1946, p. 339). Spitz studied the effect of continuous institutional care of infants under one year of age by comparing children in a nursery to children in a foundling home – as did Goldfarb before him. From his observations, Spitz concluded that (1) affective interchange is necessary for a healthy physical and behavioral development of infants; (2) this interaction is provided by reciprocity between mother (or mother substitute) and child; and (3) deprivation of this reciprocity is dangerous for the development of the personality of the child. Of the studies on hospitalization discussed here, Spitz's work on the effects of hospitalization was the most influential if we go by the number of citations, but it also came under heavy criticism.[3]

Spitz was attacked by psychologist Samuel Pinneau (1955a, 1955b; see also Karen, 1994; Spitz, 1955), who essentially pointed his arrows at four different aspects of Spitz's studies: (1) Spitz's refusal to identify the dates and locations of his observations (see Anonymous, 1952); (2) the inconsistency of the alleged number of children involved in the observations, which suggested a cross-sectional approach instead of the longitudinal study that Spitz presented; (3) Spitz's failure to account for the different cultural and racial background and socioeconomic status of the groups that were compared; and (4) the doubtful validity of the developmental scale, which jeopardized the interpretation of the test data. Despite this severe criticism, Spitz's work would be highly influential for several decades.

In addition to his scientific papers, Spitz (1947) presented the general public with a silent, black-and-white film titled *Grief: A Peril in Infancy*. Spitz filmed, amongst other children, a baby named Jane who within weeks after placement in a foundling home developed from a happy and approachable child into a distant and withdrawn one. Spitz himself described the cure for this child on one of the film's title cards: "Give mother back to baby." Jane is shown again, after her mother has returned after a three month separation, playing, clapping, and laughing. Although quite different in design (e.g., Spitz's film was not based on a single randomly chosen child and

Spitz intervenes to elicit specific behavior from the infants), reactions to Spitz's film were quite similar to the reactions Robertson would later receive for his film: those of shock and disbelieve. Karen (1994, p. 25) described how after Spitz's film was shown to physicians and psychoanalysts at the New York Academy of Medicine, a "prominent New York analyst approached Spitz with tears in his eyes. 'How could you do this to us?' he said." Apparently, people were shocked by the sight of babies pining away from grief. It was something that they had not seen or been willing to see before.

Bowlby and the WHO Report on Deprivation

So, in the first half of 1950, in an attempt to gather much needed information for his WHO report, Bowlby visited various European countries (France, the Netherlands, and Sweden) and the United States and consulted professionals in the field of psychiatric care. In France Bowlby met up with local experts and concluded that the

> most interesting work … going on in Paris is that by Madame Roudinesco,[4] a child psychiatrist who is also training to be an analyst. She and her psychologist are doing some systematic work in a residential nursery which is attached to the hospital … They get … mostly neglected children from the streets … From a research point of view the chief snag about their work is that they have very little information about the experiences which the children have had before they get to the residential nursery. (Bowlby in a letter to Noel Hunnybun,[5] January 26, 1950; AMWL: PP/BOW/B.1/11)

What catches the eye, of course, is Bowlby's interest in the history of the abandoned children's deprivation. In the same letter Bowlby expressed the "hope that the psychologist, who is a youngish girl named Mademoiselle Appelle [sic], will be able to come over to the Tavistock after Easter to discuss her work with our people" (Bowlby in a letter to Noel Hunnybun, January 26, 1950; AMWL: PP/BOW/B.1/11). Whether Appell's intended trip in 1950 was realized is unclear, she did however visit all four of the CIBA symposia organized by Bowlby between 1959 and 1965 and read a paper in 1963 (see Foss, 1961, 1963, 1965, 1969; for more details about the CIBA symposia, see Chapter 4).

The French connection is different from many of the others, because it led to collaboration and co-authored publications. In the years following their first encounter, Bowlby would cooperate closely with both Roudinesco and Appell (see Chapter 3). In several papers (Bowlby and Robertson, 1952; David, Nicolas and Roudinesco, 1952; Rosenbluth, Bowlby, and Roudinesco, 1950) on the responses of young children to separation from their mother, the work "done conjointly by the two teams" (Bowlby and Robertson, 1952, p. 131) from France and the UK were combined. Apart from these papers, Roudinesco and Appell made a film that may well have been an inspiration to James Robertson. In *Maternal Deprivation in Young Children* (Appell and Aubrey, 1951) they report of a study of institutionalized children (aged 12 to 30 months) and their impaired capacity to relate with others, which was supposedly associated with the length of deprivation of maternal care.

Also of much interest is Bowlby's five week stay in the US in March and April of 1950, where he visited people like Arnold Gesell, Milton Senn, David Levy, Margaret Ribble, Lauretta Bender, René Spitz, and "Bill" Goldfarb. In a letter to his wife Ursula, he discussed his schedule:

> As a result of my days [sic] activities I've made a huge number of appointments. On the whole I've been lucky in finding people available. Tomorrow, I'm busy morning [and] afternoon [and] in the evening have dinner with the Goldfarbs … Monday I'm busy all day [and] dine with Spitz … This means I get off to a flying start [and] don't waste time at the beginning which I'm pleased about. (Bowlby in a letter to Ursula, March 10, 1950; AMWL: PP/BOW/B.1/12)

After meeting with them both, Bowlby was particularly impressed by the work of Goldfarb and wrote about his discussions with him:

> All goes exceedingly well here – to the point where time for letter writing is hard to come by. Saturday was busy [and] fruitful, especially coffee with Goldfarb [and] his wife. I [wi]ll be writing a full description of this to Noel [Hunnybun] so will only tell you now that he is a most attractive young man of [thirty-five], American born [and] not the least Jewish, he has been doing no research for [four] years but has now nearly completed his medical studies. He dines with me tomorrow night [and] the possibility of him coming to the Tavi[stock Clinic] for a year will be discussed. That would be a great acquisition. (Bowlby in a letter to Ursula, March 13, 1950; AMWL: PP/BOW/B.1/12)

After his meetings with Goldfarb, Bowlby indeed reported to Noel Hunnybun about Goldfarb's work:

> Goldfarb is the real bright spot here, though for the past four years he has been in 'retirement' studying medicine. He is a delightful young man of 35, modest, sensitive and intelligent ... His work is not widely known, but is highly regarded in discriminating quarters. Personally he seems to be liked and respected. His studies seem to have been carried out between 1940–1946 off his own bat, and in his spare time ... He has done nothing for the past four years, though he has a great deal of interesting material ... still unpublished. I raised with him the possibility of his coming to the Tavi[stock Clinic] for 12 months ... to write his stuff up into a coherent monograph. He was greatly attracted by the idea and is thinking it over seriously. October 1951 is the earliest he could make as he has to complete a medical internship. He wants to become a psychiatrist and is already training in psycho-analysis. Though it is impossible to judge his ultimate ceiling, there is no doubt about his quality. (Bowlby in a letter to Noel Hunnybun, March 19, 1950; AMWL: PP/BOW/B.1/12)

In a staff meeting on May 11, after Bowlby had returned to England, he would add that Goldfarb would "get a senior job there [at Columbia University] ... because I think there is little doubt that he is pretty well the best chap they have got" (Travelogue given by Bowlby, May 11, 1950; AMWL: PP/BOW/F.1/1). Goldfarb's move to the Tavistock Clinic was never realized.

Although the letters discussed above give much factual information about Bowlby's travels, they contain little or no information about the views of people he encountered and foreshadow very little about his subsequent insights. Presumably, Bowlby had no time in his busy schedule to digest the information he gathered and postponed the analysis of it. Soon, however, his travels and research led to the publication of his monograph *Maternal Care and Mental Health* (Bowlby, 1951, 1952), in which he discussed the state of the art and the most recent advances in studies on deprivation. He discussed the work of Bakwin, Goldfarb, and Spitz under the heading of "direct" studies on evidence of effects of deprivation in which observations are made in institutions and in foster homes. Bowlby's own early study of 44 thieves and the work of Lowrey and Edelston were categorized as "retrospective" and "follow-up" studies. These "[r]elatively few studies taken by themselves are more than suggestive, [b]ut when all the evidence is fitted together it is seen to be remarkably consistent," Bowlby (1952, p. 46) argued. And he reached the conclusion that:

> the evidence is now such that it leaves no room for doubt regarding the general propositions – that the prolonged deprivation of the young child of maternal care may have grave and far-reaching effects on his character and so on the whole of his future life. (Bowlby, 1952, p. 46)

Bowlby's report was immediately and very favourably discussed by the editors of *The Lancet* (Editorial, 1951a). The editors considered his report "extremely impressive" (p. 1165) and summarized Bowlby's discussion of the findings by Bakwin, Goldfarb, Spitz, and others. They concurred with Bowlby that the evidence in favor of the damaging effects of mother–child separations was remarkably consistent and impressive. Quoting Bowlby's words that "knowledge of truth is always partial, and that to await certainty is to await eternity," they concluded that "in this case, to await certainty may well be to await a spreading of our present social sickness until it is beyond all cure" (p. 1166). The editors of the *British Medical Journal* followed suit and praised the "remarkably interesting and valuable report" (Editorial, 1951b, p. 1373). They, too, fully accepted Bowlby's findings and conclusions, and remarked that

> happily in children's wards and children's hospitals there is now a tendency to allow daily visiting. Admittedly this presents great difficulties to the nurses, but even the small amount of carefully controlled work which Bowlby is able to report on this limited aspect of the subject shows how worthwhile the extra trouble is. (Editorial, 1951b, p. 1374)

The reception of Bowlby's monograph in the medical journals at the time was very positive and the report exerted tremendous influence, but Bowlby's views also raised a number of questions. Winnicott (1989; see also Smuts, 1977b), for example, criticized *Maternal Care and Mental Health* because it lacked a discussion of how maternal care influences the child and what psychological processes play a role. According to Winnicott (1989), "there is a poverty of treatment in [Bowlby's] theoretical chapter ... It should be pointed out that there are very complex internal factors [at work] that cannot be dealt with in a book like this at all" (p. 425). Bowlby himself could not yet answer these questions either: "I didn't know, and I don't think anyone else knew" (Smuts, 1977b). In subsequent work, it was Bowlby's goal to get a grasp of the underlying processes. Soon afterwards, he reflected on the WHO report:

> It became clear that this hypothesis is well supported by evidence and the team is now planning to concentrate on understanding the psychological processes which lead to the grave personality disturbances – severe anxiety conditions and psychopathic personality – which we now know sometimes follow experiences of separation. (Bowlby, 1952, p. 82)

How Bowlby tackled the problem of explaining the phenomena observed will be discussed in Chapter 4.

Concluding Remarks

Although Bowlby had formed some exploratory ideas about the consequences of separation and deprivation of maternal care before World War II (as described in Chapter 1), his venture for the WHO to sum up the state of the art regarding mental health problems of homeless children was highly influential; not only for his own intellectual development, but for the field of psychology as a whole. In an interview Bowlby testified of the importance of his search for evidence supporting the ill-effects of deprivation:

> [T]hose five months I worked for World Health were very crucial ones for me, because first of all, I got to know a lot of people, secondly, I had a chance to read up the literature which I had not been able to do before and thirdly, to put my ideas together on paper. (Senn, 1977a, p. 18)

So, his assignment with the WHO gave him the chance to absorb the field and brought him in contact with leading researchers in the field of psychology and psychiatry. In this chapter, I have related how Bowlby met with René Spitz and William Goldfarb in the US, and with Jenny Roudinesco and Geneviève Appell in France. The discussions with these people confirmed Bowlby's pre-war ideas on separation and encouraged him to continue his search for evidence supporting his views on the mother–child relation.

Although Bowlby's report reaped great success after its publication, it was also controversial – certainly in psychoanalytic circles. In later years, Bowlby's ideas were heavily critiqued by Michael Rutter

(1972a, 1972b, 1979). Rutter stressed the importance of Bowlby's work done in the early 1950s, as it "stimulated a wealth of research and led to a reconsideration of the care provided for children being reared in institutions" (Rutter, 1972a, p. 120) and stated that "the concept of 'maternal deprivation' has undoubtedly been useful in focusing attention on the sometimes grave consequences of deficient or disturbed care in early life" (p. 128), but he also argued that "the term … has served its purpose and should now be abandoned" (p. 128). Rutter's main argument is that the experiences included under the term "maternal deprivation" are too heterogeneous and that the effects vary too much from child to child. That may well be true, but Bowlby's work for the WHO remains a milestone in developmental psychology and was also important for the development of his ideas on the consequences of early deprivation of maternal care. Much later, Bowlby himself would say that he had been greatly influenced by the work on maternal deprivation, because it resulted in him focusing more on separation and institutionalization (Senn, 1977a). Indeed separation had become a major theme in Bowlby's life and work and raised him for the next question: what is this bond that creates so much distress when ruptured.

Notes

1 Recent empirical studies (e.g., Rusby and Tasker, 2008, 2009) have shown long-term effects on adults' attachment styles and mental health due to temporary childhood separation by evacuation.

2 Detailed and unbroken observation meant that everyone in the nursery had to observe the children, even the boilerman. This is how Robertson, in his assigned job as conscientious objector, learned to observe (see Chapter 3).

3 A search in the Web of Science® shows that Spitz's (1945) paper alone has more citations than the other studies discussed here combined (Van der Horst, 2008).

4 "Madame Roudinesco" was born in 1903 as Jenny Weiss and married Romanian born Alexander Roudinesco in 1928. After a divorce from her first husband, she remarried Pierre Aubry in 1953. She is primarily known under the surname of her second husband – as Jenny Aubry.

5 Noel Hunnybun was a senior social worker at the Tavistock Clinic.

3
Working with James Robertson: The Importance of Observation

Research Work at the Tavistock in Post-War Years

Let us take a small step back in time from the WHO report and the issues of separation described in the previous chapter, and reflect on the resumption of Bowlby's work directly after World War II. Although the war could be seen as a blatant interruption of Bowlby's career that had just come to full steam – he had become a full member of the British Psycho-Analytical Society, had published his first scientific papers (e.g., Bowlby, 1938, 1939a, 1939b, 1939c, 1940a), and had developed a basic idea that he wanted to pursue in research – it might just as well be argued that the army years actually supplied him with several valuable assets. First of all – although Bowlby had read experimental psychology in Cambridge, was a doctoral student under Cyril Burt, and thus had a grounding in statistics and experimental design (Van Dijken, 1998) – in the army he received what he regarded as "a postgraduate education in psychology and research method" (Bowlby, 1981a, p. 3) or "the equivalent of … a Ph.D. thesis under Eric Trist's supervision" (Senn, 1977a, p. 9). This experience is clearly reflected in Bowlby's (1944, 1946) paper on 44 juvenile thieves

John Bowlby – From Psychoanalysis to Ethology: Unraveling the Roots of Attachment Theory, First Edition. Frank C. P. van der Horst.

(see Chapter 1) – a paper he had "already on the stocks" (Bowlby, Figlio, and Young, 1986, p. 39) before the war, but that he rewrote "with some statistical advice from people in the army" (Bowlby, Figlio, and Young, 1986, p. 39). So for the purpose of doing scientific research Bowlby was far better equipped than most of his psychoanalytic colleagues (Rudnytsky, 1997).

But there was another very important advantage of Bowlby's army experiences: he worked closely with many key figures in the psychiatric community of the time as a team on the War Officer Selection Board. For example, Bowlby made the acquaintance of Jack Rees, who not only was a consulting army psychiatrist, but was Medical Director of the Tavistock Clinic as well. Thus Bowlby became part of an "invisible college" consisting "of men from many hitherto scattered walks in psychiatry and psychology who met and became firm friends under the unifying and cementing influence of J. R. [Jack Rees]" (Dicks, 1970, p. 107). When Bowlby was asked to join the War Officer Selection Board – where Ronald Hargreaves was Command psychiatrist – he also worked with Wilfred Bion, Jock Sutherland, and Eric Trist. Earlier I described how these "eclectics" thought along similar lines as did Bowlby with regard to the primary needs of children and the role of real-life events in children's psychological development (see Chapter 1). So there was theoretical affinity and mutual support, but these contacts also had a more practical side to it for Bowlby: after the war he became involved in the reorganisation of the Tavistock Clinic called *Operation Phoenix* (Van Dijken, 1998). This eventually resulted in Bowlby's appointment at the "Tavi." Or to state it in Bowlby's own words:

> We were a group for which the Tavistock acted as kind of anchor so the notion was that some of the pre-war Tavistock people, together with some of the rest of us who were not Tavistock but who were in the party, should develop something or other as a post-war enterprise around the Tavistock. (Senn, 1977a, p. 9)

In January 1946, as a result of this reorganization or "post-war enterprise," Bowlby joined the staff of the Tavistock Clinic, where he would spend the remainder of his professional career. He was appointed head of the new Children's Department – which he immediately renamed to Department of Children and Parents – and in July 1947 he was elected deputy director to Sutherland. From the start of his work at the "Tavi," Bowlby was mainly concerned with three different sections: "first… to develop clinical services, second to develop training, and… third to develop research" (Bowlby, Figlio, and Young, 1986, p. 40). In the first few years he was fully occupied with setting up the clinical services and the training facilities. But, in line with senior analyst John Rickman's ideas, the Tavistock doctrine at that time was that there should be "no therapy without research; and no research without therapy" (Dicks, 1970, p. 142) – a creed that Bowlby fully supported in thought, word, and deed (Van Dijken, 1998).

As mentioned earlier, the Kleinian influence on clinical practice at the Children's Department after the war was omnipresent, so much that Bowlby sighed that he was "a stranger in his own department." For this reason, he wanted to set up a research unit of his own, one that was in no way connected to the clinical work at the department. Although Bowlby personally supported Richman's view that research and therapy should mutually enrich each other, he realized that in practice they were miles apart and required different mindsets. The work of clinicians and that of researchers almost literally formed "two different worlds [with] different frame[s] of reference … each point of view is appropriate within its own world, and is totally inappropriate in the other world" (Smuts, 1977b, pp. 7–8).

So, in 1948 Bowlby sought research support and obtained his first small grant from the Sir Halley Stewart Trust to empirically study the effects of early separation and deprivation. For this research, Bowlby "wanted to engage a psychiatric social worker" (Senn, 1977a, p. 15) and he hired James Robertson to do "observations of young children who were hospitalized, institutionalized, or otherwise separated from their parents" (Bretherton, 1991, p. 14). In subsequent years, the likes of Rudolf Schaffer (as an undergraduate intern) and Christoph Heinicke would strengthen Bowlby's research team. And in 1950 a Canadian psychologist by the name of Mary Ainsworth applied for a job at the research lab. From the start Bowlby and Ainsworth "liked each other! [They] both liked the same researchers and clinicians who were working on similar issues at the time, and … found [they] were thinking along the same lines" (Ainsworth and Marvin, 1995). As it happened, Ainsworth's work was to become very influential for Bowlby and attachment theory (see Chapter 6).

With his research team in place as the Separation Research Unit, Bowlby was ready to engage himself in observation of the consequences of separation from the mother – because "apart from institutional observations, made for instance by Spitz and Anna Freud, there was a great dearth of actual first-hand data on how young children behaved when they were separated from the mother" (Senn, 1977b, p. 11). But before turning to a presentation of the first results of this undertaking, I will describe how James Robertson – who was first and foremost in making direct observations of this kind – developed an interest in separation from his own biography.

James Robertson's Background and Interest in Separation

The eldest of five children, James Robertson was born in a poor working-class Scottish family in Rutherglen, near Glasgow, in 1911. He grew up in a family where children were cuddled, picked up, comforted and protected whenever the need. As a result, Robertson knew "that young children needed their mothers or someone else who loved them, and [was] sensitive to the pain that separation could cause" (Robertson and Robertson, 1989, p. xiii). Poverty impelled Robertson to support the closely-knit family and from age 14 to 28 he worked as a factory worker at the Glasgow steelworks (Karen, 1994; Senn, 1977b). He read voraciously at night and attended various part-time Glasgow University Extension Courses on literature, history, economics, and philosophy. In 1939, he spent a year at Fircroft College for the Higher Education of Working Men in Birmingham, studying the humanities. When World War II broke out, Robertson – a Quaker since his late teens – registered as a conscientious objector and moved to London to fulfill an alternative civilian service.

In London, Robertson helped families in neighborhoods that were heavily bombed and participated in the evacuation of children to remote parts of Britain – something that disturbed him quite severely (Karen, 1994) as he was "worried and perplexed by the distress of the little ones" (Senn, 1977b, p. 4). Soon thereafter, in 1941, he started working at Anna Freud's Hampstead Wartime Nurseries, together with his wife Joyce. She was a student worker whose task was to care for the infants that had lost family life due to the bombing of London and he had "to organize the maintenance and fire-watching services" (Robertson and Robertson, 1989, p. xiii; see also Senn, 1977b).

Interestingly, Anna Freud required that all staff members, no matter what their training or background, report their observations about the children's behavior on cards that were later used in weekly group discussions. While making observations and during the weekly sessions Robertson obtained an "impeccable training in naturalistic observation" (Bretherton, 1992).

According to the Robertsons, "the teaching [they] got from Anna Freud on the psychological development of young children fell on fertile soil" (Robertson and Robertson, 1989, p. xiii). James subsequently qualified as psychiatric social worker at the London School of Economics in 1947 and with support from Anna Freud started training in psychoanalysis. His move to the Tavistock Clinic in 1948 seemed only "a logical step" (Robertson and Robertson, 1989, p. xiv). In essence, then, James Robertson was a self-made man from the poor working class who completed his education in his late thirties. It can be surmised that he felt grateful to Anna Freud for providing him with the opportunity and stimulation to develop himself academically. At the same time, it would come as no surprise if he felt ill at ease at times in the class-conscious British medical world of the 1950s and 1960s.

Obviously, Bowlby appointed Robertson because the latter was an experienced observer and "had got a lot of experience with problems [Bowlby] was interested in and he also seemed ... to have other great merits" (Senn, 1977a, p. 15). It is important to note, however, that Robertson was extensively trained in child observation by Anna Freud herself and had acquired an orthodox Freudian psychoanalytic background. He was and remained loyal to Anna Freud and to Freudian psychoanalytic ideas that Bowlby did not share. Bowlby himself characterized his relationship with Anna Freud as "rather strange because in all matters practical ... we were in complete agreement, and all the work on separation she valued very highly. But when we came to talking theory, she had no use for my ideas at all" (Hunter, 1991, p. 170). In itself, such differences of opinion were not unusual. For example, Heinicke – a leading expert in the field of mother–child separations and a colleague of Bowlby, Robertson, and Anna Freud at the time – pointed out that his own theoretical interpretation of empirical data (Heinicke, 1956; Heinicke and Westheimer, 1966; see later in the chapter) was different from Bowlby's too. Many years later, Heinicke stressed the fact that, in a time of new and emerging developmental and clinical ideas, there was general consensus on the empirical findings, but difference in interpretation of the results. Bowlby, although he did not fully agree with Heinicke's and Westheimer's interpretation, very much supported their efforts, agreeing that providing systematic reliable observations was all-important (Heinicke, personal communication, September 15 and 19, 2008). Because Robertson shared Anna Freud's views, the earlier description of Bowlby's and Freud's views may well have been an apt description of the relationship between Bowlby and Robertson as well: agreement as to practical matters but disagreement as to their interpretation. Be that as it may, despite their different social background – working-class versus upper-middle-class – and different (psychoanalytic) viewpoints, the cooperation between Robertson and Bowlby would be highly successful and the first fruits of their work started to appear in the early 1950s (e.g., Bowlby, 1953; Bowlby, 1952; Bowlby and Robertson, 1952; Robertson, 1953; Robertson and Bowlby, 1952). It was only later that their theoretical disagreements led to personal tensions (Van der Horst and Van der Veer, 2009b; see later in the chapter).

The French Connection

In the previous chapter I have related the import of the WHO report: its publications had far reaching effects on Bowlby's career. For example, as a result, Ronald Hargreaves used his influence to get financial support for Bowlby as he regarded Bowlby's separation research highly (Van Dijken, 1998). In his position as the chairman of a review committee at the International Children's Centre, Hargreaves assigned both Bowlby in the UK and Jenny Roudinesco in France a research grant to study "the repercussions of separations from the mother among young children" (Roudinesco, David, and Nicolas, 1952, p. 66). This led the two teams to work in very close association with each other. Of course, Bowlby had visited Roudinesco's department in Paris in 1950 and had hoped for subsequent cooperation (see Chapter 2). The collaboration started fairly soon after Bowlby's visit because, according to both teams, it was of the utmost importance to gather "direct observations of children undergoing separation [as] it will become possible to understand how troubles begin and persist and to discover the effect of relevant variables"

(Roudinesco, David, and Nicolas, 1952, pp. 66–67). The systematic observations were only "at a descriptive behavioral level … [because] both teams have decided that it would be premature to expect [a deeper] understanding until we have more knowledge of how these children respond behaviorally" (Roudinesco, David, and Nicolas, 1952, p. 67). Therefore, by combining the results of Bowlby's team with those of Roudinesco and her colleagues, an attempt was made "to obtain reliable data on the development of these clinical picture and the sequences of the child's response" (Roudinesco, David, and Nicolas, 1952, p. 67). The results were published in two papers, which I shall describe in some more detail here.

In the first contribution, the French team summarised the most common reactions of children who had "temporarily been entrusted by the parents to the care of a public assistance body" (Roudinesco, David, and Nicolas, 1952, p. 67). The authors differentiated three types of response: (1) intense distress; (2) easy adjustment; and (3) partial or precarious adjustment. The children in the first category are depicted as children who "cry, moan or scream … and [who] completely surrender to their distress" (p. 68). Some of the children in this group retained the same behavior during their whole stay, others after being "inconsolable in the beginning … adjusted [them] selves progressively," i.e., the whining and whinging stopped, though changes in the nursing staff could have the effect of distress yet again. The second group of "easy adjusters" consisted of children who "do not appear to be at all affected by the change of existence brought about by their arrival in the reception ward," but "frequently they could not maintain the initial apparently carefree behavior" (p. 69). The authors emphasized that the children "all come to a point where they suddenly break down and show overt distress" (p. 69). The greatest and most diverse set comprised those children who "show signs in their behavior which are indicative of a precarious adjustment to the new environment" (p. 70). The authors describe how some of the children is this group have a lack of interest in adults, while others show a clear demand for them – for these children "the door assumes a character of great importance" (p. 72). According to the French team, there are other signs of maladjustment in this group: for example, children refuse to eat or refuse to walk, and some develop a dislike of other children. In all, the observations of children in the third category are "infinitely varied" (p. 76), but a change in behavior seems to be almost universal. Apart from the fact that all the children seem to show distress at some point during their stay, there are no general conclusions to be drawn from these descriptions; but the authors express the hope that "such a developmental study … enables us to see and understand the mechanisms that the child brings into action in response to separation" (p. 76). This is something that also echoed in much of Bowlby's work at the time: his search for explanations and the underlying mechanisms of the children's behavior. In this respect the second paper by the two teams is of great interest.

As a follow-up of the study by Roudinesco and her colleagues, Robertson and Bowlby (1952) published the results of Robertson's observations as part two of the French-Anglo cooperation. In a highly influential paper on responses of young children to separation from the mother, they described a typical sequence of three phases in response to separation from the mother: protest, despair, and denial.[1]

Identification of Typical Responses to Separation: Protest, Despair, Denial

When Robertson began working at the Tavistock Clinic in February 1948, his task was to go to "places where young children were separated from the mother and to bring back to Dr. Bowlby and his colleagues … [his] first-hand observations on their behavior" (Senn, 1977b, p. 11). Robertson's observations were part of Bowlby's so-called 'sanatorium study', a project designed to follow up young children of one to three years old who had been admitted to a (fever) hospital or a residential nursery (Karen, 1994). Right after starting his observations, Robertson "got the most enormous blow of [his] life" (Senn, 1977b, p. 12). From the beginning, it was quite obvious to him that the children he observed in paediatric wards were distressed, but that doctors and nurses were not willing to see the deteriorating emotional state of their young patients (Robertson and Robertson, 1989). Robertson was shocked by the fact that "the young children who shouted and screamed were regarded as atypical until they became settled, and uncomplaining" (Senn, 1977b, pp. 13–14). He could not understand why the hospital staff was unable or unwilling to see the things he clearly saw (Robertson and Robertson, 1989, p. 19). After observing children in hospital for several years, he identified "certain sequences of response which appear to be fairly typical of children who lose the care of their mothers at about the age of 18–24 months and who are cared for in an 'impersonal' environment" (Robertson and Bowlby, 1952, p. 131).

In their publication, Robertson and Bowlby (1952) noted for the first time how the child "commonly progresses through three phases of emotional response" (p. 132). In the first phase of protest, the anxious child has a strong need for his mother and cries in the expectation that she will respond. The child is confused and frightened by the unfamiliar surroundings and "seeks to recapture her by the full exercise of his limited resources" (Robertson and Bowlby, 1952, p. 132). This phase is gradually succeeded by the second phase of despair, characterized by an increasing hopelessness of the child. He is no longer actively seeking his mother and his crying is "monotonous and intermittent" (p. 132). Here, Robertson and Bowlby pointed to the fact that this quiet stage is "erroneously presumed to indicate a diminution of distress" (p. 132) by nurses and pediatricians. In the third and last phase of denial, the child begins to show more interest in the surroundings, which is "welcomed by the staff as a sign of recovery" (p. 132), but according to Robertson and Bowlby this apparent recovery was only a way of coping for the child. Given the circumstances – the mother is no longer available – children try to make the best of the situation, because they simply cannot tolerate the intense feelings of distress they experienced.

In retrospect, Robertson felt that, although his colleagues at the Tavistock Clinic were interested in his reports, he was the only who realized their true import, because he was the one who was "confronted daily by the inhumanity of the paediatric situation" (Robertson and Robertson, 1989, p. 13). He urgently felt he had to "humanize paediatrics" (p. 13) and doubted the possibility of finding "the correct words with which to describe objectively… a young patient in distress" (p. 23). For this reason, Robertson eventually decided to make a film record of a young child throughout a short stay in hospital, which resulted in *A Two-year-old Goes to Hospital.*

A Picture is Worth a Thousand Words

Both in the UK and in the US the field of psychology was stirred in a similar way. As we have seen, René Spitz (1947) shook the ground of psychologists in the US with his film *Grief: A Peril in Infancy* (see Chapter 2). In the UK, Robertson, after observing children pining away in hospital wards for a couple of years, "had become [so] absolutely exasperated" with the endless resistance he met during presentations to psychoanalytic, paediatric, and psychiatric audiences, that he told Bowlby he was going "to make a film to show them" (Senn, 1977a, p. 21). It was Bowlby who insisted on a careful planning of the film to ensure no one would later be able to accuse Robertson of a biased presentation: among other things, the child in the film was randomly selected – they just "st[u]ck the pin in the waiting list" (Senn, 1977b, pp. 17–18) – and a clock was always visible to show time sampling took place. In August 1952, with minimal training, minimal funds, and without artificial light, Robertson shot a deeply moving film with his handheld Bell and Howell 16 mm cine-camera: *A Two-year-old Goes to Hospital* (Robertson, 1952) – black-and-white and silent, but with spoken commentary. The protagonist of the film is Laura, an unusually composed toddler[2], who leaves home for a period of nine days to be admitted at Central Middlesex Hospital for the operation of an umbilical hernia. During that stay, she changes from a ravishing little girl to a silent and unresponsive one. Robertson's film was first shown at the Section of Paediatrics of the Royal Society of Medicine on November 28, 1952, before a large audience of doctors and nurses. The accounts of that meeting differ somewhat in their description of the way the film was received by the audience. The proceedings of the meeting (Bowlby and Robertson, 1952) just related that Bowlby and Robertson introduced the film, provided a synopsis of the film, and then added that the president of the paediatric section, Winnicott, spoke of a "highly successful first effort" that dealt with "a real problem." Winnicott continued that he himself had seen "irreversible change" as a result of "separation of small children from their mothers" and argued that "every time a child is to be taken into hospital there ought to be a careful weighing up of the value on the physical side against the danger on the psychiatric side" (Bowlby and Robertson, 1952, p. 427). Both the editors of the *British Medical Journal* and *The Lancet* favorably discussed the meeting in their issues of December 6. The editors of the *British Medical Journal* agreed that "the 2-year-old girl depicted was unhappy and that possibly her unhappiness might have been prevented" (Editorial, 1952a, p. 1249). They mentioned that this was in line with the findings in Bowlby's (1951, 1952) report and that it would be a great risk to continue to neglect these matters. The editors believed that more "friendliness and consideration" would do the children much good, but added that "the part the mother should play, and how often parents should visit, may be more controversial subjects" (Editorial, 1952a, p. 1250). The editors of *The Lancet* were equally positive but more detailed in their rendering of the reactions to the film by the audience (Editorial, 1952b). They stated that at first the audience frankly refused to admit the child was distressed at all and those who accepted that Laura was distressed were reluctant to believe it might cause long-term or even permanent emotional disturbances. These discussants argued one would need to film emotional upsets at home and hospital stays without an operation as a control. Robertson and Bowlby are said to have agreed that more research was needed but remained convinced that the child was upset, that such operations at this age should be avoided if possible, and that the isolation and lack of physical comfort in hospitals were positively bad.

Interestingly, these contemporary accounts were rather more neutral than Robertson's memory of the meeting. Robertson remembered that when "Dr. Bowlby and I presented the film … it was as if we had dropped a bomb in the hall" and that "the film encountered much resistance and rejection." Various speakers said hotly that he had filmed "an atypical child of atypical parents in an atypical ward" (Robertson and Robertson, 1989, p. 44; Senn, 1977b, p. 19).[3] The speakers supposedly also said that Robertson "had slandered paediatrics" and that the film should be withdrawn. We have no way to decide which account of the meeting is most correct, but according to Dr. Mary Lindsay (personal communication, April 7, 2008), one of the principal persons in the ensuing debate, "the film had a very hostile reception" and "the editor toned down the anger in the proceedings of the meeting." Indeed, it is very likely that the highly negative audience reactions were not reported in the minutes. The fact of the matter is that Bowlby and Robertson eventually decided to temporarily "withhold [the film] from general release" (Robertson and Robertson, 1989, p. 45) due to the massive resistance among the medical staff. For the moment it was decided that the film would only be shown to professionals, and only when either Robertson or Bowlby was present.

It should be said that the value of films as an argument in *scientific* debates is limited (that is not to say that the *emotional* effect on the viewer is not very strong). Strictly speaking, they can only show that a certain phenomenon may take place, not that it generally takes place, and under which specific circumstances. Of course, *A Two-year-old Goes to Hospital* demonstrated what had already been reported by others (e.g., Spitz, 1945, 1947; see Chapter 2). But Robertson's opponents took the film as evidence on its own, without the research context, and thus could always argue that Laura, her parents, or the hospital were somehow exceptional and that other children in (other) hospitals were perfectly fine. At any rate, they could argue with some justification that it remained far from proven that her distress was caused by the separation *per se* (see Bowlby, 1958b, 1958c; Edelston, 1955, 1958; Howells, 1958; Howells and Layng, 1955; Kräupl Taylor, 1958; Librach, 1958). Over the years, the opponents of flexible visiting in hospitals would exploit these possibilities to the utmost, with sometimes vehement debates as a result (see Herzog, 1958a, 1958b; Kidd, 1958; Robertson, 1958a, 1958b; Stephen and Whatley, 1958a, 1958b). Robertson and Bowlby's adversaries would go to great lengths to disprove them: for example child psychiatrist Fred Stone was offered research money to "prove this Bowlby stuff to be nonsense" (Hinde, 1982a, p. 60; see also Smuts, 1977a, p. 9). Such reservations about the methodological merits of films notwithstanding, Robertson campaigned for the cause of better care of children in hospital throughout the 1950s and 1960s, showing his film to many audiences, and eventually managed to persuade many people that something needed be done. Dr. Lindsay remembers how Dr. Dermot MacCarthy, who was a key figure in the debate on visiting in hospital described above, became converted:

> Dr. MacCarthy went to this meeting [the first showing of *A Two-year-old Goes to Hospital*] with his Ward Sister. Coming back in the car afterwards he went on at some length on how wrong Robertson was. However, Sister Morris said that Mr. Robertson was quite right and that these babies and young children did need their mothers; and that she used to let them stay in the ward with their children when he was not there. Dr. MacCarthy was startled by this idea, but he had great respect for Sister Morris. The next day he found that he could not walk down his children's ward without seeing Laura and her brothers and sisters. From then on, the mothers of children under five in his wards at Amersham and Aylesbury were routinely asked if they wanted to stay in the hospital with their children; most of them did, and visiting became unrestricted. (Mary Lindsay, personal communication, April 7, 2008; see also Brandon *et al.*, 2009)

A few years later, Robertson (1958c) followed up with a contrasting film: *Going to Hospital with Mother*. This time 20-months-old toddler Sally is admitted to Amersham General Hospital to be operated on an umbilical hernia, but she is admitted together with her mother. According to Robertson the film showed "the simplicity of bringing mothers into residence ... that the young patients are kept secure and in good spirits, and that ... the resident mothers continue with the bodily care through which their children experience love and security" (Senn, 1977b, pp. 24–25). Indeed, the film clearly pictured how Sally managed the hospital stay and operation without much anxiety. With this film Robertson showed "that it is the presence or absence of a mother that matters to a child of this age," as "at no time does Sally show any of the fretfulness or withdrawal commonly seen in unaccompanied young patients" (Robertson and Robertson, 1989, p. 56) such as Laura. In a discussion of the film, the editors of the influential medical journal *The Lancet* stated that "even the most sceptical audience could hardly fail to be impressed by this second film" (Editorial, 1958, p. 1112).

In later years, the Robertsons would add to these two seminal films, several documentaries regarding children in residential and foster care. In an interview Robertson once stated that "the position ... was that all the studies that had previously been published on early separation ... had been based upon children observed in hospitals and other institutions," and here the children "in addition to loss of mother ... had been subjected to multiple caretakers and many other stresses associated with institutions" (Senn, 1977b, p. 30). So in the Robertsons' next research project, *Young children in brief separation*, they wanted "to study a series of young children whose separation from the mother was free of the additional stresses which contaminate institutional studies" (Senn, 1977b, p. 31) in order to show that – in line with Anna Freud's (Burlingham and Freud, 1942, 1944) views – the effect of separation from the mother would be less profound if good substitute care was available to the child during the separation. Beginning in 1964, the Robertsons set up this new project to try and identify the variables that influence the behavior of young children during separation. For the project, Robertson filmed five children (aged 17 to 29 months) during separation from their mother, who was having a second child for which, at the time, a prolonged admission to hospital was deemed necessary. In four cases (Kate, Jane, Thomas, and Lucy), Joyce Robertson acted as a foster mother and provided the children with optimum substitute care. In the case of John this support was not available and he was sent to a residential nursery. The results of the study were that the children who were in foster care showed far less distress than did John. The film *John*, in particular, had quite an impact on the medical profession; the editors of *The Lancet* stated that the film was "a landmark … What *A Two-Year-Old* … did for paediatrics, *John* will probably do for residential care" (Editorial, 1970, p. 47). The Robertsons' interpretation of their data was that the responses shown by the fostered children were qualitatively different from those of the institutionalized children (Robertson and Robertson, 1971).

Divergence of Opinions Between Robertson and Bowlby

Following the description of the work by Robertson and Bowlby, it seems obvious that the collaboration between the two men was close and harmonious. Indeed, they shared the same views on war-time evacuations of young children – Robertson as a conscientious objector working in wartime London; Bowlby as a psychiatrist who strongly dismissed the practice in a letter to the *British Medical Journal* (Bowlby, Miller, and Winnicott, 1939; see Chapter 2). Furthermore, both men became deeply involved in the campaign to better the fate of young children in hospital. Although there are different views on the originality and decisiveness of their views (Lindsay, 2009; Robertson and McGily, 2009; Van der Horst and Van der Veer, 2009a, 2009c), their early collaboration resulted in many publications on the effects of separation from the mother, in films to support these views, and in the truly significant formulation of a sequence of responses to separation described earlier in this chapter (the phases of protest, despair, and denial or detachment). This joint work was and still is very influential in the field of (developmental) psychology.

However, the conclusion that Bowlby and Robertson cooperated in perfect harmony and basically shared the same views is actually unwarranted (Van der Horst and Van der Veer, 2009b). The fact of the matter is that they eventually disagreed on a number of theoretical issues and that their personal relationship became quite strained.

Little is known about these differences of opinion and personal tensions, although they are occasionally mentioned. Alsop-Shields and Mohay (2001) argued that "it is not possible to determine the reason for Robertson's and Bowlby's disagreement," partly also because it is "difficult to find documentation about the controversy which split the two men" (p. 55). Karen (1994) noted that the Robertsons "resented Bowlby's appropriating or getting credit for James's ideas" (p. 86), but presented no further evidence to support such a claim. Indeed, Robertson and Bowlby never displayed their theoretical divergence in public. In his books, Bowlby took pains to credit Robertson for his theoretical and practical accomplishments (e.g., Bowlby, 1953, p. 268; Bowlby, 1960a, pp. 21–22; Bowlby, 1960b, p. 89; Bowlby, 1969/1982b, pp. xvii, 26–28). In fact, it seems to have been his major concern that the disagreements would become public and that this would play into the hands of their theoretical adversaries. In one of his letters to Robertson, Bowlby expressed this concern quite explicitly:

> I do hope that we can enter into a useful discussion together, since I am afraid that if we don't misunderstanding will multiply and perhaps become public, which would give comfort only to the various people who still oppose the kind of work we are both trying to do and the kinds of social change we are both seeking to foster. (Bowlby in a letter to Robertson, September 27, 1971; AMWL: PP/BOW/B.3/25/2)

But that was not to be: after their initial very successful collaboration, in 1960 a turning-point was reached. Bowlby (1960b) then criticized Anna Freud's ideas, stating that (1) protest, despair, and detachment are habitual responses to separation from the mother *per se*, and (2) from six months children were able to grief and mourn like adults. This difference of opinion between Bowlby and Anna Freud led to a breach with the Robertsons, who identified with Freud's position. When Bowlby's paper concerning grief and mourning was published in *The Psychoanalytic Study of the Child*, he was surprised to find three devastating comments to his paper (Freud, 1960; Schur, 1960; Spitz, 1960), totaling some 40 pages. The critics all agreed that Bowlby had misinterpreted the fundamental psychoanalytic concepts, an argument that is still echoed by some psychoanalysts today (e.g., Engel, 1971; Hanley, 1978; Kernberg, 1976; Rochlin, 1971; Roiphe, 1976; Zepf, 2006; see also Cortina and Marrone, 2004).

Anna Freud struck a rather conciliatory tone, emphasizing that her team and Bowlby's team basically agreed on the facts which had been gathered by "James Robertson … a valued and important member of both teams" (Freud, 1960, p. 53). She observed, however, that "as analysts … we do not deal with the happenings in the external world as such but with their repercussions in the mind" and that here Bowlby had completely misunderstood the psychoanalytic conceptual framework. She also surmised that young children separated from their mother would show much less or no grief when they were taken care of by a substitute mother and that Bowlby's assertion that grief upon separation was inevitable was unproven.

Schur (1960), the former physician of Sigmund Freud, almost completely ignored Bowlby's article in question but criticized several of Bowlby's previous papers for their inadequate and inappropriate use of ethological concepts. He deplored the fact that Bowlby advanced concepts that were "at complete variance with basic concepts of … psychoanalysis" (Schur, 1960, p. 63) and wondered why "Bowlby felt compelled to revamp, more or less, some of the most fundamental concepts and formulations of psychoanalysis" (Schur, 1960, p. 82).

In the third and last rejoinder, Spitz (1960) agreed with Bowlby that "loss of mother figure … is responded to by the infant with grief" (Spitz, 1960, p. 93), but he also noted a "fundamental difference between Bowlby's approach and [his]" (Spitz, 1960, p. 89). According to Spitz, Bowlby had misinterpreted his findings and had failed to see the clear "difference of developmental levels which obviously exist between infants aged six months and children between three to four years of age" (Spitz, 1960, p. 89). On a theoretical level, Spitz, like Anna Freud, blamed Bowlby for using only descriptive terms and limiting himself to the behavioral level when discussing the responses of infants. In doing so, Bowlby disregarded "the structural and dynamic viewpoints which for quite some time have been accepted as cornerstones of psychoanalytic theory" (Spitz, 1960, p. 93).

In all, the critique of Bowlby's paper by his psychoanalytic colleagues was concerned mainly with (1) his descriptive approach to the behavior of children (vs. a metapsychological description); (2) the importance he placed on the role of the environment (vs. the inner world); and (3) the undermining of the concepts (e.g., infantile narcism, oral sadism) that had been around for so long and were the foundations of psychoanalytic theory. After this controversial event, theoretical differences and personal tensions between Bowlby and the Robertsons only seem to have increased (for a full account of this dispute, see Van der Horst and Van der Veer, 2009b).

Other Contributions by the Separation Research Unit: Heinicke's "Brief Separations"

Earlier I have described how James Robertson "delivered to [Bowlby's] desk this rich seam of … Robertson data" (Robertson in a letter to Bowlby, February 7, 1972; AMWL: PP/BOW/B.3/25/2). Simultaneously, there was other important work being done by a member from Bowlby's Separation Research Unit. Christoph Heinicke (1956) carried out a study that was part of Bowlby's plan to respond with additional research to criticism of Robertson's work and that had as the major purpose "to explore the general hypothesis that more extensive separation leads to more pronounced imbalance and to more extreme ways of coping with imbalance" (p. 173). According to Heinicke,

> Bowlby came to Harvard in 1952 to recruit me in the context of having been criticized for failing to support his contention that not only institutionalization… but the effect of long separations were very detrimental. Critics at Maudsley [Hospital], and particularly [Michael] Rutter, challenged these broad generalizations and I among others experienced Bowlby's and Robertson's great concern about this. [Bowlby's] theorizing and the efforts to change hospital visiting practices were confronted. It was in this context, that the initial report of my findings… were important both in modifying Bowlby's hypotheses about the effect of all separations, but particularly in that the impact of brief separations could be empirically documented. It was found that the longer the "brief separations" the greater the impact, but my studies of reunion also showed that very likely these effects could be reversed. (Heinicke, personal communication, October 6, 2008)

Whereas Robertson had mainly been concerned with children "in a hospital setting where sickness and treatment, including being confined in a cot, provide additional disturbing experiences" (Heinicke, 1956, p. 167), Heinicke compared children in residential nurseries with children in day nurseries – in order to study "the effect of differing *degrees* of separation" (Heinicke, 1956, p. 108; original italics). Although this study – and a follow-up study by Heinicke and Westheimer (1966) – consisted of only a handful of children, at the time it was "unique for the care of the design and the amount of systematic observation" (Bowlby, 1973, p. 6). In fact, it was one of the first serious attempts to gather quantitative data instead of clinical descriptions of individual children. Heinicke observed the everyday behavior of the children on several occasions during the first 27 days of their stay. Also, Heinicke administered doll play sessions early in the children's stay and towards the end of their separation. He concluded that the children who were admitted to residential care showed more signs of distress than did the children in day nurseries: for example, these "residential children" cried more, they "were in general more desperate and direct in their expression" (Heinicke, 1956, p. 167), and they "expressed not only a greater amount but also a more *intense* form of hostility" (Heinicke, 1956, p. 169; original italics). On the basis of these observations, Heinicke concluded that it is important "to think of the parents' presence as of great importance in maintaining the balance between the two-year-old's impulses and his power to organize and control these impulses in relation to the external world" (Heinicke, 1956, p. 169). In other words, "the daily affection [of the parents]... strengthens... the child's feelings" and thus helps it to overcome "the inevitable frustrations of development" and "the negative feelings" (Heinicke, 1956, p. 172) associated with it.

Concluding Remarks: Unexplained Observations

We may conclude, then, that the evidence supporting the idea that the mother-child relationship was crucial to a healthy development of children was piling up. Taken together, the observations made in Child Guidance Clinics, during the evacuations, and in residential nurseries, the discussions surrounding visits to children in hospital, and the hospitalization studies – all of which Bowlby had summarized in his WHO report (and which were described in Chapter 2) – yielded a consistent picture that was highly relevant for the proper way to deal with young children's separations. After the war, when Bowlby set up his Separation Research Unit to collect 'systematic reliable observations', he and Robertson added to the ever growing body of evidence. Their seminal description of the three phases of protest, despair, and denial and two contrasting films on children in hospital were remarkable and received quite a lot of attention. Furthermore, the Separation Research Unit, through the work of Heinicke, showed that even "brief separations" had a strong effect on children's well-being. All of these findings pointed out that separation from the parent is traumatic and potentially harmful, that children need strong emotional ties with a grown-up, and that they should be given a chance to form a new bond with a substitute parent in case they (temporarily) lose their own parents. In sum, children need to be loved, and when they lose this love, or believe they have lost it (e.g., in the case of separations they cannot comprehend), they feel very unhappy and may develop serious mental and physical problems. A growing group of psychiatrists and physicians was aware of these findings.

In all, slowly but surely, people – in hospitals, foundling homes, nurseries, etc. – were beginning to see the effects of separation and deprivation on young children. The evidence gathered led people to believe that the physical and emotional separation from a familiar environment was detrimental to the child's well-being. These new views were supported by films such as those by Spitz and Robertson (for a full overview of films on children's hospitalization and maternal deprivation, see Mason, 1967). Their cinematic contributions were a way of conveying the message to a more general public. Unfortunately, because of the retrospective and exploratory nature of most of the reported findings, there could only be speculation about the underlying mechanisms of the distress shown. It was up to others to lead the way to a theoretical and experimental validation of the consequences of maternal deprivation – and this is where Bowlby entered the stage. Or to phrase it in Robertson's words: "Dr. Bowlby was the writer, he was the theorist who was building theory and his role was to be, as agreed between us in the Tavistock, to receive my material and to write papers" (Senn, 1977b, pp. 20–21).

Bowlby was convinced at the time that (repeated) separation experiences may seriously harm the mental health of children and that the existing literature proved his point of view. He valued empirical studies and emphasized the importance of objective observation of real-life experiences (such as those by Robertson and Heinicke). However, the findings Bowlby had gathered for his WHO report were suggestive but not conclusive. What was missing was rigorous experimental investigation and, above all, a comprehensive theoretical apparatus from which to explain the findings (see Bowlby, 1982a). For a theoretical framework for the explanation of the nature of the mother–child relationship he turned to ethology, the new science of animal behavior. I will turn to this new approach in the next chapter and will argue that Bowlby's acquaintance with it was an Archimedean point in the history of attachment theory.

Notes

1 In their first description of responses of young children to separation Robertson and Bowlby (1952) used the term denial for the third phase, but Bowlby (1960b) thought that "it gave rise to many difficulties … and is now abandoned in favour of the more purely descriptive term detachment" (pp. 90–91).

2 The controlled or composed behavior of Laura would fit perfectly into the "easy adjustment" category described by Roudinesco, David, and Nicolas (1952); see earlier in this chapter.

3 This statement strangely contradicted what Robertson wrote in a letter to *The Lancet* in 1958. There he wrote that "when the film was shown to the paediatric section of the Royal Society of Medicine in November, 1952, it seemed generally agreed that … the behavior shown was common" (Robertson, 1958a, p. 1018).

4
Bowlby's Acquaintance with Ethology: The Work of Lorenz, Tinbergen, and Hinde

First Acquaintance with Ethology

In general, historians are perhaps too eager to point to turning points in history. But there are grounds to argue that the summer of 1951 was indeed pivotal in John Bowlby's thinking. It was the year Bowlby's (1951, 1952) seminal report for the World Health Organization saw the light of day. As described in earlier chapters, Bowlby had traveled the European continent and the United States for this report, in search for the consequences of separation of children from their mother (see Chapter 2). After extensively reviewing the available data, Bowlby concluded that "prolonged deprivation of the young child of maternal care may have grave and far-reaching effects on his character and so on the whole of his future life." The problem, according to Bowlby was that

> what was missing in that monograph was how comes it that those experiences can possibly have any effects. Working for the WHO for a few months I had been totally unable to cope with that part of the problem. Some reviewers pointed out that this was a sad lack. (Senn, 1977a, p. 24)

John Bowlby – From Psychoanalysis to Ethology: Unraveling the Roots of Attachment Theory, First Edition. Frank C. P. van der Horst.

So, although the findings Bowlby had gathered were suggestive, they were far from conclusive; and neither were Robertson's observations in hospitals. In fact, what was missing were rigorous experimental investigations and, above all, a comprehensive theoretical framework from which to explain the findings. According to Bowlby, "the theory was a mess – there was no suitable theory really" (Senn, 1977a). So at that point in time Bowlby was very receptive to anything that could bring him closer to solving problem of the "unexplained observations" described in the previous chapter. Bowlby was actively seeking evidence that would allow him to build a new theory and in this regard, two events in the summer of 1951 were to be decisive for Bowlby's further career.

First, a friend, psychologist Norman Hotoph, pointed out to Bowlby that German zoologist Konrad Lorenz had worked on the principle of imprinting as a process underlying the formation of affectional bonds in the 1930s. Bowlby knew Hotoph through the group of Oxford friends that included his brother Tony and Evan Durbin. Following Hotoph's suggestion, Bowlby indeed turned to Lorenz's ideas and in later publications (e.g., Bowlby, 1957, 1960c) acknowledged a deep and pervasive interest in ethology beginning in 1951, which indeed was sparked by Lorenz's (1935, 1937) gosling work. In an interview in 1979, Bowlby ranked Lorenz's *Der Kumpan in der Umwelt des Vogels* (which he read in the greatly abbreviated English translation titled *The Companion in the Bird's World*) among the 11 works which had most influenced his thinking (AMWL: PP/BOW/A.1/7; dated October 24, 1979).

A second important event occurred during the same summer. While spending a holiday in Scotland with his family-in-law, Bowlby was fortunate to meet Julian Huxley, a friend of the Longstaff family and a very prominent British evolutionary biologist. During that summer Bowlby

> took the opportunity of asking Huxley whether he knew anything about ethology and was it any use. Well, it happened that he had done some of the early work, he knew Lorenz well, [and] he was a tremendous enthusiast… So [Bowlby] thought, okay, this is scientifically alright. (Senn, 1977a, p. 25)

So, Huxley encouraged Bowlby to go into matters of ethology in more depth and actually provided him with a proof copy of Lorenz's

(1952) yet unpublished book titled *King Solomon's Ring* for which he had written the Foreword. Huxley also mentioned Niko Tinbergen's (1951) *The Study of Instinct* to Bowlby. It was partly because of Huxley's enthusiasm that Bowlby spent most of winter 1951–1952 reading his way in ethology. He later confessed: "I spent the next six months mugging up ethology – I just read everything I could get my hands on and I stuck my neck out" (Senn, 1977a, p. 25). "From that day on," Bowlby remembered, "I was completely sold on ethology" (Smuts, 1977b).

Although Bowlby's acquaintance with ethology was rather coincidental – or to phrase it in his own words, "a bit of luck" (Senn, 1977a, p. 25) – above I have described that Bowlby had an interest in nature from a very early age (see Chapter 1). As a child he had learned to value the life in the countryside during family holidays, he became an enthusiastic bird-watcher and photographer during his years at Royal Naval College in Dartmouth, and he remained a passionate naturalist throughout his life. Maybe as a result of this life-long interest in nature, Bowlby, in one of his early publications (Durbin and Bowlby, 1939; see Chapter 1), already extensively cited studies on the social life of monkeys and apes, such as Zuckermann's (1932) study of a group of baboons in the London Zoo.

Another remarkable example of Bowlby's interest in animal behavior and ethology comes from a travelogue in which Bowlby reported on his 1950 trip to the US for the World Health Organization (WHO). In New York, Bowlby was able to consult a large part of Freud's personal library. It is important to note that this was prior to his first acquaintance with ethology in 1951, at a time when Bowlby was still a psychoanalyst, albeit of a different kind than Klein or Anna Freud.

> I came across one [of Freud's] book[s] on the development of mind by [George] Romanes which is all about animals and ethology which was carefully marked... by Freud, which rather pleased me, but I unfortunately have not yet confirmed that all the markings in this book were Freud's. That I am trying to do. But I was rather pleased. (Travelog given by Bowlby, May 11, 1950; AMWL: PP/BOW/F.1/1)

Once Bowlby had found ethology to be "scientifically alright," he cast his net wide to get answers to the "unexplained observations" of children's reactions to separation, for example from Dutch animal psychologist Adriaan Kortlandt:[1]

> We are very happy to send you our reprints. Although hitherto they have not referred to ethological work we are shaping our studies increasingly in that direction, and we shall be very glad therefore to have reprints of your own work, which we already know from many references. (Bowlby in a letter to Kortlandt, dated April 28, 1954; private archive Kortlandt)

So, in the early 1950s, Bowlby was shaping his studies increasingly in the direction of ethology, though it took Bowlby quite some effort to convince his colleagues (including Mary Ainsworth) of the value of these ideas. At that time his research team was unpersuaded by his ethological ideas in relation to the mother-infant relationship.[2] Yet, for Bowlby (1953) it was clear that "the time [wa]s already ripe for a unification of psycho-analytic concepts with those of ethology" (p. 32). Of course, Bowlby's interest in ethology was based on the fact that it seemed to provide a way of thinking about the nature and function of an affectional bond between a child and its caregiver (see Bretherton, 1991, 1992).[3]

It is clear, then, that Bowlby enthusiastically embraced ethology as a new framework for his thinking; as a theoretical apparatus to explain the retrospective evidence of Bakwin, Goldfarb, Spitz, and the observations of Robertson. But before we turn to a description of how Bowlby came to "rewrite psychoanalysis in the light of ethological principles" (Dinnage, 1979, p. 325), let us for a moment wonder about the rising discipline of ethology. What was this new science of animal behavior? How did this new approach develop? Who were its key figures? And what was its state of the art when Bowlby was first introduced to it? These questions will be the subject of the next few paragraphs.

The Rise of Ethology as a Discipline

On December 12, 1973 the Nobel Prize in Physiology or Medicine was awarded to three scientists who had devoted their academic work to the study of animal behavior. Karl von Frisch, Konrad Lorenz, and Niko Tinbergen were distinguished "for the creation of a new science – ethology, the biological study of behavior" (Hinde and Thorpe, 1973, p. 346). The word ethology, from the Greek ήθος (ethos) meaning character or custom and λόγος (logos) meaning word or description, has been traced back as far as the seventeenth century, but its current meaning as the scientific study of (animal) behavior was only attributed to it in the first quarter of the twentieth century (Jaynes, 1969). According to Lorenz (1981):

> Ethology, the comparative study of behavior, is easy to define: it is the discipline which applies to the behavior of animals and humans all those questions asked and those methodologies used as a matter of course in all the other branches of biology since Charles Darwin's time. (p. 1)

Until the beginning of the previous century animal behavior was explained by using the concept of "instinct," though there was no clear description or understanding of what that concept implied. In *On the Origin of Species*, Charles Darwin (1859) already used the term as one of the pillars of evolutionary theory: instinct was a characteristic that was influenced by natural selection just as morphology was. Instincts had to be adaptive to give the organism an advantage in its environment. After Darwin though, the analogies between animals and humans were mainly studied by (comparative) psychologists in an effort to understand the behavior and psyche of animals. It was presumed, for example by behaviorists, that the regularities found in animal behavior hold for humans as well. In their studies evolution and adaptivity to the environment were largely ignored. It was only during the 1920s that zoologists put evolution and adaptivity of instincts back on the agenda. The people responsible for this change of focus, the forerunners of ethology, were Whitman and Craig in the United States, Selous and Huxley in Britain and Heinroth in Germany (Burkhardt, 2005; Kruuk, 2003; Roëll, 2000).

Charles Otis Whitman was an American biologist who, just as many other ethologists *avant la lettre*, was fascinated by animal life and ornithology from an early age. He advocated a broad approach to biological research, including observation and experimentation. His basic assumption in interpreting behavior was that "instinct and structure are to be studied from the common standpoint of phyletic descent" (Whitman, 1899 in Roëll, 2000, p. 28). Animal habits should thus be studied in the same scientific manner that anatomy and morphology were and behavior should be seen from an evolutionary viewpoint. Whitman's influence on European ethology was mainly indirect through his student Wallace Craig, who corresponded extensively with Lorenz between 1935 and 1937 on Whitman's ideas. This new approach to the study of "instinct" made no headway in the United States in this early period though (Burkhardt, 2005; Roëll, 2000).

In Europe, the new study of instincts and animal behavior did find fertile soil. In England, naturalist Edmund Selous followed Whitman's scientific tradition of studying animals: "the habits of animals are really as scientific as their anatomies" (Selous, 1905 in Burkhardt, 2005, p. 92). Selous was praised by colleagues for his detailed observations of bird behavior. His pioneering work inspired Julian Huxley in England and Tinbergen's mentor Jan Verwey in the Netherlands to do field studies of their own (Roëll, 2000). In Germany, Oskar Heinroth had great influence on the development of ethology as a scientific study through his close contacts with Lorenz. Heinroth was director of an ornithological field station and was fully devoted to making descriptions of bird behavior. In the 1930s, he and Lorenz had much contact on comparative studies of behavior; eventually it was Lorenz who would lay the theoretical foundations for their new approach (Burkhardt, 2005; Kruuk, 2003; Roëll, 2000). Lorenz (1981) attributed the founding of ethology to the decisive discovery made by Whitman, Heinroth and himself "that movement patterns [of different species] are homologous" (p. 3). From that time the study of behavior was approached in the same manner as the study of morphology of animals was. In the following years, Lorenz as the theorist and Tinbergen as the more empirically-minded researcher would lay the foundations of this new discipline.

Lorenz and Tinbergen first met at a symposium on the concept of instinct in Leiden in November 1936. They had started corresponding the year before and Tinbergen used Lorenz's (1935) very influential work *Der Kumpan in der Umwelt des Vogels* in courses he taught at Leiden University (Roëll, 2000). After their first meeting, both men felt that they were personally and intellectually kindred, especially because the work of the one so wonderfully complemented that of the other. According to Tinbergen (1974) "Lorenz's extraordinary vision and enthusiasm were supplemented and fertilised by my critical sense, my inclination to think his ideas through, and my irrepressible urge to check our 'hunches' by experimentation" (p. 198). In the year following their first encounter Tinbergen would spend some months at Lorenz's home in Altenberg where they carried out simple experiments with various animals. Their subsequent friendship was to be decisive for the development of ethology as a new approach.

Here I will discuss this development from the mid-1930s to the early 1950s – approximately the time Bowlby's attention was first drawn to its relevance for studies of human behavior – by briefly discussing Lorenz's (1935) *Der Kumpan* and Tinbergen's (1951) *The Study of Instinct*. These works give a far from complete picture of ethology, but they do account for the ethological notions Bowlby was provided with. As we have seen, it was the English translation of *Der Kumpan*, published in the American ornithological journal *The Auk* (Lorenz, 1937), that set Bowlby on track for his interest in ethology as a framework for his ideas on separation in 1951 (Ainsworth & Bowlby, 1991; Bowlby, 1969/1982b, p. xviii; Bowlby, Figlio, and Young, 1986; Hinde, 2005). Tinbergen's *The Study of Instinct* appeared in the same year as "ethology's first major text" and "a benchmark for how far ethology had come" (Burkhardt, 2005, p. 371). As I have described earlier in the chapter, Bowlby's attention was immediately drawn to it.

Lorenz's *The Companion in the Bird's World*[4]

One of Lorenz's main contributions to ethology – and his most influential in terms of attachment theory – is the formulation of several key concepts in his most influential work, *Der Kumpan in der Umwelt des Vogels* (Lorenz, 1935). It was basically Lorenz's attempt to summarize his ideas up to that point and to provide others with a theoretical framework for comparative research of animal behavior. It came to be regarded as an impressive and authoritative work, receiving very favorable reviews in the United States and England, from, amongst others, American psychologist Margaret Morse Nice, Wallace Craig, and Julian Huxley. One could say that Lorenz earned himself an international reputation with its publication.

Der Kumpan made use of many concepts – particularly the concept of the *Umwelt* or environment – that had earlier been introduced by German biologist Jacob von Uexküll, with whom Lorenz cooperated closely in the 1930s. The central concept in *Der Kumpan* is the "social releaser," a stimulus (more specifically those features of a fellow member of the same species an animal reacts to) that elicits instinctual behavior. Lorenz assumed that lower animals such as birds are not adapted to their environment by learned behavior – as humans are – but that they make use of differentiated instinctive behavior patterns. These patterns have been built up during evolution because of their survival value. These instinctive behaviors only have to be "released" or triggered by the environment. The reaction to a specific releaser is laid down in an "innate releasing mechanism" (IRM) in the organism. The structured pattern of movements that follows a releaser is called a "fixed action pattern" (FAP). This is the genetically programmed core of a species typical behavior, it is a highly stereotyped innate movement pattern based on activity in a specific coordinating centre in the central nervous system. An FAP runs to completion regardless of further stimulation. With these concepts, Lorenz linked external stimuli with the internal, innate behavior patterns of the animal. In an animal's social life Lorenz identified several releasers of instinctual behavior, so-called *Kumpane* or companions: the parent-companion, the child-companion, the sex-companion, the social-companion, and the brother-and-sister-companion. Lorenz's description of the IRM made it possible to make a clear distinction between instinctual and learned behavior (Lorenz, 1935, 1937; see also Burkhardt, 2005; Hinde, 2005; Roëll, 2000).

Probably the most interesting concept Lorenz described in *Der Kumpan* was a phenomenon that was neither instinctive nor learned. Lorenz narrated how young graylag goslings and jackdaws do not recognize members of their own species directly after birth, but show a strong following response to the first moving object in their surroundings. He named this response *Prägung* or "imprinting." The concepts of imprinting, companion, and releaser are closely related: because the animal does not instinctively recognize members of its own species, imprinting provides it with this information in a so-called sensitive period directly after birth. In this sensitive period a preference for members of the own species is established and hereby companions in the environment become able to elicit instinctive behaviors (Lorenz, 1935, 1937).

Tinbergen's *The Study of Instinct* and the Four Whys

In 1951, the year Bowlby first turned to ethology, Tinbergen published his seminal work on *The Study of Instinct*, in which he described the state of the art in ethology (see also Tinbergen, 1963). Though published while working at Oxford University, the book is a reflection of Tinbergen's ideas and research from his time in Leiden and "an extension of a series of lectures delivered at New York in February 1947" (Tinbergen, 1951, p. v). *The Study of Instinct* was of great importance to the field as "it was this book that put ethology on the map" (Kruuk, 2003, p. 149). Central in Tinbergen's book are the "four whys" or four questions regarding the behavior of animals. These four questions related to the causation, the ontogeny, the function, and the evolution of instinctive behavior. Tinbergen's focus was the question of the causation of innate behavior, mainly because up to that point it had been the focus of research by him, Lorenz, and others.

To understand the causes of innate behavior, Tinbergen proposed a hierarchical organization of instinctive behaviors. Tinbergen also differentiated between influences on the behavior of the organism by external factors (such as sensory stimuli or sign stimuli) and internal factors (what Tinbergen called "physiological mechanisms": e.g., hormones, internal sensory stimuli, and intrinsic or automatic nervous impulses generated by the central nervous system). He stated that the internal factors controlled the motivation of the organism and the so-called appetitive behavior (e.g., looking for food or courtship patterns prior to mating). Also, the internal factors determined the threshold needed to release the instinctive behavior. But the behavior is not elicited without external factors unblocking the IRM and releasing the actual consummatory act (as laid down in an FAP). Tinbergen exemplifies this reasoning with an account of the reproductive behavior of the male three-spined stickleback:

> In spring, the gradual increase in length of day brings the males into a condition of increased reproductive motivation, which drives them to migrate into shallow fresh water. Here … a rise in temperature, together with a visual stimulus situation received from a suitable territory, releases the reproductive pattern as a whole. The male settles on the territory … it reacts to strangers by fighting, and starts to build a nest. Now, whereas both nest-building and fighting depend on activations of the reproductive drive as a whole, no observer can predict which one of the two patterns will be shown at any given moment. Fighting for instance, has to be released by a specific stimulus, viz. "red male intruding into the territory." Building is not released by this stimulus situation but depends on other stimuli. Thus these two activities, though both depend on activation of the reproductive drive as a whole, are also dependent on additional (external) factors. The influence of these latter factors is, however, restricted, they act upon either fighting or building, not on the reproductive drive as a whole. (Tinbergen, 1951, p. 103)

In this example the reproductive behavior is the appetitive behavior that builds up due to internal factors and leads to a decrease of the threshold. The instinctive behavior, though, is only elicited by external factors (e.g., a male intruder) and this external stimulus unblocks the IRM and results in a FAP (namely fighting). The behavior itself takes away the motivation for the animal to strive for the stimulus. The hierarchical coordination of different IRM's results in suppression of other behavioral systems when a specific behavioral system is activated. In some instances, different and conflicting drives are activated (e.g., fleeing and fighting). In these cases displacement activities may occur (such a nest building or courting behavior toward a male intruder).

The topic of the causation of behavior took up more than half of the book. Tinbergen touched upon the three other questions, but in much less detail. Nevertheless, *The Study of Instinct* is generally seen as the work that "brought order in the perceived chaos of behaving animals" (Kruuk, 2003, p. 149) and that explained animal behavior in all its dimensions. Its huge impact was mainly due to Tinbergen's all-embracing approach. Later, many of his ideas were dismantled and replaced with new concepts and views, but for the time being Tinbergen had made ethology count.

Bowlby's Personal Relationships with Lorenz and Tinbergen

It is quite clear then that Bowlby from 1951 onward read his way into the ethological literature. He became familiar with the work of Lorenz and Tinbergen, the leading figures in ethology at the time. But what was his personal relationship with these two giants in the field of ethology?

Bowlby's first personal contact with Lorenz was during the first of the four conferences of the "World Health Organization Study Group on the Psychobiological Development of the Child," alternately held in London and Geneva between 1953 and 1956 (see Figure 4.1). It was at the suggestion of Bowlby that Lorenz was invited: Bowlby convinced the organizer of the conference, Ronald Hargreaves, of the importance of having Lorenz as a member of the study group (Smuts, 1977b). One may surmise that Bowlby looked forward to meeting Lorenz and picking his brain regarding ethological issues.

Figure 4.1 WHO study group in Geneva in 1955. From left to right: Jean Piaget, Bärbel Inhelder, Konrad Lorenz, Julian Huxley, and Frank Fremont-Smith. Courtesy of the Wellcome Library, London (AMWL: PP/BOW/L.30).

In the years after their first introduction at the conference in 1953, Bowlby and Lorenz met several times for academic discussion. Both attended the other three meetings of the WHO study group between 1954 and 1956 and visited each other's laboratories. Bowlby visited Lorenz in Altenberg in 1954 (Zazzo, 1979, p. 56) and Lorenz visited Bowlby at least twice at the Tavistock Clinic (in January 1954 and October 1957), where they had several discussions with each other, including one on "population genetics" (AMWL: PP/BOW/H.183).

Actually, the Bowlby's and the Lorenz's became quite good friends in subsequent years. Lorenz's wife Gretl and Ursula Longstaff Bowlby were both present at the first of the WHO study group meetings in 1953 (see Figure 4.2). A foundation for their friendship could have been laid here. In 1975, Bowlby received a letter from Lorenz which clearly shows their personal friendship. In the style typical of Lorenz, the letter ended with "much love from Gretl [and] myself to Ursula and you best expressed in the following diagramm [sic]" (AMWL: PP/BOW/A.6/3). A similar notation Lorenz presumably used in describing the relationships between the animals he observed. (See Figure 4.3.)

Figure 4.2 Photograph of participants in the 1953 study group of the psychology of the child. Left to right: Marcel Monnier, Grey Walter, unknown, Karl-Axel Melin, Ronald Hargreaves, unknown, Ursula Longstaff Bowlby, John Bowlby, René Zazzo, unknown, Jean Piaget, unknown, Bärbel Inhelder, unknown, Frank Fremont-Smith, Margaret Mead, Konrad and Gretl Lorenz, unknown (in background), Jim Tanner, unknown, Eduardo Krapf. Courtesy of the Wellcome Library, London (AMWL: PP/BOW/L.30).

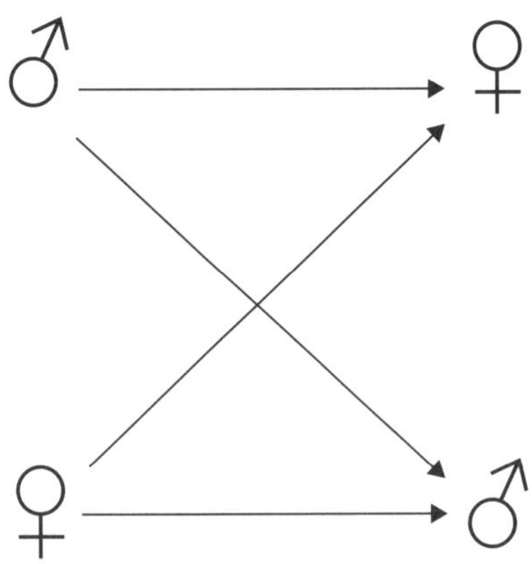

Figure 4.3 Diagram drawn by Lorenz in a letter to Bowlby.

The existing literature is silent about the personal relationship between Bowlby and one of the other founders of ethology, Niko Tinbergen. In the most authoritative work on the life of Tinbergen, Kruuk (2003) does not mention Bowlby even once. Hinde remembers that Bowlby and Tinbergen had no frequent scientific contacts; Tinbergen declined Bowlby's invitation to join the weekly meetings at the Tavistock Clinic and Hinde was asked in his place (Hinde, personal communication, March 31, 2006). Hinde later testified that Bowlby and Tinbergen did not have much academic discussion between them, at least not until later in their careers, when Tinbergen turned to the ethological study of human behavior and emphasized contact comfort in treating children with autism (Van der Horst, Van der Veer, and Van IJzendoorn, 2007). Hinde's impression is confirmed by the personal correspondence between Tinbergen and Bowlby. In a letter to Bowlby, Tinbergen acknowledged that he had not been of much help in matters of ethology:

> I often wonder, looking back, why I have in the past not been able to be of real help to you, as Robert [Hinde] has so outstandingly been. The truth is that my interest in human ethology has awakened only very recently. (Tinbergen in a letter to Bowlby, n.d.; AMWL: PP/BOW/B.3/22)

Tinbergen and Bowlby may not have had much academic discussion, but there is evidence that they had some contact on a more personal level. An inspection of Bowlby's private correspondence learns that when Tinbergen had one of his depressions in Nairobi in 1967 (see Kruuk, 2003) and had to return from Kenya, he consulted Bowlby in his role as a psychiatrist. He subsequently explained this move in a nine-page letter to his doctor:

> I was by then so off-balance, and upon return home decided, since Dr. Henderson was away on holiday, to turn to my good friend John Bowlby, who then started me on what has turned out to be the best course I could possibly have followed. (Tinbergen in a letter to his doctor, November 29, 1967; AMWL: PP/ BOW/B.3/22)

Many years earlier, in the 1950s, Tinbergen had also consulted Bowlby, this time about the mental problems of one of his children. Apparently, the child suffered from something that looked like an autistic disorder. In a letter to Bowlby, Tinbergen looked back to that episode and mentioned Bowlby's intervention:

> And above all we [Tinbergen and his wife] were concerned about these children, once we had seen the entire syndrome, temporarily, in our own children (who are now wellbalanced and integrated adults) and then some of our grandchildren. The one musical boy is the eldest son of our [...] [child], whom you were so kind to help years ago; [he/she] is now an extremely fine [schoolteacher], and a splendid [parent]. (Tinbergen in a letter to Bowlby, n.d.; AMWL: PP/BOW/B.3/22)

Apparently, these events stirred the interest of Tinbergen and his wife in the autistic syndrome and its possible cure. In their book *Autistic children: New hope for a cure*, they advocated an ethological approach to the study of children with autism and strongly supported the so-called "holding therapy" defended by Martha Welch (Tinbergen and Tinbergen, 1983; see also Kruuk, 2003). This therapy has now fallen into disrepute since it may endanger the physical and psychological health of the children and offers no clear therapeutic benefit (Chaffin *et al.*, 2006; Lieberman and Zeanah, 1999; O'Conner and Zeanah, 2003).

So at different stages in his career Bowlby was in close personal contact with ethology's founding fathers. In some of Bowlby's personal notes, he recorded that Lorenz's work "led to [his] interest in ethology and, in due course, to [his] work on *Attachment*. Tinbergen's *Study of Instinct* (1951) which [he] read soon after was also very influential" (AMWL: PP/BOW/A.1/7). But their contributions to his ideas on the development of attachment bonds do not compare to the contributions made by Robert Hinde. The acquaintanceship between Bowlby and Hinde was to become very fruitful; indeed their cooperation spurred a cross-fertilization of ideas (see Van der Horst, 2008).

Early Interactions Between Bowlby and Hinde

Just like Bowlby's acquaintance with ethology, his first encounter with Robert Hinde was rather by chance; they got to know each other in a rather curious and roundabout way. As we have seen, Bowlby suggested to Ronald Hargreaves, the organizer of the 1953 WHO study group, to invite Konrad Lorenz. At this meeting, during their first conversation, Lorenz told Bowlby about a young ethologist in Cambridge by the name of Robert Hinde. Lorenz vividly remembered Hinde's performance at a symposium at his Max Planck

Institute in Buldern in 1952, where Hinde "dropped a bombshell" with "one of the most significant papers of the conference" (Burkhardt, 2005, p. 376) on the mobbing reaction of chaffinches to owls. Lorenz was very enthusiastic about Hinde and about his work.

One year later, in February 1954, Bowlby and Hinde met for the first time during a scientific meeting on ethology and psychiatry organized by the Royal Medico-Psychological Association (RMPA) in London. They actually first met by chance (Bowlby, 1991; Hinde, 2005; see also Smuts, 1977b). Hinde (personal communication, August 22 and 26, 2005) remembered that for "the 1954 [RMPA] conference in London … they had intended to ask Lorenz and Tinbergen and neither of them would come and so it was Bowlby and me who went." Hinde and Bowlby both read a paper and afterwards had lunch together. Like Lorenz before him, Bowlby "was vastly impressed" (Smuts, 1977b, p. 24) by Hinde's expertise. As a result of their first encounter, Bowlby invited Hinde to join the weekly meetings at the Tavistock Clinic where theorists with wildly diverging views discussed case histories.

For Hinde it was a great experience to join the weekly research seminars at the Tavistock Clinic: "It is difficult to describe the excitement of those meetings. Attendance at those meetings was for me a very important scientific experience. Those discussions provided the impetus for much of the research I have done since" (Hinde, 1991, p. 155; see also Hinde, 1982b). Not unlike the WHO conferences, "the group was entirely heterogeneous." It consisted of "psychoanalysts from two schools, a Hullian learning theorist, a Skinnerian learning theorist, a Piagetian, sometimes an anti-psychiatrist, a psychiatric social worker and … an ethologist" – having "nothing theoretically in common, but [they] all had an interest in parent-offspring relationships" (Hinde, 2005, p. 3; Hinde, 2008, p. R582). Most of the members of this group can be identified, though not all: Bowlby as an analyst, Tony Ambrose as the Hullian learning theorist, Ronald Laing as the anti-psychiatrist, James Robertson as the social worker, and Robert Hinde as the ethologist.

During the weekly sessions, the participants "discussed cases of mother-child relationships brought up by the social worker and drafts of John's papers and books. It taught me that the theoretical approach must take second place to data" (Hinde, 2008, p. R582). In an interview, Hinde said about discussing these case histories with people from completely different backgrounds, that they "were willing to look at the facts and we talked about the facts and how best to explain them… [S]ome people in that group would emphasize learning theory, some would bring in Piaget, but focused on the facts as presented" (Van der Horst, Van der Veer, and Van IJzendoorn, 2007, p. 325). According to Hinde, "John's remarkable eclecticism, intellectual dynamism, and judicious enthusiasm" (Hinde, 1991, p. 155) held the group together. Nevertheless, at the end of the day, "Bowlby was taking what he wanted" (Van der Horst, Van der Veer, and Van IJzendoorn, 2007, p. 325). It was this particular broad-minded eclectic approach that characterised Bowlby's style of theorising and debating. Bowlby later applied the same format of interdisciplinary approach to the so-called CIBA symposia.[5]

The CIBA symposia followed the design for interdisciplinary discussion Bowlby had first experienced during the meetings of the WHO on the psychobiological development of the child, which he attended in the early 1950s (Tanner and Inhelder, 1971; see also Foss, 1969; see also earlier in this chapter). Bowlby was impressed by the series' innovative format: the meetings brought together a small group of researchers from different countries and disciplines for the purpose of promoting the knowledge of the subject matter and enhancing a mutual understanding of each other's work and views. Thus, following this model, Bowlby convened and chaired the Tavistock study group on mother–infant interaction, a series of four meetings at two-year intervals, held in the house of the CIBA foundation in London between 1959 and 1965. The proceedings of these meetings were published as *Determinants of Infant Behaviour* (Foss, 1961, 1963, 1965, 1969). (See Figure 4.4.)

The way the weekly Tavistock meetings and the CIBA symposia were organized is exemplary for Bowlby's eclectic approach in constructing his ideas on attachment. He arranged these meetings of infant development researchers with the specific aim to, first of all, acquaint him with current findings, and secondly, to inspire further research which might provide him with further insights about his theory. Interestingly, Bowlby also invited people that he was possibly going to disagree with. Presumably, this was because he had found out earlier – in discussions with, for example, Henry Phelps Brown and Evan Durbin about psychoanalysis (see Chapter 1) – that having to defend his ideas actually sharpened them. From 1954 onward, Hinde participated in these different meetings and thus was much influenced by Bowlby.

Figure 4.4 Robert Hinde (left) and John Bowlby (right) at the CIBA conference in 1963. Courtesy of the Wellcome Library, London (AMWL: PP/BOW/L.9).

Hinde's Early Career and Bowlby's Subsequent Influence

Robert Hinde's academic career started in 1950, when he pursued a Ph.D. with Niko Tinbergen after the latter had made the move from Leiden to Oxford (Kruuk, 2003; Tinbergen, 1991). In practice though, Hinde was supervised by David Lack. Hinde's (1952) Ph.D. thesis was an observational study of the Great Tit. Hinde described it as "a behavioral observation study in which I just wandered around the Wytham Wood with a notebook and a pencil and a pair of field glasses" (Van der Horst, Van der Veer, and Van IJzendoorn, 2007, p. 327). After completing his Ph.D., Hinde returned to Cambridge, where he had earlier earned his Master's degree, and was asked to supervise the ornithological field station in Madingley. The field station was set up in 1952 by W.H. Thorpe, who had also considered Konrad Lorenz for the job, but the latter had turned down the offer. In all modesty, Hinde commented that "various people turned down [Thorpe's] offer of the job and eventually he came down the list to me and so I was in on the start of that enterprise" (Van der Horst,

Van der Veer, and Van IJzendoorn, p. 327). During this period at the field station, Hinde worked on bird behavior and he "happened to do a study on imprinting" (Van der Horst, Van der Veer, and Van IJzendoorn, 2007, p. 327) which is how Lorenz became interested in his work and subsequently pointed Bowlby to its existence (see earlier in the chapter).

After attending the meetings at the Tavistock clinic for a couple of years, Hinde shifted his attention from studying bird behavior to research in monkeys. This move was clearly at the instigation of Bowlby, without whom Hinde "wouldn't have set up a rhesus colony to study separation" (Van der Horst, Van der Veer, and Van IJzendoorn, 2007, p. 326) in 1959. According to Hinde, Bowlby "had a very big influence on me, it influenced the subsequent course of my research" (Van der Horst, Van der Veer, and Van IJzendoorn, 2007, p. 327). Bowlby supported Hinde in acquiring enough funds to set up the rhesus colony. Clearly, it was Bowlby's hope that Hinde would "obtain experimental evidence that maternal separation could have long-term effects" (Hinde, 2005, p. 8). This becomes apparent from Hinde's application for a grant from the Mental Health Research Fund as well. The proposal (dated autumn 1958) consisted of two projects concerned with (a) "certain types of abnormal or apparently irrelevant behavior which are related to situations of stress" and (b) "the formation of the early mother-offspring relation, which is so important for mental health" (AMWL: PP/BOW/B.3/18). Especially the second project is relevant here, since it was evidently designed to support Bowlby's ideas. In his application, Hinde stated that:

> Although the importance of an adequate mother-child relationship is now recognised by psychiatrists, clinicians and pediatricians, the precise manner in which it is built up still is uncertain. In particular, the relative importance of tangible rewards, such as food and warmth, as compared with more intangible factors, such as caressing and communication, needs to be clarified. Furthermore, the relationship is essentially a dynamic one, and its growth must be studied at every stage. Here … ethologists have produced many useful pointers, since detailed studies of parent-offspring relationships in fishes, birds and lower order mammals have been made. The time is now ripe for applying similar techniques to the study of an animal rather closer to man, and the rhesus monkey is an obvious choice. Some work along these lines has already been started by Prof. Harlow at Wisconsin, who has demonstrated that an experimental approach is profitable. (AMWL: PP/BOW/B.3/18)

As we shall see, by the autumn of 1958, both Hinde and Bowlby were well aware of and highly interested in the research done in Harry Harlow's rhesus monkey laboratory. The latter's research came on the scene at almost the same time as Bowlby's, so that Bowlby was influenced by Harlow and vice versa (see Chapter 5).

In the proposal Hinde also mentioned that the origin of his "interest in the human mother-child relationship has been accentuated by contact with Dr. John Bowlby – I have acted as an ethological advisor to his research team … for the last four years" (AMWL: PP/BOW/B.3/18). About Bowlby's role in the project, Hinde wrote that he "has for some years been leading a research team concerned with human mother–offspring relations, and the present project will be closely linked with his work. He will also advise on problems related to human psychopathology" (AMWL: PP/BOW/B.3/18). From this it becomes clear, then, that at this point in time the careers of both men had become increasingly intertwined.

One remarkable example of Bowlby's influence on Hinde's subsequent ethological research is reflected in Hinde and McGinnis (1977; see also Hinde, 2005). In this study, the successive stages of protest, despair, and detachment (see Chapter 3) are experimentally studied in rhesus monkey mother-infant pairs. In four different procedures the young rhesus monkeys (aged 30–32 weeks) are separated for a 13 day period: (1) the mother is removed, but the infant stays in its familiar surroundings (as if the mother goes to hospital); (2) the infant is removed while the mother stays in the group (as if the infant goes to hospital); (3) mother and infant are both removed from the group and are separated (as if mother and infant go to different hospitals); and (4) mother and infant are removed from the group, but are not separated (as if mother and infant go to the same hospital). Results of this study indicated that infants who were separated from the group but not from the mother (procedure 4) were less affected by the separation than the infants in the other procedures; and that the protest phase lasted longer for infants that were removed from both their mothers and their familiar surroundings (procedures 2 and 3) as compared to those who were not (procedure 1), but that the latter group after a brief period of protest showed profound despair. These findings seemed to support the view that reactions to separation from the mother are differentiated (i.e. that optimal substitute mothering during separation should ameliorate the child's distress) and not Bowlby's (1960b) claim that protest, despair, and detachment are habitual responses to separation from the mother *per se* (see Chater 3).

Later in his career, Hinde turned to working with human families with his wife Joan Stevenson-Hinde. After his retirement, he "wanted to come to terms with some issues of the past" (Van der Horst, Van der Veer, and Van IJzendoorn, 2007, p. 328) and focused on religion (Hinde, 1999), on the sources of ethics (Hinde 2002, 2007), and on war and its causes (Hinde, 1997; Hinde and Rotblat, 2003). Interestingly, Hinde's interest in the origins of war echoed an early interest of Bowlby – of which he testified in his publication on *Personal Aggressiveness and War* (Durbin and Bowlby, 1939; see Chapter 1).

Hinde's Influence on Bowlby

Just as Hinde avowed Bowlby's influence on his own thinking and career, Bowlby in several places was very clear about Hinde's influence on his work (e.g., Ainsworth and Bowlby, 1991; Dinnage, 1979; Senn, 1977a; Smuts, 1977b). Bowlby mentioned Hinde as one of the persons who was crucial in his personal and scientific development in the 1950s and 1960s. Hinde succeeded, so to speak, Evan Durbin, who was influential in the 1930s, and wartime colleague and clinical psychologist at the Tavistock clinic Eric Trist, who was important for Bowlby in the 1940s. This explains why Bowlby – after dedicating the first volume to his wife Ursula – dedicated his second volume of *Attachment and Loss* (Bowlby, 1973) to those three friends (Smuts, 1977b). Bowlby would later comment on Hinde's influence and the influence of ethology on his thinking:

> Ethology I regard as immensely important. What I've been trying to do, really, is to rewrite psychoanalysis in the light of ethological principles. Hinde has had a particularly strong influence on me; I've known him since 1954 – he's vetted my work and criticized it ever since. (Dinnage, 1979, p. 325)

Bowlby appreciated Hinde's advice to the extent that he always asked Hinde to comment on his drafts (Smuts, 1977b). That it was not always easy for him to cope with these criticisms emerges from his private correspondence. In a letter to his wife Ursula, for example, he wrote:

> Frank Beach has read *Separation anxiety* and seems interested. Both he and Robert Hinde, whose comments I read yesterday, make a number of criticisms. I suspect they are not of great substance, but they'll need careful insight and that takes time. Naturally I'm very grateful for them fundamentally, but I confess I hate them initially and feel anxious until I have grasped their full significance. (Bowlby in a letter to Ursula, June 3, 1968: AMWL: PP/BOW/B.1/20)

Thus, during the 1950s and 1960s Hinde became more or less a tutor to Bowlby with regard to matters of ethology. According to Bowlby (1969/1982b) "a main reason for valuing ethology [was] that it provide[d] a wide range of new concepts to try out in our theorising" (pp. 6–7). In his reworking of psychoanalytical theory and the integration of ethological findings and concepts into attachment theory, Bowlby introduced a number of concepts. Hinde (2005) emphasized that Bowlby "examined every concept critically for validity and relevance before assimilating it" (p. 2) and he did so with "meticulous care" (p. 9). Since these ethologically based attachment concepts still play such a central role in attachment theory and have stirred so much debate, in the next two paragraphs I will discuss their theoretical importance, origin, and intellectual authorship. Subsequently, I will provide the reader with an overview of how Bowlby (1969/1982b) applied ethology to attachment behavior in the first volume of *Attachment and Loss*.

Theoretical Issues: Instinct and Psychoanalysis

In the discussions Hinde and Bowlby had over the years, the former often criticized Bowlby for devoting too much energy to aligning his views with the Freudian ones. Hinde later confessed that "that was almost a joke between John and me. When I was reading the manuscript of his books, I said, what do you want to say with all this stuff about psychoanalysis anyway?" Of course, at that point Bowlby was trying to sell his ethologically oriented version of psychoanalytic theory to the psychoanalytic world. Actually, he was in a rather precarious position, because he was severely criticized by the British Psycho-Analytical Society because of his renegade views on defence, for example (see Van der Horst and Van der Veer, 2009b). But, according to Hinde, Bowlby "was not just defending his back against psychoanalytic criticism, he was producing a true amalgam" (Hinde, 2005, p. 9). In this connection, Hinde's critical stance towards psychoanalytic theory resembled that of Bowlby's friends in the 1920s (see Chapter 1).

Hinde described his own viewpoint as that of "an angry young man [who] criticized libido models … and [Lorenz's] concept of instinct" (Van der Horst, Van der Veer, and Van IJzendoorn, 2007, pp. 329–330). That is why Hinde titled his book *Animal Behaviour* (Hinde, 1966) and not *Animal instinct*.[6] The term "instinct" is not used once in that book, particularly because it was more or less out of use ever since Frank Beach wrote a paper in *Psychological Review* called "The descent of instinct." In this paper, Beach (1955) argued against the use of instinctive behavior, because "to prove that behavior is unlearned is equivalent to proving the null hypothesis" (p. 405). The dichotomy between inherited and acquired behavior was, according to Beach, "narrow and naive" (p. 409). He ends by stating that "instinct will disappear, to be replaced by scientifically valid and useful explanations" (p. 409).

From Bowlby's personal papers it becomes evident that it was Hinde who suggested to him to dismiss the concept of instinct[7] and opt for the terms "environmentally stable" and "environmentally labile." In a letter to Bowlby, Hinde wrote: "I think you are right in attributing the terms environmentally stable and labile as applied to behaviour to me … [though] they were used earlier in other contexts by Smallhausen" (Hinde in a letter to Bowlby, September 6, 1965; AMWL: PP/BOW/K.4/15). Hinde later remembered "discussing the pros and cons with [Bowlby]. It is very easy for me to claim more than I ought to claim, but I do know that those terms came from me" (Van der Horst, Van der Veer, and Van IJzendoorn, 2007, p. 329).

Bowlby used the term environmentally stable behavior for all instinctive behaviors that are little influenced by the environment, if at all. Instinctive behavior that is much influenced by the environment was termed environmentally labile. As long as an organism lives in its environment of adaptedness (see next paragraph), its behaviors are stable; under these circumstances all members of a species show the same species specific behavior. Bowlby mentioned parents' care for their children and childrens' attachment to their parents as just two examples of human environmentally stable behavior (Bowlby, 1969/1982b, pp. 38–40). By adopting these new concepts,

Bowlby recognized that children have the potential to develop certain behavioral patterns, but that the course of development is dependent upon the environment (see Hinde, 2005). Another significant concept related to these issues is that of the environment of evolutionary adaptedness, to which I will now turn.

Theoretical Issues: Environment of Evolutionary Adaptedness

Another concept Bowlby introduced is that of the environment of evolutionary adaptedness (EEA); a concept that is central to the argument of attachment theory (Bowlby, 1969/1982b; Hinde, 2005; Hrdy, 1999; see also Sable, 2004). Bowlby used the concept of the EEA to explain how humans inherited form their primate ancestors a propensity for attachment behavior as a survival strategy. Mary Main (personal communication, June 28, 2005) has suggested that it was not Bowlby but Hinde who came up with the idea of the EEA. In an interview Hinde once commented:

> I certainly think it was something that came up between us, but which of us actually coined the term, I don't know. If you look at the orienting attitudes of ethology, the environment to which the animal is adapted is critical for understanding its behavior and certainly I took that idea to Bowlby. Whether he or I thought of the term is another issue. It's a concept that's come in for a good deal of criticism, as you know, because human environments were diverse and so on, but that's another issue. I think the criticism by Kevin Laland is misguided really, I mean, he doesn't understand the historical context in which it first arose. (Van der Horst, Van der Veer, and Van IJzendoorn, 2007, p. 330)

Here, Hinde is referring to Laland and Brown (2002), who wrote a critical review of the concept of the EEA. Their criticism primarily concerns the stereotypical description of the EEA as a Pleistocene African savannah. According to the authors, the environment in which humans lived during a large period of time was very different for different groups of hunter-gatherers. Hence, one cannot argue that humans adapted their behavior to one specific environment. Similar criticism had been voiced previously by evolutionary anthropologists (e.g., Foley, 1996; Irons, 1998). Hinde is not impressed by these critiques:

> The critics [of the EEA] are a pity actually, I have to say that. The point is this, Bowlby talked about the EEA primarily as those aspects of the environment of the young child which involve the mother. It was then used by other people and it was pointed out that environments are very different, but Bowlby's real point was that all babies need to be near their mother, all babies need to suckle, all babies need contact comfort. It was mainly the things that universally mattered in the mother-child relationship when he talked about the EEA. The fact that humans have lived in all sorts of physical environments is another issue. (Van der Horst, Van der Veer, and Van IJzendoorn, 2007, p. 331)

Elsewhere, Hinde (1982a, 1987) has expressed the view that the generic concept of the EEA was of particular importance during the development of attachment theory, but that now that attachment theory has become established, the discussion concerning the EEA is no longer relevant: "[T]hat battle is now won: we are no longer concerned with broad principles but with the nature of individual differences between mother-infant relationships" (Hinde, 1982a, p. 72; see also Irons, 1998). However, within evolutionary psychology the notion of the EEA is still relevant, where it refers jointly to the problems hunter-gatherers had to solve and the conditions under which they solved them (including their developmental environment; Buss, 2004, 2005).

Applying Ethology to Attachment Behavior: Tinbergen's Four Whys

A way of assessing ethology's influence on John Bowlby and attachment theory is to look at it from a theoretical perspective, i.e., to investigate how Bowlby used certain ethological ideas or notions in attachment theory. There is vast evidence in *Attachment and Loss* (Bowlby, 1969/1982b, 1973, 1980a) that he was indeed heavily influenced by the ethological framework. For example, in Volume 1 Bowlby addressed each of Tinbergen's four whys of behavior: evolution, causation, function, and ontogeny. In his work, Tinbergen (1951, 1963) had argued that for ethologists the question what explains animal behavior can be asked and answered in four different ways (see Chapter 4). By describing how Bowlby answered these ethological questions for attachment behavior, I will here demonstrate this influence.

Earlier in this chapter I addressed the issue of the concept of the "environment of evolutionary adaptedness," which Bowlby used to answer Tinbergen's question of the *evolution* of behavior. Bowlby (1969/1982b, p. 47) leaves no doubt about the central role of this concept in attachment theory: "the concept EEA is vital to the argument of this book." According to Bowlby, the behavior that ensures a tight bond between mother and child evolved into instinctive behavior as a result of natural selection: children attach themselves to their caregivers because of the survival value in man's environment of evolutionary adaptedness. According to Bowlby:

> *the only relevant criterion by which to consider the natural adaptedness of any particular part of present day man's behavioural equipment is the degree to which and the way in which it might contribute to population survival in man's primeval environment* ... [i.e.,] the one that man inhabited for two million years until changes of the past few thousand years led to the extraordinary variety of habitats he occupies today ... It is against this picture of man's EEA that the environmentally stable behavioural equipment of man is considered. Much of this equipment... is so structured that it enables individuals of each sex and each age-group to take their place in the organised social group characteristic of the species. (Bowlby, 1969/1982b, pp. 59/63–64; original italics)

In their environment of adaptedness humans had to be equipped with instinctive behavioral systems to be able to cope with the dangers of predators or aggressive members of their own species. The bond between mother and child is the consequence of such an essential behavioral system. So attachment behavior is the behavior that promotes and maintains proximity to caregivers to ensure safety against such dangers. With this description of the EEA and the evolution of attachment as instinctive behavior, Bowlby answered one of Tinbergen's four whys.

Bowlby's (1969/1982b, pp. 85–103) description of the *causation* of instinctive behavior, or the activation and termination of it, followed ideas proposed by Hinde and Tinbergen and is based on animal research. As causes for instinctive behavior, Bowlby named hormone levels, organization and autonomous action of the nervous system (CNS), and environmental stimuli. Bowlby (1969/1982b, pp. 124–140) clearly distinguished causation, the immediate causes of a system's activation, from the *function* of a behavioral system: "The function of a [biological] system is that consequence of the system's activity which led to its having been evolved, and which leads to its continuing to remain in the equipment of the species" (1969/1982b, p. 127). Finally, Bowlby (1969/1982b, pp. 145–174) addressed the issue of the *ontogeny* of instinctive behavior, which "usually take[s] at first a primitive form and proceed[s] thence to undergo an elaborate process of development" (1969/1982b, p. 145). Bowlby (1969/1982b, pp. 199–204) largely based his description of the ontogeny of attachment behavior in human infants on Ainsworth's (1963, 1967) Uganda reports. As we shall see, her observations in Africa were a confirmation of Bowlby's theoretical ideas and of the results of Harlow's observations of and experiments with monkeys (see Chapters 5 and 6). Thus Bowlby satisfied Tinbergen's four criteria for the satisfactory explanation of a biological phenomenon: he provided an account of the evolution, causation, function, and ontogeny of attachment behavior.

Concluding Remarks

In this chapter, I have pointed out that from 1951 Bowlby was in personal and scientific contact with leading European scientists in the field of ethology, namely Niko Tinbergen, Konrad Lorenz, and Julian Huxley. From 1954 onward, "with Robert Hinde's generous and stern guidance" (Bowlby, 1980b, p. 650), Bowlby was introduced to the theoretical principles of ethology and studies in animal behavior. It became clear that from that point in time it was his goal 'to rewrite psychoanalysis in the light of ethological principles,' because, according to Bowlby, "the theory was a mess – there was no suitable theory really" (Senn, 1977a, p. 26). For this theoretical purpose, Bowlby introduced new concepts such as 'environmentally stable' and 'environmentally labile', and the concept of the 'environment of evolutionary adaptedness'. Also, he adopted an ethological approach to explain the nature of affectional bonds. At the same time it was Bowlby's "belief that problems of method and theoretical interpretation are best approached from a firm base in empirical data" (Bowlby, 1961d, p. xiii). However, his problem was that the empirical basis to support his new view of the mother–child bond was exactly what he was lacking.

Therefore, Bowlby started collecting evidence that could support his new views. The interdisciplinary approach he took to accomplish this fact is reflected in four symposia held in the late 1950s and early 1960s (see earlier in the chapter). For these symposia Bowlby preferred to invite a small number of people

> who were already engaged in first-hand studies of the behavior of infants and young children in a social setting … representatives of those making similar studies in animals, … [and] a number of clinicians who could contribute from their experience of what seems pathologically and therapeutically relevant. (Bowlby, 1961d, p. xiv)

During these meetings Bowlby emphasized the need for an exchange of ideas between different fields of study and the fact that "an understanding of mother-infant interaction in humans will come soonest if the knowledge and skills of several different groups of workers are pooled" (Bowlby, 1965, p. xiii).

During these so-called CIBA conferences it was important that priority was given to "empirical studies, especially those that utilize first-hand observations of what actually happens between infant and mother. In the past these have been scarce, but an increasing number of investigators are now awakening to their interest and value" (Bowlby, 1963b, p. xi). After the symposia, Bowlby recapitulated that it was interesting to see "how the work … reported had been influenced or even initiated as a result of discussions that had occurred at … previous meetings or as a result of visits or correspondence that had been started at them" (Bowlby, 1969, p. xiv).

In an interview, Bowlby once stated that "in 1957 I started tackling theory" (Senn, 1977a, p. 28). In that year he proposed "a new theoretical framework for understanding problems of personality development and pathology" (Bowlby, 1980b, p. 650) but "because this framework [wa]s radically different to the frameworks adopted by psychoanalysts and learning theorists, it remain[ed] controversial" (Bowlby, 1980b, p. 650). The controversiality of the theory would diminish though, "thanks in large part to the related studies of rhesus monkeys undertaken by Harry Harlow in the US and Hinde over here" (Bowlby, 1980b, p. 650). Harlow and Hinde were to carry out the experimental developmental research that Bowlby needed for the empirical validation of his ideas. The cross-fertilization of the work and ideas of Harlow and Bowlby is the subject of the next chapter: attention will be drawn to what happens "when strangers from strange disciplines first meet" (Bowlby, 1969, p. xiii).

Notes

1 The correspondence between Kortlandt and Bowlby was very brief and consists of only nine letters. They stopped writing in 1957 and this may have had something to do with the fact that Hinde (1957) was very critical of Kortlandt's (1955) publication on "aspects and prospect of the concept of instinct" (see A. Kortlandt, personal communication, April 8, 2006).

2 This explains why ethology is not mentioned by Bowlby, Ainsworth, Boston, and Rosenbluth (1956), even though Bowlby had already published an article about his ethological ideas elsewhere.

3 Vicedo (2009b) has argued that "child analysts turned to Lorenz for three main reasons: studies of child deprivation showing the need for mother love faced increasing criticism; analysts saw an opportunity to flesh out the concept of instinct; and they were able to capitalize on the higher status and authority of biological studies" (p. 291).

4 This discussion of *The Companion in the Bird's World* does not include Lorenz's later modification and sophistication of the concepts introduced here.

5 The four CIBA symposia (organized in 1959, 1961, 1963, and 1965) were funded by the CIBA foundation, a foundation formed in 1949 by the Swiss company CIBA (now Novartis) that promotes scientific excellence by arranging scientific meetings. The four meetings are often also referred to as meetings of the Tavistock study group.

6 Hinde mentions a change of title of the book in a letter to Bowlby (October 27, 1965; AMWL: PP/BOW/B.3/18).

7 Bowlby dismissed the concept of instinct, but retained the idea of instinctive behavior.

5
From Theoretical Claims to Empirical Evidence: Harry Harlow and the Nature of Love

Toward Empirical Confirmation

In the previous chapter, we have seen that from 1951 Bowlby made increasing use of ethological findings and theorizing guided by British ethologist, colleague and life-long friend Robert Hinde. Bowlby's talk to the members of the British Psycho-Analytical Society on June 19, 1957 (published as Bowlby, 1958d) testified of his growing confidence in the relevance of ethology (see later in the chapter). Clearly, then, he had put forward bold theoretical claims, but was urgently looking for empirical evidence that would support these claims. Of course, Hinde – with Bowlby's support – had set up a rhesus colony with the specific aim to get the empirical confirmation of Bowlby's ideas, but the much needed results were not yet available. It would take Hinde a considerable amount of time to establish the rhesus colony from 1959 onward, as becomes clear from a letter from Hinde to Harlow in 1961:

> Our own monkey work is progressing slowly. We felt it worthwhile to make fairly detailed studies of the noises and gestures of rhesus monkeys first and the noises turned out to be a good deal more complicated than

John Bowlby – From Psychoanalysis to Ethology: Unraveling the Roots of Attachment Theory, First Edition. Frank C. P. van der Horst.

> we had at first suspected. As the babies arrive, we are hoping to do some detailed studies of normal mother/baby interaction. One of our difficulties has been obtaining fully adult females. If you can give me any advice on sources of either pregnant females or fully adult females I should be more than grateful. (Hinde in a letter to Harlow, April 20, 1961)

Eventually, the first results from Hinde's field station would only be available in published form from 1964 onwards (e.g., Hinde, Spencer-Booth, and Bruce, 1966; Rowell, Hinde and Spencer-Booth, 1964; Spencer-Booth and Hinde, 1966; Spencer-Booth, Hinde, and Bruce, 1965). For this reason, it was of great value that on the other side of the Atlantic, American animal psychologist Harry Harlow had been doing very relevant experiments on the 'nature of love'. Today, in almost any introductory, general, or developmental psychology textbook (e.g., DeHart, Sroufe, and Cooper, 2004; Lightfoot, Cole, and Cole, 2009) the work of Bowlby and Harlow is discussed in tandem. Despite their rather different backgrounds – Bowlby a clinician by training and Harlow an experimentalist – the two men had several things in common. One of them was that they showed no hesitation in expressing views that went against the prevailing *Zeitgeist*. In the 1950s and 1960s, both men formulated new ideas on the nature of the bond between child and caregiver. They defied the prevailing psychoanalytic and learning theoretical views that dominated psychological thinking from the 1930s. Although it has been argued (Singer, 1975) that Harlow's experimenting had no influence on Bowlby's theorizing, here I will make clear that Bowlby used Harlow's surrogate work with rhesus monkeys as much needed empirical support for his emerging theory of attachment. Interestingly, in his turn, Harlow was influenced by Bowlby's thinking and tried to model his rhesus work to support Bowlby's new theoretical framework (e.g., Seay, Hansen, and Harlow, 1962; Seay and Harlow, 1965).

In this chapter, I will describe the personal and professional relationships between these two giants in the field of psychology and will attempt to delineate the cross-fertilization of their work during the most active years of their acquaintance from 1957 through the mid-1970s. I will demonstrate that Bowlby and Harlow's interests converged as Harlow shifted his focus to a developmental approach shortly before the two met. Their introduction at a distance by Hinde was the beginning of an exchange of ideas that resulted in groundbreaking experimenting and theorizing that affects the field of developmental psychology to this day. At times, I will discuss other influence besides Harlow, for example the contributions of other "ethologists." Also, I will end this chapter by providing the reader with a sociogram illustrating the interpersonal relations of proponents of attachment and ethology.

Harlow's Early Career

Harry Harlow received a Ph.D. in psychology from Stanford University in 1930 and spent the remainder of his academic career as a professor at the University of Wisconsin-Madison. Harlow was educated in the psychological tradition of the 1920s and 1930s, a time when psychology was making an effort to become a "real" science. Studying behavior was a case of controlling the environment and varying one particular condition. It was a time when behaviorist views carried the day and the conditioned responses of Norwegian rats were the key to understanding mental life. So, when Harlow was appointed at Wisconsin in 1930 and found that the psychology department's chairman had the rat laboratory dismantled and that it was not about to be replaced, he was greatly inconvenienced (Harlow, 1977; Suomi and LeRoy, 1982).

It was at the suggestion of the chairman's wife that Harlow decided to study primates at the local zoo and he soon found out that the intellectual capabilities of the monkeys were far greater than those of rats (Suomi and LeRoy, 1982). To study these capabilities more rigorously and effectively, Harlow developed the Wisconsin General Test Apparatus (WGTA) (Harlow and Bromer, 1938). (See Figure 5.1 for a prototype.) Through the WGTA it was possible to present the monkeys with a large number of learning tests in a highly standardized way. With it he tested the monkeys with discrimination learning and memory tasks (e.g., Harlow, 1943, 1944). Harlow's next step was to study cortical localization of learning capabilities by doing lesion studies with monkeys (e.g., Harlow and Dagnon, 1943; Harlow and Settlage, 1947; Moss and Harlow, 1948). By lesioning different areas of the brain, Harlow noted that each of the operated monkeys performed differently on the WGTA tests. This work was basically similar to the work done by Karl Lashley (1950), who forwarded the principle of mass action: the reduction in learning is proportional to the amount of tissue removed and the more complex the learning task the more disruptive the lesions are, but the location of the removed cortex

Figure 5.1 Original delayed response apparatus used at Vilas Park Zoo. Courtesy of Helen LeRoy.

had no effect. Lashley concluded that memories could not be localized, but that they are widely distributed across the cortex.

In the late 1940s, Harlow achieved "a major conceptual and methodological breakthrough" (Suomi and LeRoy, 1982, p. 321) by identifying the formation of learning sets in monkeys (Harlow, 1949). Harlow demonstrated that his monkeys "learned to learn" and that they acquired a strategy for problem-solving. As methods of studying processes underlying monkey learning were exhausted, Harlow in the early 1950s turned to studying motivation and the ontogeny of learning. This type of developmental research required the establishment of a breeding colony of rhesus monkeys. It was at this point that Harlow's attention was drawn to the phenomenon of affection.

Harlow had always had problems importing monkeys: apart from being very expensive, they were often ill upon arrival and infected the other monkeys in the laboratory (Harlow, 2008). In 1956, following Van Wagenen's (1950) procedures, he decided to raise his own rhesus monkeys, and thus the Wisconsin lab became the first self-sustaining colony of monkeys in the US. The monkeys were kept in separate cages at all times to avoid any spread of disease. The results of this procedure were remarkable for those who could see it: the monkeys Harlow raised were physically perfectly healthy, but their social behavior was very awkward. They were simply unable to socially interact with each other. Another striking observation Harlow made, was that the infant monkeys "clung to [the folded gauze diapers on the floor of their cage] and engaged in violent temper tantrums when the pads were removed and replaced for sanitary reasons" (Harlow, 1958, p. 675). Harlow wondered whether these observations could mean anything for the needs of human children.

Just two months prior to Bowlby's British Psycho-Analytical Society address, which discussed in great depth the child's tie to the mother, Harlow spoke on April 20, 1957 at a conference in Washington, D.C. The title of his address was the "Experimental Analysis of Behavior" and it included a discussion of trends in this area. Harlow (1957) began his address by stating that "no behavior is too complicated to analyze experimentally, if only the proper techniques can be discovered and developed" (p. 485). He went on to emphasize the importance of a developing trend toward longitudinal studies (psychology had traditionally been concerned with a cross-sectional approach), and he told how:

> I have followed with interest the changes in my own research programs and the development of these programs. The experimental *S* that has consumed almost all my research time has been the rhesus monkey. When I initially approached the experimental analysis of this animal's behavior, I approached it in the classical, cross-sectional manner … If it had not been for the fact that my monkey *Ss* continued to live after they had solved a problem and that they were not expendable in view of the available financial support, I might still be engaged in cross-sectional studies of the monkey's behavior. (Harlow, 1957, p. 487)

These comments clearly indicate that Harlow was moving toward experimental developmental research, the type of research that Bowlby so badly needed at the time. Harlow was now on the threshold of the affectional studies, for which he would become famous. He explained that:

> More recently we have planned and initiated much more extensive longitudinal studies in which we have separated infant rhesus monkeys from their mothers at birth and raised them under the controlled conditions of the laboratory. We have been successful in raising over fifty of these

> young animals, and we have obtained data on their learning development from birth through three years of age ... We have found the longitudinal approach to the experimental analysis of behavior interesting and even exciting, and we are now extending this type of analysis to other areas than learning, perception, and motivation ... [W]e are planning and conducting systematic longitudinal studies on the development of emotional responses. (Harlow, 1957, p. 488)

Just like Bowlby before his fellow psychiatrists of the British Psycho-Analytical Society, Harlow, before an audience of clinical psychologists, stressed the importance of observational methods in this process, something that was of course very obvious to him.

> At the present time ... we are interested in tracing the development of various patterns of emotional behaviour ... We began by looking for response patterns which might fit ... But this observational study ... is gradually taking on the characteristics of an experiment. As we gain sophistication about the monkey's emotional responses, we become more selective in the patterns which we observe. (Harlow, 1957, p. 490)

It was because of their mutual interest in this area of emotional behavior and responses that Harlow and Bowlby became acquainted. In Harlow's words: "It is an understatement to add that we have research interests in common" (Harlow in a letter to Bowlby,[1] January 27, 1958).

Ethology and Animal Psychology: Contrasting Approaches to Animal Behavior

However, it was not a foregone conclusion that a British ethologically oriented psychiatrist and an American animal behaviorist would have an opportunity to meet in those days. In the 1950s, there was a great barrier between ethologists (who were mostly biologists by training) and students of animal behavior (mostly psychologists). Ethologists emphasized observation of animals in their natural habitat, whereas comparative psychologists relied on rigorous experimentation in the laboratory. The culmination of this debate was a 1953 critique by Theodore Schneirla's student Daniel Lehrman of Lorenz's concept of instinct, at that time the central theoretical construct of ethology (Lehrman, 1953). But in contrast to what might be expected, when

Lehrman visited Europe in 1954 and met with leading ethologists, he was very well received. Just like many of the ethologists, Lehrman had a background in evolutionary biology and ornithology and this may have been essential in bridging their differences. Although Lorenz never acknowledged Lehrman's ideas, they later became mainstream ethology (Griffiths, 2004). Eventually Hinde (1966) wrote his authoritative book *Animal Behaviour* which was essentially "a synthesis of ethology and comparative psychology" (Van der Horst, Van der Veer, and Van IJzendoorn, 2007, pp. 9–10; see also Timberlake, 1993).

In this climate of contrasting views, Hinde and Harlow met for the first time in Palo Alto in early 1957 at a conference organized by Frank Beach that was intended to bring together a group of European ethologists (Niko Tinbergen, Gerard Baerends, Jan van Iersel, David Vowles, Eckhardt Hess, and Robert Hinde) with a group of mainly North-American comparative and experimental psychologists (Frank Beach, Donald Hebb, Daniel Lehrman, Jay Rosenblatt, Karl Lashley, and Harry Harlow). Hinde has good memories of the event: "It was a wonderful conference, about three weeks, [where you had] nothing to publish, and if you did not finish what you had to say today there was always tomorrow" (Robert Hinde, personal communication, March 14, 2007; see also Hinde 2008). After their first encounter, Hinde and Harlow met several times in the late fifties and sixties. Although they influenced each other and their relationship was very cordial in the days they interacted, Hinde in retrospect remembers that at that time their approaches were still rather far apart:

> I must have next met Harry when I visited Madison and was appalled by this room full of cages with babies going 'whoowhoowhoo' and Harlow had no sensitivity at that point that he was damaging these infants. At that time I was beginning to work on mother-infant relations in monkeys myself, but I already knew enough about monkeys to know that that "whoo"-call was a distress call. These experiments had their restrictions, but they did show certain important things. After that I saw him at least once a year for a while as he asked me to join his scientific committee. Of course his results influenced my way of thinking, but I was then an ethologist and not keen on his laboratory orientation. And I could never have attempted to do the sort of research that he did because our colony only had six adult males and two or three females in each group. We attempted to create an approximation to a normal social situation: it was a long way off, of course, but at least it was social. (Robert Hinde, personal communication, August 22 and 26, 2005; March 14, 2007)

Hinde's ideas about laboratory studies also become clear from one of his research proposals (dated summer 1962), in which he wrote of a study of "the behavior of adults separated from their group companions." Hinde reasoned that "since monkeys, like humans, are social animals, separation from the group is a mildly stressful situation, and it is one which, unlike the electric shocks and air blasts so often used in laboratory studies, is relevant to natural conditions" (AMWL: PP/BOW/B.3/18).

Despite these differences in theoretical orientation, it was Robert Hinde who would eventually establish contact between Bowlby and Harlow. At the Palo Alto conference, Hinde and Harlow had a discussion on motherhood and after returning home Hinde informed Bowlby that Harlow was interested in Bowlby's recent work on this subject (Blum, 2002; Hrdy, 1999; Karen, 1994; Suomi, Van der Horst and Van der Veer, 2008; Van der Horst *et al.*, 2007).

Harlow and Bowlby Become Acquainted in 1957

It was just several months later that Bowlby and Harlow introduced themselves by letter. The written record of their relationship commenced with a letter dated August 8, 1957 in which Bowlby expressed his interest:

> Robert Hinde tells me that you were interested in my recent paper when he showed it to you at Palo Alto and at his suggestion I am now sending you a copy. I need hardly say I would be most grateful for any comments and criticisms you cared to make. I shall be at the Center at Palo Alto from mid-September and will be preparing it for publication then. Robert Hinde told me of your experimental work on maternal responses in monkeys. If you have any papers or typescripts I would be very grateful for them. If there were a chance, I would try to visit you next Spring when I hope to be moving around U.S.A. (Bowlby in a letter to Harlow, August 8, 1957)

The paper which Bowlby sent to Harlow at the time was a draft of "The nature of the child's tie to his mother" (Bowlby, 1958d). Harlow replied by return of post, thanking Bowlby for the paper, which he several years later (in a letter to Bowlby, March 25, 1959) would refer to as a "reference bible":

> [Y]our interests are ... closely akin to a research program I am developing on maternal responses in monkeys. I certainly hope that you can pay a visit to my laboratory sometime during this forthcoming year. At the moment our researches are just getting underway, and I hope to use these materials for my American Psychological Association Presidential Address in September, 1958. This address will be the first formal presentation of these researches. (Harlow in a letter to Bowlby, August 16, 1957)

Mutual Referencing after 1957

After the two men began corresponding in August, 1957, they also began referring to each other's writings. A review of Bowlby's publications from 1951 to 1957 (Bowlby, 1951, 1953, 1957; Bowlby, Robertson, and Rosenbluth, 1952; Bowlby *et al.*, 1956; Bowlby and Robertson, 1952; Robertson and Bowlby, 1953) yields no mention of Harlow's work. Likewise, we find no reference to Bowlby's work in Harlow's first developmental writings (Harlow, 1957).

The early correspondence resulted in the planning of mutual visits and in the exchange of reprints.[2] Seven of Bowlby's publications (Bowlby, 1958d, 1960a, 1960b, 1960c, 1961c; Bowlby, Robertson, and Rosenbluth, 1952; Bowlby *et al.*, 1956) have been found in Harlow's reprint collection, in addition to two volumes on *Attachment and Loss* (Bowlby, 1969/1982b, 1973). It is especially interesting to see Harlow's notes jotted in the margins of Bowlby's papers.

As a result of the interchange, the first reference to Harlow's work appears in Bowlby's work (Bowlby, 1958d). This paper was an expanded version of an address Bowlby gave before the British Psycho-Analytical Society on June 19, 1957. The paper is concerned with conceptualizing the nature of the young child's tie to his mother, the dynamics which promote and underlie this tie. Bowlby described four alternative views found in the psychoanalytic or psychological literature at the time. He then went on to present his own theoretical perspective. He emphasized that his view was based on direct observation of infants and young children, rather than on retrospective analysis of older subjects as was the typical base for psychoanalytic theorizing at the time. Bowlby went on to state:

> The longer I contemplated the diverse clinical evidence the more dissatisfied I became with the views current in psychoanalytical and psychological literature and the more I found myself turning to the ethologists for help. The extent to which I have drawn on concepts of ethology will be apparent. (Bowlby, 1958d, p. 351)

The four then contemporary views he described were, first of all, the cupboard-love theory of object relations, according to which the physiological needs for food and warmth are met by the mother, through which the baby gradually learns to regard the mother as the source of all gratification and love. Secondly, primary object sucking, which states that the infant has a built-in need to orally attach to a breast and subsequently learns the breast is attached to the mother and then relates to her also. Thirdly, primary object clinging, according to which the infant has a built-in need to touch and cling to a human being, independent of food, but just as important. And finally, there is the primary return-to-womb craving, which holds that the infant resents its removal from the womb at birth and wants to return there.

Bowlby then described his own hypothesis, one of much greater complexity, as "Component Instinctual Responses." He believed that five responses comprise attachment behavior – sucking, clinging, following, crying, and smiling – also acknowledging that many more may exist. He explained that his theory was "rooted firmly in biological theory and requires no dynamic which is not plainly explicable in terms of the survival of the species" (Bowlby, 1958d, p. 369). This amalgam of psychoanalysis and ethology, Bowlby's rejection of the theory of cupboard love, and his lack of attention to the child's inner world were all quite controversial at the time, at least in psychoanalytic circles (Hrdy, 1999; Karen, 1994). Psychoanalysts reacted that "a baby … isn't a duckling" (Karen, 1994, p. 107).

A main point of Bowlby's argument was that no one response was more primary than another. He believed it was a mistake to emphasize sucking and feeding as the most important. Pointing out the inadequacy of human infant studies to date in terms of illustrating his hypothesis, Bowlby turned to observation of animals. It was in this context that Bowlby first cited Harlow's research. He clearly used Harlow's findings to undermine the psychoanalytic idea that all attachment develops through oral gratification. Harlow had specifically investigated the importance of clinging. Bowlby cited Harlow's yet unpublished nonhuman primate data "on the attachment behavior of young rhesus monkeys" (later published as Harlow, 1958):

> Clinging appears to be a universal characteristic of primate infants and is found from the lemurs up to anthropoid apes and human babies ... Though in the higher species mothers play a role in holding their infants, those of lower species do little for them; in all it is plain that in the wild the infant's life depends, indeed literally hangs, on the efficiency of his clinging response ... In at least two different species ... there is first-hand evidence that clinging occurs before sucking ... We may conclude, therefore, that in sub-human primates clinging is a primary response, first exhibited independently of food. Harlow ... removed [young rhesus monkeys] from their mothers at birth, they are provided with the choice of two varieties of model to which to cling and from which to take food ... Preliminary results strongly suggest that the preferred model is the one which is more 'comf[ortable]' to cling to rather than the one which provides food. (Bowlby, 1958d, p. 366)

Harlow and Bowlby Finally Meet in 1958

After the first two letters in August, 1957, eight additional letters were exchanged during the period Bowlby spent at the Palo Alto Center from mid-September, 1957 through mid-June, 1958. In these letters, the two men discussed their mutual interests and made arrangements for Bowlby to visit Harlow's lab in Madison as Bowlby was finally able to carry out the plans of a visit he had mentioned in his first letter. Bowlby attended one of Harlow's lectures on April 26, 1958: "I heard him speak and I saw his films, which had a very powerful effect on me" (Smuts, 1977b, p. 27). Bowlby also visited Harlow's laboratory for two days in June of that same year (Smuts, 1977b; Zazzo, 1979). In a letter to his wife Bowlby shows his enthusiasm after their first encounter:

> You may remember I went to hear the final paper of the [Monterey] conference – an address by Harry Harlow of Wisconsin on mother infant interaction in monkeys. His stuff is a tremendous confirmation of the Child's Tie paper, which he quoted. Afterwards Chris[toph Heinicke] heard him remark, in very good humour, to a friend: "You know, I thought

> I had got hold of a really original idea [and] then to find that bastard Bowlby had beaten me to it!" This is not really true [and] I think we can say it's a dead heat – the work of each supports the other. We had a very amiable chat [and] arranged to meet in June. (Bowlby in a letter to Ursula, April 28, 1958; AMWL: PP/BOW/B.1/20)

The lecture Bowlby attended was a presentation Harlow gave at the meetings of the American Philosophical Society (published as Harlow and Zimmermann, 1958) on the development of affectional responses in infant monkeys. There Harlow touched upon, in contrast with Bowlby's earlier in-depth analysis of the same matter, the various psychoanalytic theoretical positions concerning the bond of the infant to the mother. Referring to their personal contacts, Harlow mentioned that "Bowlby has given approximately equal emphasis to primary clinging (contact) and sucking as innate affectional components, and at a later maturational level, visual and auditory following" (Harlow and Zimmermann, 1958, p. 501). This was Bowlby's first appearance in a Harlow publication.

Bowlby visited Madison in June, 1958 and wrote to Harlow on the 26th, thanking him for his hospitality, and adding: "I shall look forward to keeping in touch … I hope too you will put me on your list to send mimeograph versions as and when your stuff goes further forward. We will reciprocate." By June of 1958, the earlier formal salutations and closings "Dear Professor Harlow" and "Yours sincerely" or "Dear Dr. Bowlby" and "Cordially" had changed to a much more informal tone, becoming "Dear Harry" and "Yours ever, John," or "Dear John" and "Best personal wishes, Harry."

Two months later, on August 31, 1958, Harlow delivered his famous presidential address on "The nature of love" to the American Psychological Association. "The recent writings of John Bowlby" (Harlow, 1958, p. 673) are mentioned in the published paper, to the effect that he recognized the mother's importance in providing the infant with intimate physical contact, as well as serving as a source of nutrition. Harlow also positively discussed Bowlby's notion of "primary object following," i.e., the tendency to visually and orally search the mother. The fact that Bowlby is cited twice in the presidential address is of some significance given that Harlow referred to but six names of researchers and hardly discusses their ideas.

Ethology Further Emphasized in Bowlby's Work

It was in July, 1959, that Bowlby (1960c) read a paper on ethology before the Congress of the International Psychoanalytical Association in Copenhagen. Bowlby began his paper by remarking that eight years had now passed since his interest in ethology had been aroused, initially by Lorenz's gosling work.

> From this time forward the further I read and the more ethologists I met the more I felt a kinship with them. Here were first-rate scientists studying the family life of lower species who were not only making observations that were at least analogous to those made of human family life but whose interests, like those of analysts, lay in the field of instinctive behavior, conflict, and the many surprising and sometimes pathological outcomes of conflict … A main reason I value ethology is that it gives us a wide range of new concepts to try out in our theorizing. (Bowlby, 1960c, p. 313)

At the same time, Bowlby was cautious about extrapolating or generalizing from one species to another. He shared this restraint with Harlow who often reiterated that "monkeys are not furry little men with tails." Both, however, were convinced of the importance of animal research in providing a better understanding of human social behavior. Bowlby expressed his view thus:

> Man is a species in his own right with certain unusual characteristics. It may be therefore that none of the ideas stemming from studies of lower species is relevant. Yet this seems improbable … [W]e share anatomical and physiological features with lower species, and it would be odd were we to share none of the behavioural features which go with them. (Bowlby, 1960c, p. 314)

Carrying the notion further, Bowlby explained his efforts to use ideas gleaned from ethology in order to understand the ontogeny of what psychoanalysts called "object relations." For a specific example of instinctual response systems present in the young, which facilitate the attachment of the infant to a mother figure without the mother's active participation, Bowlby (1960c) referred to and cited Harlow's surrogate mother research: "a newborn monkey will cling to a dummy provided it is soft and comfortable. The provision of food and warmth are quite unnecessary. These young creatures follow for the sake of following and cling for the sake of clinging" (p. 314).

Several pages later, in discussing the consequences of disrupting the mother-infant bond, Bowlby mentioned the substitution of one behavior for another due to frustration when the normal event was blocked, e.g., thumb sucking or overeating when denied maternal access. He drew a parallel with non-nutritive sucking in chimpanzees and rhesus monkeys:

> In Harlow's laboratory I have seen a full-grown rhesus female who habitually sucked her own breast and a male who sucked his penis. Both had been reared in isolation. In these cases what we should all describe as oral symptoms had developed as a result of depriving the infant of a relationship with a mother-figure … May it not be the same for oral symptoms in human infants? (Bowlby, 1960c, p. 316)

In his conclusions, Bowlby once again stated that an understanding of biological processes is required in order to understand the psychological concomitants of biological processes. Two months later, in September 1959, the first symposium organized by Bowlby was held at the Tavistock Clinic and Harlow was an invited participant.

Mutual Contacts: The CIBA Symposia from 1959 to 1965

The initial introduction by Hinde and Bowlby's visit to Harlow's laboratory led to a fruitful cooperation during the following years. Just prior to a Chicago meeting, Harlow invited Bowlby to visit the University of Wisconsin again, but Bowlby replied with regrets on March 30, 1961, stating that he was already booked up with engagements relative to a forthcoming Chicago trip and would hope to visit Harlow's lab in 1962 or 1963 during a "more leisurely trip in the States. Looking forward to seeing you in the Autumn" (Bowlby in a letter to Harlow, March 30, 1961). Bowlby was undoubtedly referring to the second of four CIBA symposia to be held in London in the autumn of 1961 (see Chapter 4).

Figure 5.2 CIBA conference group photograph 1965. From left to right: Jay Rosenblatt, Brian Foss, Martin Richards (at back), Mavis Gunther, unknown, Harriet Rheingold, unknown, David Hamburg (in centre), unknown, Jack Gewirtz (at back), Harry Harlow, Mary Ainsworth, Lou Sander, Tony Ambrose (in center), Dorothy Heard, Peter Wolff, Miriam David, Genevieve Appell, Henry Ricciuti, John Bowlby, and Daniel Freedman. Courtesy of the Wellcome Library, London (AMWL: PP/BOW/L.31).

Harlow was a major participant of and contributor to the CIBA symposia in 1959 (Harlow, 1961), 1961 (Harlow, 1963), and 1965 (Harlow and Harlow, 1969) (Figure 5.2), but was unable to attend the third session in 1963. In his introduction to the proceedings of the last meeting, Bowlby contended that his early hopes had come true:

> As the series of meetings proceeds, reserves and misconceptions, inevitable when strangers from strange disciplines first meet, will recede and give place to an increasing grasp of what the other is attempting and why; to cross-fertilization of related fields; to mutual understanding and personal friendship. (Bowlby, 1969, p. xiii)

It is clear that both Harlow and Bowlby shared these positive feelings about the effectiveness of the symposia and that Bowlby was very pleased with the way things worked out. During the second study group, on September 7 and 9, 1961, Bowlby wrote to his wife Ursula:

> There is widespread enthusiasm at the way the study group is going, regrets we have so little time, [and] shows demand we meet again in [two] years time – (after our holiday next time). The atmosphere is much less tense this time – Jack Gewirtz no longer a problem child – [and] communication is quick, spontaneous [and] effective. The two year gap, I'm sure, is better than one year. It has given plenty of time for everyone to digest the lessons of the first meeting, [and] there has been much private visiting [and] private communication between the members since. The result is that this time it is the atmosphere of a house-party. Harry H[arlow] has got to London last night so missed the first two days but is now with us … Tomorrow he is on the platform [and] we should probably have some firework. I confess I feel rather proud of this party, both as a convener [and] chairman, I can take much credit for the party atmosphere, [and] also because so much of the work reported owes its origin to my stimulation. We have had [three] excellent presentations (Mary Ainsworth, Peter Wolff [and] Heinz Prechtl) [and] two that were too long (Jack Gewirtz [and] Tony Ambrose). In addition, Robert [Hinde] has shone [and] Rudolf Schaffer did very well in a brief contribution. They say Thelma [Rowell] is on the best of things [and] presents her Cambridge monkeys tomorrow. (Bowlby in a letter to Ursula, September 7, 1961; AMWL: PP/BOW/B.1/24)

> The study group is over [and] has been a tremendous success. Everyone has enjoyed it [and] feel they have profited from it. It has been extremely friendly [and] intense, together with cautious and effective discussion. We managed to cover a lot of ground without hurry. It is striking how far [and] fast people have developed in the two years since we last met. In a sense it has become a kind of club [and] seems likely to have far reaching effects. (Bowlby in a letter to Ursula, September 9, 1961; AMWL: PP/BOW/B.1/24)

After the last of the CIBA symposia, Bowlby wrote to Harlow that he was "very glad indeed that you were able to be with us last week and to give us such a stimulating account of your work" (Bowlby in a letter to Harlow September 21, 1965). Bowlby's sentiments concerning the ultimate success of the four-part series are echoed in a letter Harlow wrote to Bowlby:

> It was my personal opinion that the last [CIBA symposium] was more informative than the first two … I was impressed by the fact that the people who reported both in formal papers and in discussion were far more sophisticated about the problems … and I think I can include myself

> within this generalization. Furthermore, I thought that members of the conference communicated with each other far more effectively than they had ... and I believe that this was a result of increasing sophistication in the nature of the problems attacked and in the development of adequate measurement and techniques. I personally believe that the Tavistock series ... achieved a great deal. (Harlow in a letter to Bowlby, October 18, 1965)

There is no doubt, then, that the CIBA symposia achieved their goal. By bringing together major figures in the field, such as Mary Ainsworth, John Bowlby, Jack Gewirtz, Harry Harlow, Robert Hinde, Harriet Rheingold, and Theodore Schneirla, they were able to further the mutual understanding of animal psychologists, ethologist, and learning theorists, and to advance the understanding of infant behavior (Foss, 1961, 1963, 1965, 1969). In particular, they allowed Bowlby and Harlow to meet on a regular basis and to discuss each other's ideas thoroughly.

Bowlby's Writings in the Early 1960s: Using Harlow's Empirical Findings as a Secure Base

In the early 1960s, in several papers, Bowlby (1960a, 1960b, 1961a, 1961b, 1961c) expanded upon the theme of separation anxiety. He intended it as companion pieces to his earlier treatise on the child's tie to the mother (Bowlby, 1958d). In a review of the literature (Bowlby, 1961a; see also Bowlby, 1960a), he presented his new conceptualization of separation anxiety in the same detailed manner as he elaborated on the nature of the child's tie to the mother in that previous paper. Before presenting his own theory, Bowlby delineated five different theories of anxiety related to the child's attachment to the mother. First, he described "transformed libido" theory, a view held by Freud until 1926, where he attributed anxiety to a child's unsatisfied libido upon separation from an attachment figure. Second, he mentioned the view that separation anxiety may mirror birth trauma and is the counterpart to the craving of the infant in the "return-to-the-womb theory" met before. The third view Bowlby discussed was that of "signal theory," which held that anxiety behavior has a function and results from a safety device to ensure that the separation will not be long and implied that the child's tie to the mother derives from a secondary drive. The fourth view presented was that of "depressive anxiety," after Melanie Klein, who suggested the infant felt responsible for destroying his mother and believed he had lost her forever. Finally, Bowlby discussed "persecutory anxiety," also after Melanie Klein, where the young child feels the mother has left him, because she is angry with him.

Fifth and finally, Bowlby then described his own theory as "primary anxiety" theory, defining anxiety as:

> a primary response not reducible to other terms and due simply to the rupture of the attachment to his mother. / The child is bound to his mother by a number of instinctual response systems, each of which is primary and which together have high survival value … I wish to distinguish it sharply from states of anxiety dependent on foresight. (Bowlby, 1961a, pp. 253/267)

Bowlby emphasized that his theory involved a new and ethologically inspired approach:

> The heart of this theory is that the organism is provided with a repertoire of behaviour patterns, which are bred into it like the features of its anatomy and physiology, and which have become characteristic of its species *because of their survival value to the species.* (Bowlby, 1960a, p. 95; original italics)

But Bowlby now also clearly relied on the careful experiments by comparative psychologists such as Harry Harlow. In discussing fright and an animal's escape from a fearful situation to a secure situation, he referred to the latter as a "haven of safety," a term which he took from Harlow and Zimmermann (1958). Bowlby quoted Harlow and Zimmermann as follows:

> In describing their very interesting experiments with rhesus monkeys they write: "One function of the real mother, human or sub-human, and presumably of a mother surrogate, is to provide a haven of safety for the infant in times of fear or danger." (Bowlby, 1960a, p. 97)

Later in the same paper, Bowlby compared the behavior of the young child, Laura (filmed by Robertson, 1952; see Chapter 3), who pretended to be asleep when a strange man entered her room, to the behavior of the rhesus infants, who froze in a crouched posture when introduced to a strange situation in the absence of the surrogate mother. That remarkable comparison too was a reference to Harlow

Figure 5.3 John Bowlby lecturing at the 117th Annual Meeting of the American Psychiatric Association in Chicago, 1961. Courtesy of the Wellcome Library, London (AMWL: PP/BOW/L.5).

and Zimmermann's paper. Bowlby also discussed the infants' rushing to the mother (if she was present) as a source of security, describing the response as so strong "it can be adequately depicted only by motion pictures" (Bowlby, 1960a, p. 101). Here, again, the *emotional* impact of films is evident; something that can not be conveyed by the language used in scientific papers. With his comment, Bowlby was no doubt referring to Harlow's film, *The Nature and Development of Affection* (Harlow and Zimmermann, 1959b), a film that has been shown to thousands of introductory psychology classes over the years and received an award for excellence at a European film festival in 1960.

In three other papers Bowlby (1960b, 1961b, 1961c) of that period discussed maternal separation and the processes of grief and mourning: according to his views separation from the mother-figure would lead to separation anxiety and grief and would set in train processes of mourning. Bowlby described the three stages of protest, despair, and detachment. One of the papers was based on a lecture Bowlby (1961c) read at a meeting of the American Psychiatric Association in Chicago in May, 1961 (see Figure 5.3). There Bowlby once again presented his new ideas to an audience of psychiatrists. He stressed the importance of observation instead of using retrospective evidence, described the analogous course of grief and mourning in children and adults as well as in animals, and finally pointed to the evolutionary basis of the process of mourning. To buttress his claim that "in the light of phylogeny it is likely that the instinctual bonds that tie human young to a mother figure are built on the same general pattern as in other mammalian species" (Bowlby, 1961c, p. 482), Bowlby referred once again to the work of Harlow (Harlow and Zimmermann, 1959a). There was no discussion of Harlow's work beyond that, but Bowlby's own description of the stages of protest, despair, and detachment was to greatly influence Harlow's experimenting.

Harlow's Research in the 1960s: Seeking Empirical Evidence for Bowlby's Theoretical Claims

Bowlby's influence on Harlow's work becomes evident after the first two CIBA conferences. In two studies on mother–infant separation Harlow modelled his experiments with rhesus monkeys on the human separation syndrome described by Bowlby (Stephen Suomi, personal communication, August 27, 2006). In his experiments Harlow either physically (Seay, Hansen, and Harlow, 1962) or totaly (not just physically but also visually and audibly) separated (Seay and Harlow, 1965) the infant rhesus monkeys from their mothers for three and two weeks respectively. In both studies, the rhesus infants initially responded with "violent and prolonged protest" and then passed into a stage of "low activity, little or no play and occasional crying" (Seay and Harlow, 1965, p. 439). These stages were similar to the phases of protest and despair described by Bowlby. The third phase of detachment was not found in either study, presumably because of the relatively short period of separation. Overall, Harlow reported considerable similarity in the responses to mother-infant separation in human children and infant monkeys, explicitly referring to Bowlby's (1960b, 1961a) studies on the subject.

Bowlby's Continuing Interest in Harlow's Work

Ten years after their first publications on the mother-child bond (Bowlby, 1958d; Harlow, 1958), Bowlby (1968) published a paper on the effects on behavior of the disruption of an affectional bond. In this paper he stated that "[t]here is now abundant evidence that, not only in birds but in mammals also, young become attached to mother-objects despite not being fed from that source" (p. 96), and referred to Harlow's work with rhesus monkeys (Harlow and Harlow, 1965). This statement made clear that there no longer was any empirical support for psychoanalytic and learning theorist explanations for attachment behavior.

In 1969, four years after the fourth and last CIBA symposium, the first volume of Bowlby's trilogy on *Attachment and Loss* was published. In that volume, Bowlby drew heavily on the results of Harlow's experiments as an empirical confirmation of his ideas. Throughout this book, Bowlby made ample use of animal evidence and biological theorizing (e.g., Lorenz, Tinbergen). Among the students of animal behavior Bowlby referred to, Harlow figured prominently. We shall mention but a few examples.

In discussing motor patterns of primate sexual behavior, Bowlby (1969/1982b) claimed there is clear evidence that they are subject to a sensitive developmental phase and pointed out Harlow's extensive series of experiments in which rhesus infants were raised in differing social environments, "all differing greatly from the environment of evolutionary adaptedness" (p. 165). Pointing out the deficits in adult heterosexual behavior displayed by the Wisconsin isolate-reared monkeys, Bowlby cited a personal communication in which Harlow wrote he was "now quite convinced that there is no adequate substitute for monkey mothers early in the socialization process" (Harlow in a letter to Bowlby dated October 18, 1965).

A chapter on the nature of attachment behavior contained a reiteration by Bowlby (1969/1982b) of the four principal theories of the child's tie to the mother that he had disputed in his earlier paper (Bowlby, 1958d). This time he prefaced his own view with the interesting phrase: "Until 1958, which saw the publication of Harlow's first papers and of an early version of the view expressed here, four principal theories regarding the nature and origin of the child's tie were ... found" (p. 178). With that phrase, Bowlby seemed to at least implicitly make two points: first, that he and Harlow simultaneously and independently arrived at similar views, and, second, that Harlow's findings were of fundamental importance for attachment theory and hence for his own thinking.

In a discussion of primate infant and mother roles in their joint relationship, Bowlby (1969/1982b) referred to the tenacity of primate infants brought up in human homes to cling to their foster parents and added: "Of the cases in which an infant has been brought up on an experimental dummy the best-known reports are those of Harlow and his colleagues (Harlow, 1961; Harlow and Harlow, 1965)" (p. 194). The next sub-topic was the infant's ability to discriminate the mother, and Bowlby again cited Harlow and Harlow (1965) pointing out that Harlow believed a rhesus infant learned attachment to a specific mother during the first week or two of life.

In his chapter on the nature and function of attachment behavior, Bowlby connected Lorenz's work on imprinting to Harlow's rhesus monkey work. To support his views on the nature and function of attachment behavior, Bowlby (1969/1982b) used Harlow's experiments to undermine "the secondary drive type of theory." He meticulously described Harlow's (Harlow, 1961; Harlow and Zimmermann, 1959a) experiments with the cloth and wire mother illustrating "that 'contact comfort' led to attachment behavior whereas food did not" and that "typical attachment behavior is directed to the non-feeding cloth model whereas no such behavior is directed toward the feeding wire one" (Bowlby, 1969/1982b, pp. 213–216).

In developing a control systems approach to attachment behavior, Bowlby (1969/1982b) applied Harlow's (Harlow and Harlow, 1965) views on the object and social exploratory behavior of young monkeys to that of human children: just as infant monkeys, human children have an exploratory system that is "antithetic to [their] attachment behaviour" (p. 239), because it takes them away from their mother.

From these few examples, it becomes clear that in the first volume of his magnum opus *Attachment and Loss*, Bowlby used Harlow's empirical data on rhesus monkeys as uncontested evidence for his own views on the nature and development of the attachment relation which is formed between children and their caregivers in the first year of life. Harlow's findings provided Bowlby with independent empirical evidence, which he could use to argue the superiority of his ideas over those of psychoanalysts and learning theorists.

Sociogram

At this point, it seems feasible to summarize Bowlby's interaction with ethologists and animal psychologists as discussed in previous chapters. These interactions are summarized in a sociogram or "sociometric chart plotting the structure of interpersonal relations in a group situation" (Merriam-Webster Online Dictionary). It is no coincidence that the interactions in this sociogram, leading to Bowlby's introduction to ethology, start with Julian Huxley, Niko Tinbergen, and Konrad Lorenz. Bowlby acknowledged them in his *Attachment and Loss* and claimed he was "grateful to all three for continuing education and for encouragement" (Bowlby, 1969/1982b, p. xviii). Tinbergen and Lorenz, as the proponents of continental ethology in the 1930s, met with their British counterpart Huxley at separate ornithological conferences in Amsterdam in 1930 and Oxford in 1934, respectively (Burchardt, 2005; Kruuk, 2003). Later, both Lorenz and Huxley would attend the World Health Organization (WHO) conferences in Geneva and London from 1953 to 1956, meetings Bowlby also participated in. In 1936, Lorenz visited Leiden and during a symposium on *Instinct* was first introduced to Tinbergen (Roëll, 2000). As we have seen, their interactions would have great impact on the field of biology and they were awarded the Nobel Prize in Physiology or Medicine (together with Karl von Frisch) in 1973. In the 1940s, it was mostly Tinbergen who interacted with leading researchers in British ethology, much more so than did Lorenz. For example, Tinbergen corresponded with Hinde's later Ph.D. supervisor David Lack from 1940 onward and met Lack for the first time at a conference in Leiden in 1946 (Burchardt, 2005). Tinbergen and William Thorpe had their first encounter when Tinbergen was travelling through Great-Britain with Lack in 1946, right after their first encounter in Leiden (Kruuk, 2003). In 1950, although he was officially supervised by Lack, Robert Hinde started his Ph.D. with Tinbergen after the latter had made the move to Oxford (Kruuk, 2003; Tinbergen, 1991). Eventually, Thorpe set up an ornithological field station in Cambridge and asked Hinde to supervise the enterprise. Meanwhile, Hinde and Lorenz first met at a symposium in Buldern in 1952, where Hinde impressed Lorenz with a paper on the mobbing reaction of chaffinches to owls (see Chapter 4). Thus, in the 1930s and 1940s, a network of European ethologists was created, which quickly resumed its activity after the war. It was in the early 1950s that Bowlby became acquainted with many of them.

After his attention was drawn to ethology, Bowlby's first interaction with this network of ethologists was during a vacation with his family-in-law in 1951, where he met with Huxley, who encouraged him to go into ethology in more depth and referred him to the work of Tinbergen. After reading his way into ethology, Bowlby suggested to invite Lorenz to the first WHO conference on "the psychobiological development of the child" (Tanner and Inhelder, 1971) in Geneva in 1953. At this meeting, Lorenz spoke highly of Hinde's work and Bowlby became interested in meeting Hinde. The first encounter between Hinde and Bowlby was rather by chance, though, during a scientific meeting on ethology and psychiatry organized by the Royal Medico-Psychological Association in London in 1954. The organizers had intended to invite Tinbergen and Lorenz, but they were both unavailable, so Hinde and Bowlby were asked to participate instead (see Chapter 4).

A couple of years later, in 1957, Tinbergen, Hinde, and Harry Harlow attended the same conference in Stanford, where European ethologists and American animal psychologists, on the invitation of Daniel Lehrman, attempted to bridge their differences of opinion. After returning to England, Hinde drew Bowlby's attention to the work of Harlow, and Harlow and Bowlby corresponded from 1957 onward and visited each other's laboratories in subsequent years (see Chapter 5). Finally, Steve Suomi was introduced to Harlow by his father after the latter met Harlow on an airplane and through Harlow Suomi was later introduced to both Bowlby and Hinde at a scientific meeting in New York (Suomi, Van der Horst, and Van der Veer, 2008).

The sociogram (Box 5.1) summarizes the interactions Bowlby had with many influential ethologists and animal psychologists from the 1930s to the 1970s. Many of these interactions have been discussed in previous chapters and have been documented. I present this sociogram as evidence of a cross-fertilization of ethological and attachment ideas.

Concluding Remarks

In this chapter, I have taken a closer look at the cross-fertilization of the work of John Bowlby and Harry Harlow. I quoted from their correspondence and showed their joint presence at professional

Box 5.1

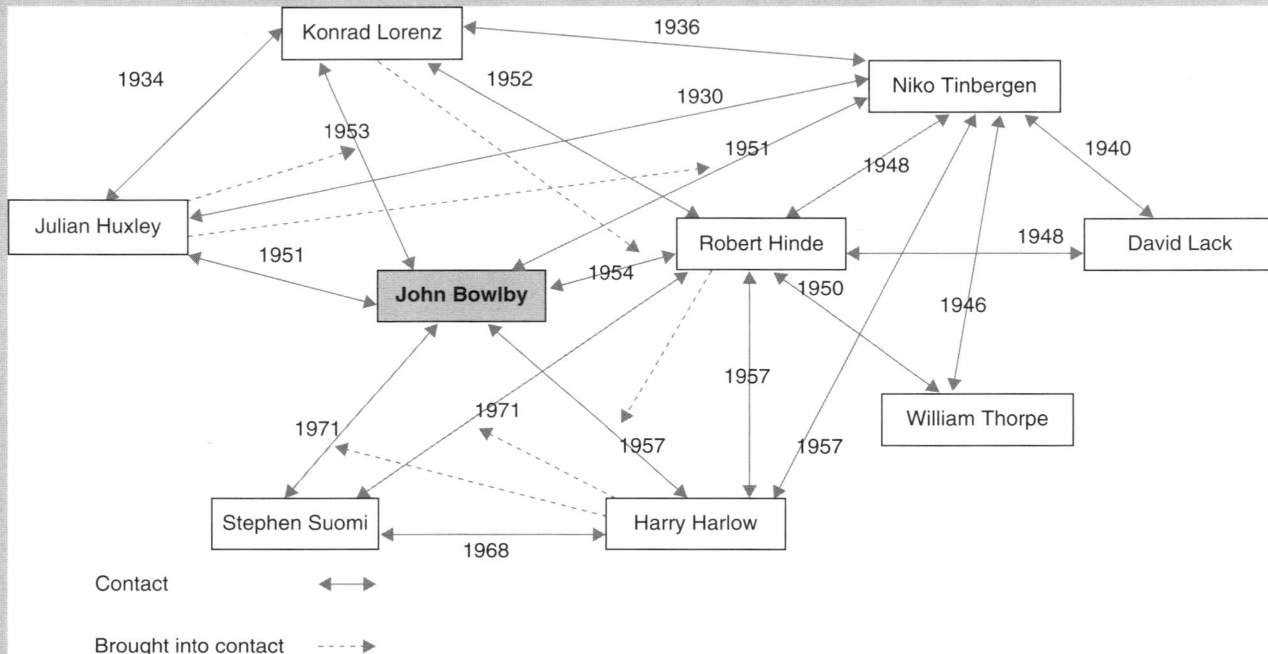
Konrad Lorenz
Niko Tinbergen
Julian Huxley
Robert Hinde
David Lack
John Bowlby
William Thorpe
Stephen Suomi
Harry Harlow
1934
1936
1952
1930
1953
1951
1940
1948
1951
1948
1954
1950
1946
1957
1971
1971
1957
1957
1968
Contact
Brought into contact

meetings. The two men wrote dozens of letters to each other and met at least five times between 1958 and 1965. Instances in which Bowlby cited Harlow's work as evidence for his own theoretical views, or as illustrative documentation of a behavior or phenomenon, have been noted. We may conclude that Harlow's scientific influence on Bowlby has been demonstrated beyond reasonable doubt: Harlow's experiments showed in a remarkable way what Bowlby had been theorizing about since his introduction to ethology in the early 1950s. These findings make abundantly clear that Singer (1975) was wrong in asserting that Harlow's empirical work had no impact on Bowlby's theory whatsoever. A careful analysis shows that Harlow provided an important part of the solid empirical foundation for Bowlby's theoretical construction.[3]

In his turn, Harlow was influenced by Bowlby's new theorizing. I have described how in two studies on separation (Seay, Hansen, and Harlow, 1962; Seay and Harlow, 1965) Harlow modeled his experiments on Bowlby's ideas. Harlow's own assertion that he and his colleagues used one of Bowlby's paper as something of a "reference bible" (see earlier), his frequent requests in their correspondence for offprints of Bowlby's papers, and his references to Bowlby's ideas make it clear that he regarded Bowlby as one of the major theoreticians. It was Harlow's student Suomi (1995) who acknowledged Bowlby's major influence in three areas of animal research: (1) descriptive studies of the development of attachment and other social relationships in monkeys and apes; (2) experimental and naturalistic studies of social separation in nonhuman primates, and (3) investigations of the long-term consequences of differential early attachments in rhesus monkeys.

The scientific and personal contact between Bowlby and Harlow that started in 1957 lasted through the 1960s and early 1970s until Harlow's retirement in 1974. They kept each other informed about their work and cited each other's work extensively. Although they came from widely diverging backgrounds and differed in many respects they found a common denominator in their interest in the origin of affectional bonds. Together they reached the introductory psychology textbooks and influenced the lives of many children around the world.

Meanwhile, Mary Ainsworth had returned from Uganda with highly relevant observational material of young Ganda children.

Although reluctant at first, she would, at the strong insistence of Bowlby, make her observation public at one of the Tavistock symposia (Ainsworth, 1963). We will turn to Ainsworth's contributions to attachment theory in the next chapter.

Notes

1 The correspondence between Harry Harlow and John Bowlby (thus far twenty letters were recovered) resides with Helen A. LeRoy, who was Harlow's executive assistant at the Primate Lab at the University of Wisconsin-Madison from her arrival in 1958 until his retirement in 1974.

2 Note that reprints at the time had to be typed anew, because the Xeroxing machine was still a luxury of the future. In order to make multiple copies to exchange their writings, researchers had to resort to having papers typed several times or to reproducing them by mimeograph. On the mailing list for Harlow's papers we find among others the names of Mary Ainsworth, Gerard Baerends, John Bowlby, Julian Huxley, and René Spitz.

3 Recently, Vicedo (2009a) criticized what she called "Harlow's legend" and has pointed to Harlow's more complex views about affectional systems and the role of peers that appeared in his later research. Here, I have restricted myself to a description of Bowlby's use of Harlow's work.

6
Mary Ainsworth's Role in the Study of Attachment

Ainsworth's Contributions to Attachment Theory

In 1950, Mary Salter Ainsworth gave up her assistant professorship at the University of Toronto and moved to England together with her husband Leonard Ainsworth, where the latter was given the opportunity to do graduate work at London University College. At that time Mary Ainsworth herself had yet not found a job in England and at the suggestion of a friend, she applied for a position with John Bowlby at the London Tavistock Clinic. This decision would "reset the whole direction of her research career" (Ainsworth, 1983; see also Bretherton, 2003), "while at the same time incorporating some of its earlier threads" (Ainsworth and Bowlby, 1991, p. 3). Although the direct cooperation between Ainsworth and Bowlby at the Separation Research Unit (see Chapter 3) lasted only three years, the result was indeed of great consequence. It brought together Bowlby's ideas on the importance of early-life experiences for later child development, his emphasis on naturalistic observation, and his interest in ethology with Ainsworth's ideas on security – ideas she

John Bowlby – From Psychoanalysis to Ethology: Unraveling the Roots of Attachment Theory, First Edition. Frank C. P. van der Horst.

acquired while studying and working with William Blatz in Toronto in the 1930s and 1940s.

In the preceding chapters the contacts between Bowlby and various ethologists have been discussed. I have tried to show how these contacts influenced attachment theory and subsequent animal research. I do not want to give the impression, however, that in discussing the interchange between attachment theory and ethology, I assumed that Bowlby was the sole founder of attachment theory. Attachment theory as it eventually evolved also owes much to the conceptual and empirical work of Mary Ainsworth, and to date her contribution may have been somewhat underestimated by historians of science.

In this chapter, I will describe Ainsworth's early life and career, her early interactions with Bowlby, and I will relate the importance of Ainsworth's contributions to Bowlby's ideas and to attachment theory. It is of special importance to trace the origin of the "secure base" phenomenon that Bowlby incorporated as a central concept into attachment theory and to delineate the scientific influences on the development of one of Ainsworth's most important methodological contributions to attachment theory: the Strange Situation Procedure (SSP).

Ainsworth's Early Life and Career

Mary Dinsmore Salter was born in Glensdale, Ohio, in 1913, the eldest of three sisters. Since her parents "placed high value on a good … education" (Ainsworth, 1983, p. 2), it was assumed she and her sisters would go to college. Her choice for psychology was prompted by her reading of William McDougall's (1927) *Character and the Conduct of Life*. As a result, Ainsworth entered the University of Toronto as an undergraduate in psychology in 1929 – when she was only 16 – "hoping… to understand how she had come to be the person she was, and what her parents had to do with it" (Ainsworth and Bowlby, 1991, p. 2). After obtaining a Bachelor's degree in 1935, she earned a Master's degree in 1936 with Sperrin Chant. Her thesis which was an investigation of the relationship between attitudes and emotional response resulted in her first publication (i.e., Chant and Salter, 1937). In a time of international turmoil and the threat of war, Chant and Ainsworth assessed the subjects' attitude toward war and simultaneously used the galvanic skin response to assess their emotional response. The authors concluded that the data gathered in their study did not support "the general belief that attitudes are highly emotional" (p. 289). Ainsworth later emphasized that during her time with Chant, she had a lot of training in experimental methods (Bretherton, personal communication, March 1, 2010).

Apart from working with Chant, who taught her "that research can be fun" (Ainsworth, 1983, p. 3), and Edward Bott, for whom she worked as a teaching assistant in his introductory psychology course for medical students, Ainsworth started taking undergraduate and graduate classes with William Emet Blatz and soon became impressed by his work and ideas. Through Blatz, who was head of the Toronto Institute of Child Study, Ainsworth was introduced to 'security theory' (Blatz, 1966; see also Ainsworth, 2010). In security theory, Blatz both reformulated and challenged Freudian ideas, though he tried to hide any connection between his ideas and Freud's, because of the anti-Freudian climate at the department at the time (Ainsworth, 1983; Bretherton, 1992). Ainsworth eventually took her Ph.D. in psychology with Blatz and her dissertation, titled "An evaluation of adjustment based on the concept of security" (Salter, 1940), contained the first publication of the secure base concept (Bretherton, 1992; Bretherton and Main, 2000). Although Blatz is often mentioned as the source of inspiration for Ainsworth's secure base concept, his influence has, until now, never been fully investigated. It is therefore of great interest to look at Blatz's ideas on security in more detail.

William Blatz and Security Theory

The most comprehensive overview of Blatz's security theory is his posthumously published work *Human Security* (Blatz, 1966) – a book based on tape recorded notes and published with the help of his former students. In it, Blatz formulated ideas he had been working on since the early 1930s, when he began to develop the concept of security, by which he meant "the state of mind which accompanies the willingness to accept the consequences of one's acts – without equivocation of any sort. The feeling accompanying this state may be called serenity. Security is the basic goal of all living beings" (p. 13). Blatz made a clear distinction between security and safety: those who seek safety are insecure. Hence, security is akin to feeling self-confident and competent. Also, Blatz used security as a concept and an operational definition of mental health.

On the basis of his experience with neglected and deserted children, Blatz hypothesized that "early care of the infant is most important in establishing a secure basis for later experience. This care should not be interrupted too frequently by change in the persons who are caring for the child" (Blatz, 1966, p. 7). Clearly, according to Blatz, security is acquired through early experience, namely, a loving and, above all, consistent relationship with parents.

Blatz reasoned that no one can feel insecure for a long time and be mentally healthy. Children typically develop an 'immature dependent security' from their parents, depending on and trusting in them. According to Blatz, "from familiarity and warmth the child learns to depend upon the agent" (Blatz, 1966, p. 37). He described the interaction between a child and its "agent" thus:

> Held in his mother's arms, he feels that he may explore and seek adventure, but suddenly he seems to have reached a limit, his laugh dries up, he cuddles closer and buries his face in his mother's breast, and the game is over. The accepting of the new, the potentially fearful, is exciting, but there must be a familiar, trusted world from which he can foray, and to which he can always return. The dependable agent is a must if early security is to be established. (Blatz, 1966, p. 39)

The mother, or the "agent", is referred to by Blatz as a "jumping-off platform" (p. 39). This relationship with the mother and the security that the child derives from it, according to Blatz, has far-reaching consequences for later life and relationships: "the best insurance against a later mental illness is an early and sound security pattern" (p. 43).

Developmentally, a person gradually enters a state of insecurity and then moves in one of four possible directions. Ideally, the adult may turn to a love partner and develop a "mature dependent security." Blatz saw this form of security as clearly superior and especially desirable since this is a two-way relationship with each providing security for the other. If, for what kind of reason, an adult is unable to form a "mature dependent security" there are several other possibilities.

However desirable for the child, Blatz saw moving back to immature dependent security as a clear sign of regression in adulthood – a one-way relationship would be maladaptive with an adult partner. As an alternative, the adult may become "independent secure," believing he can solve everything himself. He may also avoid insecurity by forming "pseudo-security," relying on so-called "deputy agents" (e.g., postponement, denial, intolerance of other views, blaming others for one's own shortcomings, etc.) to avoid being confronted with problems – an apparent but only temporary solution. Clearly, Blatz used the term "deputy agent" instead of Freud's "defence mechanism," for reasons stated above.

In conclusion, Blatz believed that infants should be taken care of consistently, in order to develop a dependent security, i.e., a basic self-confidence to wander into new and unfamiliar situations based on the fact that the other is always there to help. The trusted other is a jumping platform from which to explore the environment. Also, when children get into a frightening situation, they have to feel free to retreat to the other for comfort and reassurance. Blatz emphasized that the other (i.e., caregiver) should not be replaced too often. Gradually, persons need to form a secure relationship with another adult; this is much easier when they developed immature dependent security in childhood.

During her time in Toronto as a Ph.D. in the 1930s, Ainsworth became familiar with Blatz's ideas on security. Ainsworth's dissertation research included "an analysis of students' autobiographical narratives in support of the validity of her paper-and-pencil self-report scales of familial and extrafamilial security, foreshadowing her later penchant for narrative methods of data collection" (Bretherton, 1992, p. 760). In her thesis, Ainsworth stated that "familial security in the early stages is of a dependent type and forms a basis from which the individual can work out gradually forming new skills and interests in other fields" (Salter, 1940, p. 45). In the case "familial security is lacking, the individual is handicapped by the lack of what might be called a secure base from which to work" (p. 45). So already in Ainsworth's early work as a Ph.D. student with Blatz the notion of the secure base is present – albeit related to the family, not a specific attachment figure. Nevertheless, it is quite clear that Ainsworth found inspiration in Toronto during her collaboration with Blatz and took these valuable experiences to the Tavistock Clinic in 1950.

Working on Separation at the Tavistock Clinic with Bowlby and Robertson

After World War II, when Ainsworth reached the rank of major in the Canadian Women's Army Corps, she returned to the University of Toronto as an assistant professor of psychology to give, among other things, a course on clinical assessment. She was trained in the Rorschach Test by Bruno Klopfer and prepared a manual for her students that impressed Knopfler so much, that he asked her to co-author a volume of *Developments in the Rorschach Technique* (Klopfer *et al.*, 1954). Ainsworth also continued to work with Blatz, as did her future husband Leonard. Earlier we have seen how Mary Ainsworth then followed her husband to London and applied for a job at the Tavistock Clinic. During her time there, she worked very closely with John Bowlby and James Robertson on "the effects on personality development of separation from the mother in early childhood" (Ainsworth and Bowlby, 1954, p. 105). It was perhaps then that Ainsworth learned about ethology as a new framework – or at least a framework that could be used when studying children and explaining the mother-child relation – but Ainsworth and Bowlby seem to have had quite different memories about this episode.

In an interview, Ainsworth once stated that she "was in London … at the time [Bowlby] first discovered ethology" (Rudnytsky, 1997, p. 396). Just as Bowlby, she had developed an early interest in animal studies, in Ainsworth's case through her reading of Earnest Thompson Seton's (1899) story about Lobo the Wolf. Ainsworth claimed to have been familiar with ethology even before Bowlby was: "As a matter of fact, I had been ahead of him, in a way, because I had read *King Solomon's Ring* before he had ever heard of Konrad Lorenz" (Rudnytsky, 1997, p. 396). This may be doubted, however, as we have seen that Bowlby read *King Solomon's Ring* in a proof copy version provided to him by Julian Huxley (see Chapter 4). Also, we know that Bowlby was familiar with Lorenz's work before Ainsworth came to London. Be that as it may, Ainsworth was at first very sceptical about the applicability of this new theoretical framework as applied to human mothers and infants – Ainsworth even warned Bowlby that "using baby chicks' behavior to argue against an entrenched psychoanalytic position might *ruin* his reputation!" (Ainsworth and Marvin, 1995, p. 7; original italics) – but in her later work she would actually accept and emphasize Bowlby's ethological ideas. According to Bowlby, this was due to *his* influence on her as he would later state that Ainsworth "must have known a bit about [ethology] before she left [for Uganda], because I was getting enthusiastic about it ... when she was [at the Tavistock Clinic]" (Smuts, 1977b, p. 29). Bowlby vividly remembered that "she must have shown quite a lot of interest in it ... I remember having quite prolonged debates on paper ... and that's how she became ethologically oriented" (Smuts, 1977b, pp. 29–30). In Uganda, Ainsworth experienced what she described as a "Eureka" experience: she suddenly realized how well Bowlby's notions fit with what she observed.

The ethological orientation at the Separation Research Unit becomes clear from an early paper by Ainsworth and Bowlby (1954) – one of only three publications that they ever published together. In it, they stated that psychoanalysis provided "an invaluable body of working hypotheses for those responsible for the treatment of psychogenic disorders," (p. 106) but they also argued that psychoanalysis had "serious shortcomings as a basis for scientific research" (p. 106). As an alternative, they provided object relations theory as formulated by Klein and Fairbairn and "the work of ethologists, notably Lorenz and Tinbergen" (p. 160). Ethology, in their view, offered great possibilities "to those who are concerned with research into the influence of early mother-child relationships on personality" (p. 160). It could well be that, at that time, this was mainly Bowlby's position. Ethology did not come up in another paper they wrote (Bowlby *et al.*, 1956), because Bowlby's "collaborators did not accept these newfangled ideas at the time" (Inge Bretherton, personal communication, March 29, 2010).

At the Tavistock, Ainsworth's closest colleague was James Robertson, who had been charged with observing young children before, during and after being separated from their mother (see Chapter 3). One of Ainsworth's tasks was to assist Robertson with the analysis of his detailed observational notes. With regard to these observations, Ainsworth "was deeply impressed by their value" (Ainsworth, 1983, p. 8). Since it was Anna Freud who had taught Robertson about the value of observation, one could argue that she indirectly influenced Ainsworth as well. When Ainsworth's time at the Tavistock Clinic was drawing to a close – Leonard Ainsworth having finished his Ph.D. work in the autumn of 1953 – she resolved that "wherever she went next she would undertake research into what goes on between an infant and its mother that accounts for the formation of its strong bond to her" and that she would "base her study on the direct observation of infants and mothers in the context of home and family" (Ainsworth and Bowlby, 1991, p. 4), because she was "entranced with the prospect of a future study … in which I would employ simple, direct, naturalistic observation, and to use simple descriptive statistics to deal with its findings" (Ainsworth, 1983, p. 8). Clearly, her work with Bowlby and, in particular, Robertson had influenced her interest in these research methods. The opportunity to do naturalistic observations came, sooner than expected, when Ainsworth – again – followed her husband and moved to Kampala, Uganda in 1954.

Naturalistic Observation in Uganda

In Africa, Ainsworth began observations of interactions of young Ganda children and their mothers (e.g., Ainsworth, 1963, 1967), which highly influenced her further career and theoretical thinking on attachment. At the start of her project, Ainsworth's aim was to study the infants' responses to weaning (a clearly psychoanalytic theme) and to separation. Soon, however, it became apparent that the ancient Ganda practice of separating a child from his mother and sending it to relatives – usually the grandmother – at the time of weaning, had passed into disuse. Instead, Ainsworth decided to shift the focus of her study to the development of the children's attachment and "to ascertain the effect of variations in infant-care practices upon the course of development, particularly upon the growth of attachment" (Ainsworth, 1967, p. 6). During her observations of infant–mother interactions, Ainsworth experienced a real change in her thinking – a Eureka experience: "The transition I made from thinking in psychoanalytic terms to thinking in terms of ethology felt much like … a paradigm shift" (Ainsworth and Marvin, 1995, p. 4). So, after a false start, Ainsworth decided to give Bowlby's ideas a chance and it didn't take her long to realize that he had been right.

According to Bowlby, "the approach [Ainsworth] adopts is the natural history approach typical of the social anthropologist and of the ethologist" (Ainsworth and Marvin, 1995, p. v). Ainsworth also adopted an ecological approach, evident in the case studies for each family (some were polygamous, in others the husband was not living with the family most of the time, because he had a job somewhere else). Her approach can best be described as simple, direct, naturalistic observation – just as Ainsworth had envisioned when working at the Tavistock Clinic with Robertson. These observations led to the first mother–child study from an evolutionary perspective – a study that even antedated Bowlby's presentation of his revolutionary ideas in a lecture to the British Psycho-Analytical Society in 1957 (published as Bowlby, 1958d; see Chapter 5 in this volume).

Ainsworth linked her data from the observational study in Uganda, carried out in 1954–1955, to the new theoretical framework that Bowlby had been working on since the early 1950s, when they collaborated at the Tavistock Clinic. Her experiences in Uganda and her early publications on mother-child interaction resulted in "cross-cultural" data that supported the notion of a biologically grounded attachment between mothers and their children (see Van IJzendoorn and Sagi, 2008).

How best to summarize Ainsworth's project in East Africa? The sample of her study consisted of 28 Ganda children – 15 boys and 13 girls – aged 1–24 months. In fact, Ainsworth did not really want to include the older children, but they were the children of the chief whose permission was necessary to undertake the research. The observations Ainsworth made of these children spanned up to nine months. The families were visited at home every two weeks for two hours. During these home-visits, Ainsworth made observations of the interaction between mother and infant and she interviewed the mothers with the help of a field worker who acted as a translator and a collaborator. During the informal visits, information was gathered about feeding, sleeping, and crying of the child, and factors connected to rearing practices such as the mother's sensitivity.

It was in Uganda, during these very detailed home-observations, that Ainsworth was for the first time able to ascertain the crucial role of maternal sensitivity in the development of attachment. Ainsworth (1967) related that "development is an interactional process – an interaction between constitutional elements and environmental circumstances" (p. 388). As one of these environmental influences "sensitivity of the mother in responding to the baby's signals" (Ainsworth, 1967, p. 397) emerged as highly significant. According to Ainsworth, "sensitivity of response to signals implies that signals are perceived and correctly interpreted and that the response is prompt and appropriate" (p. 397). She noticed that the amount of care given by the mother was significant to the development of attachment and believed that this was due to the fact

> that interaction and sensitivity to signals have as a necessary condition that the mother is available to the child. If the mother is elsewhere, she obviously cannot respond to and interact with the baby, although her mere presence is no guarantee of sensitivity or interaction. (Ainsworth, 1967, p. 397)

In fact, this is the first statement of Ainsworth's ideas on availability of the mother and of maternal sensitivity as an antecedent of attachment development. It would become a crucial concept in Ainsworth's Baltimore Study as well (see later in this chapter).

During her time in Uganda, Ainsworth accumulated rich and detailed qualitative data and her attempt to describe Ganda children during their first year of life was impressive. At the same time, she used a rigorous approach to synthesize her observations into overall constructs. Ainsworth's observations and the general patterns of attachment that she identified were to prove very relevant and important for attachment theory. But for the time being the results were not available to others, though Bowlby encouraged her to write up her data. Eventually, it took Ainsworth more than a decade to analyze her observational material in terms of a coherent framework and to publish them in the form of the monograph: *Infancy in Uganda: Infant Care and the Growth of Love* (Ainsworth, 1967). It is an open question to what extent her theoretical understanding of the observational findings changed over these years, for example, by theoretical discussions with colleagues during the CIBA meetings (see later in this chapter).

Back to Baltimore and Back in Touch with Bowlby

After returning from Uganda in 1955, Ainsworth was appointed, first as a lecturer and later as assistant professor of psychology, at Johns Hopkins University. Professionally, Ainsworth was involved in teaching and was working as a clinical psychologist doing diagnostic work as well. Privately, she suffered marital problems, problems that also affected her work (Isaacson, 2006). Due to these difficult circumstances, Ainsworth was unable to work on her Uganda data for several years. It was in this stressful period that Bowlby wrote to her: "You have been very silent in these past months and we are wondering how you are faring. I hope all goes well" (Bowlby in a letter to Ainsworth, January 5, 1956). After a short reply by Ainsworth, Bowlby answered: "Your silence was so out of character that I was beginning to wonder if anything was wrong" (Bowlby in a letter to Ainsworth, February 21, 1956). For a couple of years, Ainsworth and Bowlby "sort of lost touch" (Rudnytsky, 1997, p. 397) and were working in their own spheres, but they finally met again in 1960 – for the first time since Ainsworth had left the Tavistock Clinic for Uganda. This was after Bowlby sent Ainsworth his recently published article on "The nature of the child's tie to his mother" (Bowlby, 1958d; see Chapter 5 earlier in this book) and Ainsworth invited him to come to Baltimore. Their reunion after years of relative silence took place when, during a trip through the US, Bowlby visited the Ainsworths for the weekend in their home in Baltimore. In a travelogue upon his return to England, Bowlby spoke to the staff of the Tavistock Clinic about his stay with the Ainsworths.

> I had a long crack with Mary Ainsworth, a lot of interesting things which I will try to retail to you. She would like to come to Great Britain. The possibility that I mentioned to her … that we are looking for someone, it was quite clear that Mary herself would be more than interested in this job, but I doubt very much whether in fact they will both come back because I strongly suspect that Len would not wish to do so, and I suspect he would not get so good a job in this country as he has got there … We compared a lot of notes and found our thinking was along very similar lines and we planned various liaisons in the future along research lines which I will perhaps tell you about. (AMWL: PP/BOW/F.1/1, Travelogue given by Dr. Bowlby at the Staff Meeting on May 11, 1960)

In the intervening years, Bowlby and Ainsworth had only been in contact by letters sent across the Atlantic. But when they met after five years, they were indeed both pleasantly surprised by their "encouraging convergence of ideas" (Ainsworth and Marvin, 1995, p. 7). Although Ainsworth's appointment at the Tavistock Clinic was not to be, their meeting led to more intensified cooperation. Their "long distance relationship … picked up impetus"

(Ainsworth, 1983, p. 13) and Bowlby and Ainsworth frequently exchanged letters and drafts (Isaacson, 2006). Bowlby also invited Ainsworth to attend the CIBA symposia in 1961, 1963, and 1965. According to Ainsworth, "the renewal of contact with John led to [her] inclusion in the Tavistock Mother-Infant Study Group which established a basis of communication with leading developmental scientists of various nationalities and disciplines" (Ainsworth, 1983, p. 13). This interaction with these leading scientists would prove very fruitful to her.

Ainsworth at the CIBA Symposia in the 1960s

For the first meeting of the CIBA study group in 1959, Bowlby had not asked Ainsworth as a "charter member of the Tavistock Group" because he "thought [Ainsworth] had gone off in other directions" (Rudnytsky, 1997, p. 397). But after their reunion, it became obvious that her presence at these meetings was "pertinent" (Rudnytsky, 1997, p. 397). During the first session she attended, in September 1961, Ainsworth gave the first public presentation of her data from Uganda in front of an audience consisting of psychoanalysts (e.g., Tony Ambrose, James Robertson, Ruth Thomas), psychologists (e.g., Marion Bernstein, Harriet Rheingold, Rudolph Schaffer), psychiatrists (e.g., John Bowlby, Miriam David, Peter Wolff), ethologists (e.g., Mavis Gunther, Robert Hinde), and a learning theorist (Jack Gewirtz). The reception of her work quite exceeded her expectations as she had not "expect[ed] experts to find it so original and stimulating" (Ainsworth in a letter to Leonard Doob, October 12, 1961).[1]

In her presentation, Ainsworth (1963) reported on the identification of "patterns of attachment behavior" (p. 75). She stated that "the judgement that the infant had formed an attachment to his mother as a special person rested on no single criterion," but that there is "a variety of behavior patterns that may be used as criteria of attachment" (p. 76). Ainsworth discerned no less than 12 behavioral patterns in the first year of life: differential crying, smiling, and vocalization, visual-motor orientation toward the mother, crying when the mother leaves the room, following, scrambling, burying the face, exploration from a secure base, clinging, lifting arms in greeting, and clapping hands in greeting. With regard to exploration – a concept that she borrowed from Blatz, but that was also important to Bowlby via ethology – Ainsworth was able to link her data to Harlow's studies with rhesus monkeys. This is an example of her interpretation of the data being influenced by subsequent work, since the Ganda study predated Harlow's work.

> As Harlow (1960) has observed with infant monkeys … the baby, once attached to his mother, can use her as a secure base from which to explore the world, can use her as a "haven of safety" from which he can face an external threat without panic. (Ainsworth, 1963, p. 78)

On the basis of her observations, Ainsworth divided the children into three groups "according to the strength and quality of the attachment to their mothers" (pp. 83–84): a secure-attached group, an insecure-attached group and a non-attached group – classifications that were later replaced by secure, insecure-resistant, and insecure-avoidant respectively (see Van IJzendoorn and Sagi, 2008). Ainsworth suggested that

> a major consideration from now on will be to examine the relationships between variations in infant-care practices and the distribution of the babies into these three groups to see which practices seemed to facilitate the development of a secure attachment and which did not. (Ainsworth, 1963, pp. 84–85)

Ainsworth concluded that, although there are individual differences in the development of attachment, "there is enough consistency in the responses that mediate attachment and enough regularity in the developmental sequence to lend support to Bowlby's (1958d) hypothesis of component instinctual responses as the basis of the child's tie to his mother" (Ainsworth, 1963, p. 101).

In the discussion following Ainsworth's presentation, Schaffer asked Ainsworth if she could "say something more about the behavioral distinction between attachment and security," as he was "not really happy about the use of words like security and anxiety as applied to early infancy" (pp. 104–105). Ainsworth replied that "babies classed as insecure were those that cried a lot, even if the mother was present. The secure ones only cried when sick, tired, hungry or left alone" (p. 105). Bowlby then suggested to determine security directly by measuring "the extent to which an infant will explore away from its mother" (p. 105), but Ainsworth replied that "exploratory behavior depends very much on age, whereas crying can be used as an indicator at any age" (p. 105). "Given that crying is a measure of security," learning theorist Gewirtz subsequently wondered, "how would a mother's milk supply relate to crying?" To his surprise, the secure-attached babies were given the breast for comfort and he was clearly astounded to learn that these babies cried less: "They were reinforced for crying, yet they did not cry?"[2] Essentially, the discussion centered around the question of how to determine whether a child is attached or not. This question was very useful, because it led Ainsworth (1977) to "scrutinize the decision-making processes involved in such a judgement" (p. 51).

Just as Harlow valued these CIBA meetings highly (see Chapter 5 earlier in this book), Ainsworth later acknowledged that she "got an awful lot out of those discussions" (Rudnytsky, 1997, p. 398). In the Foreword to *Infancy in Uganda*, she stated that "not the least of [Bowlby's] contributions was the convening and directing of the four Tavistock Seminars on Mother-Infant Interaction. It was of immeasurable help to meet the members of the study group and to exchange findings and ideas" (Ainsworth, 1967, p. xi). The study group brought Ainsworth repeatedly in contact with the likes of Jack Gewirtz, Harry Harlow, Robert Hinde, James Robertson, Thelma Rowell, Rudolph Shaffer, and others. For Ainsworth, the meetings served the purpose of sharpening her mind with respect to attachment issues and further developing her ideas, for example those on the concept of the "secure base."

The Origin and Development of the Secure Base Concept

Earlier I have described William Blatz's ideas on security and demonstrated Ainsworth's use of this concept in her thesis and subsequent writings. Quite remarkably, in subsequent years, the origin of the secure base concept somehow got lost. Although Ainsworth used the concept in her own dissertation (Salter, 1940), she did not know where to trace the term in Blatz's writings. The reader may remember that in security theory, as discussed in an earlier part of this chapter under the heading titled "William Blatz and Security Theory," Blatz emphasized the need for the infant of a basic self-confidence and the possibility to use the parent as a jumping platform from which to explore the world. As we have seen, the concept of security came under some criticism during the CIBA symposium in 1961. Shortly afterward, Ainsworth, while discussing the use of psychoanalytic theory in Bowlby's ideas, wrote to him about the intellectual authorship of the concept of security. From this letter it also becomes clear how Ainsworth valued her own theoretical contributions to attachment theory in-the-making.

> I am gratified that you find "secure" and "security" useful terms – since I have been using them since 1936! And essentially in the same way. I too have distinguished between "safety" and "security" although in a somewhat different way. I have thought a person felt "secure" when he was unafraid – and indeed when no threat of danger occurred to him. He could feel "safe," however, under circumstances when he was well aware of the threat of danger and perhaps just recently escaped from it or perhaps would be subjected to it if he ventured from his present "haven of safety." Harlow's infant rhesus thus flees to his "mother" as a haven of safety, but after having clung to her for a while he can venture forth using her as a secure base. (Ainsworth in a letter to Bowlby, April 10, 1962)

What catches the eye here is that Ainsworth, just as Blatz, made a clear distinction between security and safety. Also, it is of great interest to see how Ainsworth linked Blatzian theory to the experimental work of Harlow. This is, of course, very similar to the way Bowlby earlier applied Harlow's empirical results to his own theoretical ideas in the late 1950s and the 1960s (see the previous chapter in this volume).

Two years later, in 1964, when asked about the origin of the secure base concept by Harry Harlow himself, Ainsworth remembered the construct of secure base in relation to Blatz, but could not directly trace the idea and the exact term in his writings. In a letter to Harlow, she explained:

> I very much enjoyed both your lecture last Monday and our visit afterwards. It has been in my mind ever since to trace the "secure base" concept back to Blatzian writings. I suspect that it is entirely oral tradition. I cannot locate an example in Blatz's writings where he uses that specific term – although he has published his viewpoint very inadequately.

> Indeed, the best places to find an account of Blatzian "security theory" are in my own monographs … You may have wondered … why I did not acknowledge you when I used the phrase "secure base" [from which to explore the world] in my recent papers. It was not through lack of appreciation of your work, but merely because I felt as though I had always used this concept … I am … sure that Blatz … and I had the notion in mind back in the 1930s and 1940s. (Ainsworth in a letter to Harlow, March 26, 1964)

Indeed, at the time of writing, in books such as *The Management of Young Children* (Blatz and Bolt, 1930), *The Five Sisters: A Study of Child Psychology* (Blatz, 1938), and *Understanding the Young Child* (Blatz, 1944), one did not find traces of the security concept. As I have shown above, it was only after his death and with the help of his former students that Blatz's (1966) ideas were published more extensively in *Human Security* (see earlier in this chapter).

Still, years later, Ainsworth wrote along similar lines to Bowlby about the acknowledgement of the notion of the secure base:

> I myself have puzzled how to acknowledge the origins of "exploration from a secure base" or "secure base from which to explore." I certainly used the term explicitly at CIBA II [in 1961] for the first time. The concept was certainly implicit in Harlow's work, but I didn't get it from him. But I originally got the concept from Blatz. I have scoured his publications for an explicit statement of the concept but can't find one – it was oral tradition. I clearly had this concept in mind when I undertook my Ph.D. dissertation, but it is not explicitly stated in… my thesis publication… Blatz … was so foolish as not to write up his ideas properly. (Ainsworth in a letter to Bowlby, February 23, 1971; AMWL: PP/BOW/B.3/3)

Clearly, Ainsworth was well aware of the fact that "there is so much of [my approach] that relates pretty directly to Blatzian theory" (Ainsworth in a letter to Northway, August 31, 1965) and that the concept of security originated from Blatz's ideas. Yet she found no evidence in his early writings supporting that idea, i.e., she was unable to show that Blatz used the term secure base. There are, however, examples in Ainsworth's own writing that indicate that the notion of the term secure base was present in her thinking before Harlow (1958) wrote that "one function of the … mother … is to provide a haven of safety for the infant in times of fear and danger" (p. 678). Earlier, I described that the idea of "a secure base from which to work" was present in Ainsworth's dissertation (Salter, 1940). Also, in

Figure 6.1 Mary Ainsworth and John Bowlby in Charlottesville in 1986. Picture courtesy of the Wellcome Library, London (AMWL: PP/BOW/L.19, nr. 23).

her work with her husband Leonard, Ainsworth stated that "given the generally secure basis from which to work, the young child gradually learns skills through which he can independently gain satisfactions" (Ainsworth and Ainsworth, 1958, p. 5).

So, although Blatz failed to take ownership of his ideas in writing, there is ample evidence that the secure base concept originates in his work. Also, the fact that Blatz's ideas influenced Ainsworth's later ideas on attachment and security now seems quite evident. Ultimately, Blatz's ideas on security were of great consequence for attachment theory. Through Blatz, Ainsworth was, for the first time, exposed to the idea that security and exploratory behavior are related. Ainsworth shared these ideas with Bowlby, who incorporated the notion as a basic assumption in the attachment paradigm. (See Figure 6.1.)

Developing the Strange Situation Procedure

During the 1960s and 1970s, Ainsworth worked on the Baltimore Study, a replication study based on her experiences in Uganda. Families in this study were recruited through pediatricians before the birth of the infant and visited monthly for four hours until the infant was one year old. Data collection started in 1963 and was completed in 1966. Observers dictated detailed narratives into a tape recorder, based on their shorthand notes, directly after the visit ended. The transcripts of these narratives served as the basis for data analysis. Analyses of mother–infant interaction confirmed Ainsworth's earlier finding based on her observations of Ganda children: when a mother responded to her child with sensitive responsiveness during the first three months of life, the pair had a more harmonious relationship during the last quarter of the first year. The intensive home-observations – in both Ganda and Baltimore families – were the firm basis for the development of the development of an experimental instrument to observe and assess children's attachment relationship with their caregivers. Without the home-observations it would not have been possible to assess the quality of the *relationship* between mother and child.

This important yet serendipitous result of the Baltimore Study was named the "Strange Situation Procedure" (SSP) and was first described by Ainsworth and Wittig (1969) and more extensively in the classic work *Patterns of Attachment* (Ainsworth *et al.*, 1978) where the findings are placed in the context of the home-observations. In the SSP the child is observed playing for 20 minutes while caregivers and strangers enter and leave the room. By alternating familiar and unfamiliar situations, Ainsworth tried to simulate situations in the child's daily life and, thus, to increase the ecological validity of her instrument. During the whole procedure, the child is carefully observed. Specific points of interest are the amount of exploratory behavior shown by the infant, the anxiety shown toward the stranger, and the child's reactions to the departure of and especially the reunion with the caregiver. On the basis of their behaviors, children are grouped into three categories: secure, insecure-resistant, and insecure-avoidant. Each of these groups reflects a different kind of attachment relationship with the caregiver. The securely attached children will explore the environment in the presence of the mother, they will engage with the stranger if the mother is present, they will be upset when the mother leaves, but are happy when she returns and are easily comforted by her. Insecure-resistant children are reluctant to explore the room even in the presence of the mother, they are extremely distressed when the mother leaves and will show ambivalence towards her when she returns (they remain close to her, yet do not find solace, sometimes they show aggression, such as hitting her).

Insecure-avoidant children basically ignore the mother and show little emotion when she leaves the room or returns. These children show some exploratory behavior and are seemingly preoccupied with toys, but it is superficial play, as if to distract themselves from the distress.

It is of great interest to reflect on the development of the SSP, as it has become the most relevant measure of attachment in infants in current attachment research. The creation of the SSP is described by Ainsworth in several letters to Bowlby. These letters have not been published before but they are highly relevant to trace the different influences on its development.

In February 1965, Ainsworth for the first time mentioned her new procedure for measuring attachment behaviour in letters to colleagues. The first two she informed were Bowlby and Robertson. In one of her letters, Ainsworth stated that she had "introduced a little experimental situation – a "strange situation" – to which we introduce the baby at 51 weeks of age. This takes place at JHU, and we can observe it through a one-way-vision mirror" (Ainsworth in a letter to Robertson, February 28, 1965). In a letter to Bowlby, Ainsworth compared her new procedure to "the Harlow and Arsenian situations." Here, Ainsworth referred to Harlow's (1958) experimental situation in which rhesus monkeys are placed in a new environment with and without their surrogate mother (see Chapter 5 in the present volume) and to Arsenian's (1943) study of "young children in an insecure situation." In this study, Arsenian placed young children – aged 11 to 30 months – in a strange room with toys. Those children who were left alone in this strange environment behaved in a highly 'insecure' fashion, while those who were accompanied by their mothers typically approached the toys and played with them, thus behaving 'secure'. Indeed, the original purpose of Ainsworth "strange situation" was to study exploration in the presence and absence of the mother, just as Arsenian had done. Using the SSP, Ainsworth wanted to test her hypothesis about the usefulness of "following, crying when mother leaves the room, and using mother as a secure base to explore" (Ainsworth in a letter to Bowlby, February 29, 1965).

At about the same time – their letters probably crossed in the mail – Bowlby stated: "The account of all your work on attachment patterns and responses to minor separations make my mouth water for more" (Bowlby in a letter to Ainsworth, February 26, 1965), which is conceivable since he was at that time writing his first part of *Attachment*. Also, Bowlby informed Ainsworth about Hinde's work on the responses of monkeys to brief periods of separation – which Hinde would report on at the forthcoming Tavistock meeting (published as Hinde, 1969). Bowlby wrote that the "initial findings seem very interesting – especially the response to mother's return" (Bowlby in a letter to Ainsworth, February 26, 1965). It is unclear whether Hinde's findings sparked Ainsworth's interest in the reunion phase of the strange situation, or that perhaps they reminded her of the reunions after severe separations during hospitalization reported by Robertson, but these reunion episodes were to become the most important parts for the measurement of attachment security.

Concluding Remarks

In this chapter, I have described Mary Ainsworth's contributions to attachment theory as it evolved in the 1950s and 1960s. Bowlby and Ainsworth were in close contact with each other during most of this period and shared their ideas. Through Ainsworth, Bowlby was for the first time introduced to ideas from Blatz's security theory; ideas he subsequently incorporated – in a highly adjusted form – into the attachment theory. It is remarkable to see how Blatz's ideas resembled those of Bowlby. Blatz's emphasis on consistent care, his concept of the caregiver as a jumping-off platform from which to explore the environment and to which one can return as a haven of safety, and his idea that early relationships form a blueprint for later ones, all these ideas found a place in one form or another in attachment theory. To have acquainted Bowlby with the ideas of her mentor, ideas she elaborated and for which found ways to study, is definitely one of Ainsworth's great contributions.

Very important to the development of attachment theory was Ainsworth's study in Uganda. During her time at the Tavistock Clinic, before she left for Africa, Ainsworth was inspired by Robertson's naturalistic observations of children in hospitals and residential nurseries. It is likely that Ainsworth, just as others, was vastly impressed by *A two-year-old*, which was first shown publicly when Ainsworth was working with Bowlby and Robertson in London. Influenced by her direct cooperation with Robertson, analyzing some of his impressive observational work, Ainsworth set up and executed the first mother-child study from an evolutionary perspective. In her study, published with much delay in 1967, she was able to unravel different patterns of attachment and was able to group children in securely-attached and insecurely-attached categories. Also, largely due to her intensive home-observations, she was able to describe the crucial role of maternal sensitivity for the development of attachment. And only through these home-observations was it possible to show that the individual differences in the SSP were linked to the mother–infant relationship.

Ainsworth's subsequent work in Baltimore resulted in the development of the Strange Situation Procedure (Ainsworth and Wittig, 1969). With this powerful but simple procedure, it was now possible to assess the quality of a child's attachment relationship with the caregiver in a laboratory situation. Ainsworth corresponded regularly with Bowlby and Robertson about the development of the SSP. She acknowledged the influence of Arsenian, Harlow, and Hinde in this process. Her contributions were grist to Bowlby's mill and made, as he expressed it, his 'mouth water for more'. Also Bowlby sent chapters of his theoretical work to her for comment, which she did – extensively.

Apart from these early contributions (the notion of the secure base, maternal sensitivity, intensive home-observations, a method for assessing the quality of attachment, and the original tripartite classification system of attachment relationships), Ainsworth would further develop her ideas and, at the same time, keep contributing to the development of attachment theory. Other examples of Ainsworth's contributions – in fact, contributions that preceded and validated the SSP – are research establishing the link between maternal sensitivity and attachment security, and acknowledgement of the fact that the mother needs to be "free enough of preoccupations and anxieties of her own" (Ainsworth, 1967, pp. 397–398) to foster the establishment of a secure attachment relationship. These themes have been central in research on individual differences in attachment ever since.

This overview allows us to draw the following conclusions. First of all, Ainsworth's contributions were highly important and influential in the construction of attachment theory. Secondly, these contributions were in large part formed in interactions with Bowlby, Hinde, Harlow, Robertson, and others, who were in one way or another involved in the Tavistock study group. Drawing on her experiences working with Blatz, Robertson, and Bowlby, Ainsworth started the Baltimore study in 1963. She reached the summit of her career while working at the Johns Hopkins University and was able to merge different elements (the importance of early experience, the notion of the secure base, the need for naturalistic observation, and an ethological point of view) into a coherent framework. This resulted in many publications (e.g., Ainsworth and Bell, 1970; Ainsworth, Bell, and Stayton, 1971; Ainsworth and Wittig, 1969; Bell and Ainsworth, 1972) and ultimately resulted in her seminal work on *Patterns of Attachment* (Ainsworth *et al.*, 1978). In this publication, Ainsworth and her colleagues described the development of the Strange Situation Procedure and the classification system for the different types of reactions to this separation from and reunion with the mother. In this chapter, I have described how this 'little experimental situation' evolved and how the work and ideas of Blatz, Bowlby, Harlow, and Hinde, amongst others, shaped its development. The SSP and the accompanying classification system are still used in attachment research today. The notions of security and the caregiver as a secure base from which to explore the environment and a safe haven to which to flee when afraid have become entrenched in attachment theory. Finally, the concept of maternal sensitivity has become part of mainstream psychology. With Bowlby, Mary Ainsworth was a founder of the attachment paradigm.

Notes

1 If not specified otherwise, letters by Ainsworth are quoted via Isaacson (2006).

2 Several years later, Ainsworth and Gewirtz would have a fierce debate in *Child Development* about exactly this issue (Ainsworth and Bell, 1977; Bell and Ainsworth, 1972; Gewirtz and Boyd, 1977a, 1977b). In a replication study by Hubbard and Van IJzendoorn (1991) the results of the Ainsworth and Bell study were not supported. Hubbard and Van IJzendoorn use the concept of differential responsiveness to explain that severe distress calls need a prompt reply whereas mild distress vocalizations do not.

Conclusions

In this book, I explored the roots of attachment theory and focused on what I called the "ethological era" of attachment theory – the period from the publication of *Maternal Care and Mental Health* in 1951 to the publication of the first part of *Attachment and Loss* in 1969. I started with an elaborate description of Bowlby's early life and career. It became clear that Bowlby's formative years had a profound influence on his choice of career. His interest in separation and in the caregiver-child relationship was stirred by his own upbringing and childhood. Also of consequence was Bowlby's early interest in nature, as it anticipated his later focus on ethological methods and concepts. During the pre-war years, Bowlby gradually developed the view that early experiences influence later personality development and that the child has a primary need for the mother. Bowlby was an independent thinker within the psychoanalytic movement and held views that were at variance with those of Melanie Klein and Anna Freud. He considered himself to be a psychoanalyst nonetheless.

After this account of the formative years of Bowlby's career, I reviewed Bowlby's (1951) monograph on maternal deprivation for

John Bowlby – From Psychoanalysis to Ethology: Unraveling the Roots of Attachment Theory, First Edition. Frank C. P. van der Horst.

the WHO and the different issues of separation that Bowlby reported in his study. I drew attention to observations made during wartime evacuations and in residential nurseries, to the discussion concerning visiting of children in hospital, and to results of clinical studies and hospitalization studies. During his trip for the WHO, Bowlby met with leading researchers in the field, such as William Goldfarb and René Spitz, and had a chance to discuss with them the consequences of separation. Contrary to general belief, Bowlby was only one of many who were concerned about potentially harmful effects of temporary mother–child separations. I concluded that the publication of his WHO monograph was an Archimedean point in the construction of attachment theory.

At the time of publication of the WHO report, Bowlby was clearly dissatisfied with psychoanalytic theory, because in his view it could not account adequately for the responses of young children to separation from their mothers and to deprivation of maternal care (Van Dijken, 1998; Van Dijken *et al.*, 1998). So, when Bowlby's attention was drawn to ethology in 1951, he quickly saw its potential as a new theoretical approach. Ainsworth later stated that Bowlby's "discovery of ethology was the key that released the main structure of attachment theory all at once" and that "attachment theory began with a sudden flash of insight, sparked by ethology, that led to a scientific revolution, the understanding of personality development" (Southgate, Ainsworth, and Southern, 1990, p. 13).

I have argued that Bowlby's interactions with key players in the field of ethology such as Huxley, Lorenz, Tinbergen, and especially British ethologist Robert Hinde were decisive in constructing a new framework to explain mother-child interactions in early life. Almost as crucial was the work of American psychologist Harry Harlow, who provided Bowlby with evidence on separation in rhesus monkeys, at a time when Bowlby was looking for empirical confirmation of his ideas. I used the hitherto undiscovered correspondence between Harlow and Bowlby to illustrate the importance of this solid empirical foundation for Bowlby's theoretical construction. However, not only was Bowlby influenced by ethologists and animal psychologists, in his turn he also influenced the work of many in the field of animal behavior studies. Bowlby (1976) wrote in this respect: "there has been a most rewarding two-way process of mutual influence in which those of us working with humans have applied concepts and methods derived from colleagues working with animals, whilst they in turn have focused experimental attention on problems and variables identified by clinicians" (p. 28). I have discussed Bowlby's influence on Tinbergen, Hinde, and Harlow, and have thus illustrated the cross-fertilization of attachment theory and primate research.

The Role of Observation and Experiment

Ethological studies were and still are characterized by the emphasis on observation of (animal) behavior in a natural environment (see Tinbergen, 1951, 1963). Bowlby valued this emphasis on observation of real life events – even before his acquaintance with ethology – but early in his career he encountered much resistance from psychoanalysts in the British Psycho-Analytical Society, particularly the Kleinian school. When he addressed the members of the Society to become a full member, Bowlby stressed the need for observation of real life events (see Bowlby, 1940a). The fact that Bowlby preferred to do observations in natural situations also becomes clear from his cooperation with James Robertson, resulting in the scientific films *A Two-year-old Goes to Hospital* (Robertson, 1952) and *Going to Hospital with Mother* (Robertson, 1958c). Bowlby had appointed James Robertson as a psychiatric social worker of the Separation Research Unit in 1948 – three years before he stumbled across ethology as a new framework. Robertson had had an "impeccable training in naturalistic observation" while working in Anna Freud's Hampstead Nurseries. Robertson's highly detailed observations of children in nurseries and hospitals led to the discovery of the three phases of protest, despair, and denial.

Bowlby not only criticized psychoanalysts' neglect of observation, but their lack of what he called scientific training as well: "Unfortunately some of the leading people in psychoanalysis have had no scientific training. Neither Melanie Klein nor Anna Freud knew the first thing about scientific method. They were totally ignorant" (Bowlby, Figlio, and Young, 1986, p. 45). Obviously, Bowlby valued observation and experiment in his research form early on in his career. Bowlby did have the scientific and experimental background others within the psychoanalytic movement lacked: as a medical student at Cambridge he read experimental psychology and thus had a grounding in statistics and experimental design. Also, Bowlby was in the Research and Training Centre of the Officer's Selection Board during World War II, which he described as a practically oriented centre where he worked with three academic psychologists. "In the army I received what was really a postgraduate training in psychology" (Senn, 1977a, p. 9). So, although Bowlby was a clinician at heart, he did know about experimental procedures and when he went to the Tavistock Clinic after the war in 1946, his brief was to provide three strands – not only a clinical service and a training program, but a research program as well.

The importance of real-life, naturalistic observations also became influential in attachment theory in another way. Robertson influenced Ainsworth as she was vastly impressed by the former's observations when she was working with him at the Tavistock Clinic between 1951 and 1954. Ainsworth was determined to use "simple, direct, naturalistic observation" in her next project, which eventually resulted in her cross-cultural study in Uganda. In Chapter 6, it became clear that attachment theory was not a one-man job by Bowlby, and that Ainsworth's theoretical contributions make her a co-founder of attachment theory. Her introduction of the notion of the secure base, the discovery of the concept of maternal sensitivity as an antecedent of attachment, the use of intensive home-observations, the development of a method for assessing the quality of attachment, and the original tripartite classification system of attachment relationships, were all essential to the development of attachment theory.

With regard to the importance of experimentation, it is clear that Bowlby valued empirical confirmation of ideas he had developed in his interaction with children in clinical practice and that led to the formulation of his theoretical model of attachment behavior. Bowlby found support for his ideas in the work of Harlow, but also actively stimulated studies that provided evidence for attachment ideas. Bowlby helped Hinde set up a rhesus colony in the late 1950s to test the effects of long-term effects of maternal separation. In the US, Harlow sought empirical evidence for Bowlby's and Robertson's description of the stages of protest, despair, and detachment. Eventually, Ainsworth's Baltimore studies would establish empirical research as an integral part of attachment theory.

Bowlby's Method of Theory Construction

I have described the development of attachment theory as a stepwise process. First, Bowlby's attention was drawn to the severe consequences of separation from the mother – fueled by experiences in his own childhood and experiences in his professional career (e.g., Priory Gate School, 44 thieves). When Bowlby subsequently wrote his report for the WHO, he had seen enough separation to make the next step in the development of his theory: to wonder about the *nature* of the relationship between mother and child. Apparently, this bond was so strong that when it was disrupted it led to very serious emotional difficulties. Bowlby felt that psychoanalysis did not explain the consequences of separation adequately. He especially disliked Melanie Klein's emphasis on "phantasies" and the internal world of the child, whereas he himself tried to take the objective environment into account and to focus on observable facts. At this point in time, he chanced upon the work of Lorenz and ideas on imprinting. Ethology provided Bowlby with the explanations and mechanisms underlying attachment behavior. What Bowlby took from ethology was, first, that the strong relationship between mother and child was independent of food, and second, the basic notion that the relationship between child and mother was somehow prepared before birth because of its survival value. With the publication of his paper on "The nature of the child's tie to his mother," Bowlby (1958d) for the first time made his ethological ideas public, but he still needed the empirical evidence to support these ideas. This was when he met with Harry Harlow, whose experiments with rhesus monkeys of course were a remarkable confirmation of his theorizing. Bowlby's subsequent approach to theory construction was clearly eclectic: Bowlby used ideas and theories of others from all kinds of disciplines to explain the importance of mother–child attachment. He incorporated not only psychoanalytic and ethological ideas, but ideas from Jean Piaget, Ludwig von Bertalanffy,[1] and, of course, Mary Ainsworth as well.

I have stated that Bowlby more or less "stumbled" upon ethology as a new framework. His discovery of ethology was indeed serendipitous, but Bowlby immediately recognised its significance. One could question whether his coincidental acquaintance with this new discipline in 1951 was crucial in the construction of attachment theory. Or would Bowlby sooner or later have found an evolutionary framework for his ideas anyway? There is abundant evidence that Bowlby had a firm conviction from very early on in his career – that an infant primarily needs a warm and loving mother, and that separations from the mother are potentially damaging (see Chapter 1; see also Van der Horst and Van der Veer, 2010). In the 1930s, Bowlby adopted this fundamental idea and never substantially changed that basic notion in later years. His first and foremost goal – and his lifelong undertaking – was to convince certain others (e.g., orthodox psychoanalysts, psychiatrists, clinicians, and medical doctors) of the importance of this idea by theorizing and gathering empirical evidence. To stimulate his and others' work and theorizing, Bowlby had found an interdisciplinary approach to be highly successful (see Chapter 4).

In the early 1950s, Bowlby for the first time experienced the value of an interdisciplinary approach during the WHO study group meetings on the psychobiological development of the child. Here, he was able to discuss his ideas with a small group of experts with very different backgrounds for the purpose of exchanging views and ideas. This is where Bowlby met with leading researchers such as Erik Erikson, Julian Huxley, Konrad Lorenz, Margaret Mead, Jean Piaget, and others. Bowlby would later apply this interdisciplinary approach to the weekly meetings at the Tavistock Clinic (which included Robert Hinde, Ronald Laing, and James Robertson, for example) and to the biennial CIBA conferences on mother-infant interaction he organized (for which Bowlby invited Mary Ainsworth, Jack Gewirtz, Harry Harlow, and Rudolph Schaffer, amongst others).

Through these meetings Bowlby was introduced to the latest research findings and the state of the art in the field. Being a theorist by nature of training, he carefully weighed the evidence and tried to integrate the findings into a coherent framework. He was quite systematic about using evidence from different fields; even when seemingly coincidental snippets of information came his way. If they fit the larger picture, and he found additional validation, he incorporated them. In areas that were not his specialty, Bowlby consulted others about the value of new ideas he had come across – as he had done with Huxley when he was first referred to ethology (see Chapter 4). Bowlby took evidence from other fields and investigators, and contributed to the generation of such evidence (see Suomi, 1995), but he melded it into a coherent theory. Most of his papers and books he wrote alone, without inviting others to become co-authors (i.e., he did not make Ainsworth a co-author, for example). Constantly rewriting and polishing his manuscripts, he incorporated other people's ideas into this framework. Whereas he always gave them credit initially, after a while these new ideas blended into his own – something that went against the grain with Robertson (see Van der Horst and Van der Veer, 2009b). It was this eclectic approach that would eventually become Bowlby's trademark.

Bowlby's approach to theory construction resembles the approach Darwin claimed to use in a letter to his son Horace (quoted by Bowlby in his biography of Darwin):

> I have been speculating last night what makes a man a discoverer of undiscovered things; and a most perplexing problem it is. Many men who are very clever – much cleverer than the discoverers – never originate anything. As far as I can conjecture the art consists in habitually searching for the causes and meaning of everything which occurs. This implies sharp observation, and requires as much knowledge as possible of the subject investigated. (Darwin in a letter to his son, quoted by Bowlby, 1990, p. 411)

As we have seen, Bowlby invited clever people with very different backgrounds to his study group with the specific goal of acquiring knowledge as well as new viewpoints. But it was he, filled with the same boundless ambition and curiosity Darwin described, who grew into the major theorist of attachment.

Another striking observation is one made by Bowlby himself. As early as 1958, in one of many letters Bowlby wrote to his wife Ursula over the years, Bowlby compared himself to both Freud and Darwin:

> It pleases me to believe I have some of Darwin's characteristics, tho[ugh] by no means all! He was a tremendously good observer [and] of course a full-time research worker all his life. I'm not that good an observer [and] very far from full-time. However I believe I have some of his capacity to live with a problem over many years, mulling over the data until the theory begins to take shape [and] also keeping the theory close to the data. None of this vicious speculation! But broad bold theory when it comes. Two other characteristics I'm pleased to share with him – very systematic note making [and] drafting at top speed with plenty of revisions later. So however good a scientist I may or may not be, I think I'm the same sort of scientist as Darwin – [and] not the least like Freud. (Bowlby in a letter to Ursula, May 19, 1958; AMWL, PP/BOW/B.1/20; original underlining)

With these perceptive comments Bowlby expressed his great admiration for Darwin – an admiration that becomes clear from his biography of Darwin as well (Bowlby, 1990). Bowlby devoted the last years of his life to this substantial work, which was published just three months before his death. According to Ursula, "the publication of the Darwin book … made the end of his life full of interest and enjoyment" (Ursula in a letter to Joan Stevenson-Hinde, September 24, 1990; private archive Stevenson-Hinde). In the book, Bowlby put forward the thesis that "Darwin's long lasting troubles … can be understood as responses to stressful events … [and] as a result of a childhood shadowed by an invalid and dying mother" (Bowlby, 1990, pp. 1–2).[2] In other words, Bowlby explained Darwin's enduring mental problems by referring to events that took place in his childhood and that were connected with his attachment figure. By writing this biography, Bowlby completed the circle: he started with a passion for nature, turned to clinical practice and mental health studies and finished with a clinically inspired work on "the most influential biologist to have lived" (Bowlby, 1990, p. 1).

Theory Construction and the Nature of Theory Change

Looking at Bowlby's approach to theory construction from the perspective of the philosophy of science, his development of attachment theory in the 1950s and 1960s can best be explained by concepts forwarded by Kuhn (1962) in *The Structure of Scientific Revolutions.*[3] According to Kuhn, science does not evolve in a linear way, but there are paradigm shifts that advance our scientific understanding. At the same time, each paradigm shift brings about new concepts and instruments that make it difficult to understand the adherents of the old paradigm. Adherents of different paradigms live, so to speak, in different, incommensurable worlds. This is approximately what happened when Bowlby turned psychoanalysis into attachment theory. Bowlby (1982a) described his move to ethology in these terms and realized that "any novel framework is difficult to grasp, especially so for those long familiar with a previous one" (p. 668). Yet Bowlby (1981b) saw possibilities for psychoanalysis to become a natural science. He believed that "psychoanalysts will be wise to employ the procedures [of biologists]" and that "the criteria to which our science should strive to conform, are close to those adopted by our neighbours of the biological sciences" (p. 253). Bowlby felt closely associated with (evolutionary) biologists, who deal with phenomena "of vastly greater complex" (p. 253). Ironically, Freud himself considered psychoanalysis to be a natural science and often speculated about the neurological processes underlying the phenomena he described.

Bowlby's Scientific Descent

Finally, I will address the issue of Bowlby's scientific descent. Experts of attachment theory still differ in opinion whether attachment theory at bottom is a psychoanalytic (e.g., Fonagy, 1999, 2001; Fonagy, Gergely, and Target, 2008; Slade, 1999, 2008) or an evolutionary theory (e.g., Belsky, 1999; Simpson, 1999; Simpson and Belsky, 2008). Bowlby himself stated that his "own position, regarding Freud's work, is that the phenomenons to which [Freud] called attention are immensely important; but the theories which he came up with are very dated and inadequate" (Bowlby, Figlio, and Young, 1986, p. 45). What Bowlby was trying to do was to get psychoanalysts on a more empirical track, to ask them not to neglect real life experiences, and to gather evidence for their views: "If they come up with some interesting and hard data ... I shall be interested, but not until then" (Warme *et al.*, 1980). Bowlby specifically stated that he "didn't happen to go along with the particular theory that Freud had advanced – not because [Freud] was convinced of it, but because [Freud] couldn't think of anything better" (Bowlby, Figlio, and Young, 1986, p. 42). So, Bowlby concluded that "as long as you define psychoanalysis in terms of traditional theories, i.e., Freud's theories and not the phenomena he was trying to explain, (a) my ideas are not psychoanalysis; and (b) no new ideas can ever be psychoanalysis – by definition" (Bowlby, Figlio, and Young, 1986, p. 57). "If psychoanalysis is to attain full status as one of the behavioural sciences," Bowlby (1969/1982b) added, "it must add to its traditional method the tried methods of the natural sciences" (p. 9). This is exactly what Bowlby saw as his mission.

Bowlby became involved in the debate between adherents of an intuitive, hypothetical approach with emphasis on the unconscious and psychoanalytic interpretation versus advocates of an empirical-analytical approach with emphasis on real-life experiences and observable data. I have made clear that Bowlby chose the empirical approach and wanted psychoanalysts to make the move to a more scientific, empirically based approach to psychology and the study of personality development.

However, it would not be entirely fair to say that Bowlby discounted all of psychoanalytic theory. On several occasions, Bowlby testified that he never discarded all of psychoanalytic theory, but that he only wanted to "utilise ethological principles to reformulate clinical theory" (Bowlby, 1976, p. 4) or to "rewrite psychoanalysis in the light of ethological concepts" (Dinnage, 1979, p. 325). Maybe this was because he thought that "the phenomena of psychoanalysis are far too important to be left to the psychoanalytic *movement*" (Bowlby, Figlio, and Young, 1986, p. 57; original italics). Be that as it may, to this day some experts of attachment theory emphasize "the psychoanalytic core of attachment theory: that part of attachment theory that sees emotion regulation as central to healthy development" (Steele, personal communication, October 12, 2007). Others, however, state that "it was John Bowlby's great merit to include the evolutionary basis of attachment into his framework of thinking" (Keller, 2008). I consider both the psychoanalytic foundation of attachment and the ethological mainstay to be of great importance; the cross-fertilisation of these ideas is one of Bowlby's great merits. Indeed, Bowlby succeeded in what he called "an experiment in interbreeding" (Bowlby, 1980b). Bowlby remained loyal to at least part of Freud's heritage. In the preface to the first volume of *Attachment and Loss*, Bowlby (Bowlby, 1969/1982b) noted "that the field [he] had ploughed so light-heartedly was not less than the field Freud had started tilling sixty years earlier, and that it contained all those same rocky excrescences and thorny entanglements that he had encountered" (p. xi). By using ethological theory, Bowlby realized that "from a new viewpoint a familiar landscape can sometimes look very different" (p. xi).

It was Bowlby's passion to understand and help children that suffered from a lack of love and understanding, a passion that originated in his own childhood. He was a skilled and amiable clinician who saw countless children in the Tavistock Clinic and the London Childhood Guidance Centre and was committed to help them by all possible means. But it was his ultimate belief that these children would be helped best not by speculating about their internal conflicts and drives, but by observing and explaining their behavior in their real-life circumstances in the spirit of ethology.

In his comparison with Freud and Darwin, Bowlby stated that with respect to theory-building he placed himself in the tradition of Darwin. Careful observation, note making, and theory formation on the basis of hard data were to be preferred over facile armchair speculation.

Notes

1 How Bowlby used ideas from Piaget's theory of cognitive development and from Von Bertalanffy's systems theory is outside the scope of this book.

2 Bowlby's daughter Mary Gatling and other members of the Bowlby family believe that there is an autobiography contained within his biography of Charles Darwin (Mary Gatling, personal communication, April 27, 2009).

3 The reader may remember that Kuhn's (1962) book *The Structure of Scientific Revolutions* figured prominently on Bowlby's list of books that most influenced him (see Chapter 1).

References

Adams, J. (1924). *Modern Development in Educational Practice.* London: University of London Press.

Adrian, E. D. (1946). The mental and physical origins of behaviour. *International Journal of Psycho-Analysis*, 27, 1–6.

Ainsworth, M. D. S. (1963). The development of infant-mother interaction among the Ganda. In B. M. Foss (ed.), *Determinants of Infant Behavior II* (pp. 67–104). London: Methuen.

Ainsworth, M. D. S. (1967). *Infancy in Uganda: Infant Care and the Growth of Love.* Baltimore, MD: The Johns Hopkins University Press.

Amsworth, M. D. S. (1977). Attachment theory and its utillity in cross-cultural research. In P. H. Leiderman, S. R. Tulkin, and A. Rosenfeld (eds), *Culture and Infancy: Variations in the Human Experience* (pp. 49–67). New York: Academic Press.

Ainsworth, M. D. S. (1983). Mary D. Salter Ainsworth. In A. N. O'Connel and N. F. Russo (eds), *Models of Achievement: Reflections of Eminent Women in Psychology* (pp. 200–219). New York: Columbia University Press.

Ainsworth, M. D. S. (2010). Security and attachment. In R. Volpe (ed.), *The Secure Child: Timeless Lessons in Parenting and Childhood Education* (pp. 43–53). Toronto: University of Toronto Press.

Ainsworth, M. D. S. and Ainsworth, L. H. (1958). *Measuring Security in Personal Adjustment.* Toronto, Canada: University of Toronto Press.

John Bowlby – From Psychoanalysis to Ethology: Unraveling the Roots of Attachment Theory, First Edition. Frank C. P. van der Horst.

Ainsworth, M. D. S. and Bell, S. M. (1977). Infant crying and maternal responsiveness: A rejoinder to Gewirtz and Boyd. *Child Development*, 48, 1208–1216.

Ainsworth, M. D. S., Bell, S. M., and Stayton, D. (1971). Individual differences in strange situation behavior of one-year-olds. In H. Schaffer (ed.), *The Origins of Human Social Relations*. London: Academic Press.

Ainsworth, M. D. S., Blehar, M. C., Waters, E., and Wall, S. (1978). *Patterns of Attachment: A Psychological Study of the Strange Situation*. Hillsdale, NJ: Erlbaum.

Ainsworth, M. D. S. and Bowlby, J. (1954). Research strategy in the study of mother-child separation. *Courrier du Centre International de l'Enfance*, 4, 105–131.

Ainsworth, M. D. S., and Bowlby, J. (1991). An ethological approach to personality development. *American Psychologist*, 46, 333–341.

Ainsworth, M. D. S. and Marvin, R. S. (1995). On the shaping of attachment theory and research: An interview with Mary D. S. Ainsworth. In E. Waters, B. E. Vaughn, G. Posada, and K. Kondo-Ikemura (eds), *Caregiving, Cultural, and Cognitive Perspectives on Secure-base Behavior and Working Models: New Growing Points of Attachment Theory and Research. Monographs of the Society for Research in Child Development*, 60(2–3), 3–21.

Ainsworth, M. D. S. and Wittig, B. A. (1969). Attachment and exploratory behavior of 1-year-olds in a strange situation. In B. M. Foss (ed.), *Determinants of Infant Behavior, IV* (pp. 111–136). London: Methuen.

Alsop-Shields, L. and Mohay, H. (2001). John Bowlby and James Robertson: theorists, scientists and crusaders for improvements in the care of children in hospital. *Journal of Advanced Nursing*, 35(1), 50–58.

Anonymous (1952, May 5). Milk. *Time*, 59(18), 51.

Appell, G. and Aubrey, J. (1951). *Maternal Deprivation in Young Children* [Film]. New York: New York University Film Library.

Arsenian, J. M. (1943). Young children in an insecure situation. *Journal of Abnormal Social Psychology*, 38, 225–249.

Bacciagaluppi, M. (1994). The influence of Ferenczi on Bowlby. *International Forum of Psychoanalysis*, 3(2), 97–101.

Bakwin, H. (1942). Loneliness in infants. *American Journal of Diseases in Children*, 63, 30–40.

Batten, L. W. (1945). A parent at hospital. Letter to the editor. *The Lancet*, June 30, 834.

Beach, F. A. (1955). The descent of instinct. *Psychological Review*, 62, 401–410.

Beekman, D. (1977). *The Mechanical Baby*. Westport, CT: Lawrence Hill & Company.

Bell, S. M. and Ainsworth, M. D. S. (1972). Infant crying and maternal responsiveness. *Child Development*, 43, 1171–1190.

Belsky, J. (1999). Modern evolutionary theory and patterns of attachment. In J. Cassidy and P. R. Schaver (eds), *Handbook of Attachment: Theory, Research and Clinical Applications* (pp. 141–161). New York: The Guilford Press.

Bender, L. and Yarnell, H. (1941). An observation nursery. A study of 250 children on the psychiatric division of Bellevue Hospital. *American Journal of Psychiatry*, 97, 1158–1174.

Bennett, V. and Isaacs, S. (1931). *Health and Education in the Nursery*. London: Routledge.

Beverly, B. I. (1936). The effect of illness on emotional development. *Journal of Pediatrics*, 8, 533–543.

Blatz, W. E. (1938). *The Five Sisters: A Study of Child Psychology*. New York: William Morrow.

Blatz, W. E. (1944). *Understanding the Young Child*. Toronto: Clarke, Irwin.

Blatz, W. E. (1966). *Human Security: Some Reflections*. Toronto: University of Toronto Press.

Blatz, W. E. and Bolt, H. M. (1930). *The Management of Young Children*. Toronto: McClelland & Stewart.

Bliss, T. (1945). A parent at hospital. Letter to the editor. *The Lancet*, June 2, 704.

Blum, D. (2002). *Love at Goon Park*. Wisconsin: Perseus Publishing.

Boring, E. G. (1950). *A History of Experimental Psychology*. New York: Appleton-Century-Crofts.

Bowlby, J. (1938). The abnormally aggressive child. *The New Era*, 19, 230–234.

Bowlby, J. (1939a). Jealous and spiteful children. *Home and School*, 5(5), 83–85.

Bowlby, J. (1939b). Subsititute homes. *Mother and Child*, April, 3–7.

Bowlby, J. (1939c). Hysteria in children. In R.G. Gordon (ed.), *A Survey of Child Psychiatry* (pp. 80–94). London: Oxford University Press.

Bowlby, J. (1940a). The infleunce of early environment in the development of neurosis and neurotic character. *The International Journal of Psycho-Analysis*, 21, 154–178.

Bowlby, J. (1940b). Visiting in children's wards. Letter to the editor. *The Lancet*, February 10, 291.

Bowlby, J. (1944). Forty-four juvenile thieves: Their characters and home-life. *The International Journal for Psycho-Analysis*, 25, 19–53, 107–128.

Bowlby, J. (1946). *Forty-four Juvenile Thieves: Their Characters and Home-life*. London: Ballière, Tindall & Cox.

Bowlby, J. (1951). Maternal care and mental health. *Bulletin of the World Health Organization*, 3, 355–534.

Bowlby, J. (1952). *Maternal Care and Mental Health*. Geneva: World Health Organization.

Bowlby, J. (1953). Critical phases in the development of social responses in man and other animals. *New Biology*, 14, 25–32.

Bowlby, J. (1957). An ethological approach to research in child development. *British Journal of Medical Psychology*, 30, 230–240.

Bowlby, J. (1958a). *Can I Leave My Baby?* London: The National Association for Mental Health.

Bowlby, J. (1958b). Separation of mother and child. Letter to the editor. *The Lancet*, March 1, 480.

Bowlby, J. (1958c). Separation of mother and child. Letter to the editor. *The Lancet*, May 17, 1070–1071.

Bowlby, J. (1958d). The nature of the child's tie to his mother. *International Journal of Psycho-Analysis*, 39, 350–373.

Bowlby, J. (1960a). Separation anxiety. *International Journal of Psycho-Analysis*, 41, 89–113.

Bowlby, J. (1960b). Grief and mourning in infancy and early childhood. *The Psychoanalytic Study of the Child*, 15, 9–52.

Bowlby, J. (1960c). Symposium on psycho-analysis and ethology II: ethology and the development of object relations. *International Journal of Psycho-Analysis*, 41, 313–317.

Bowlby, J. (1961a). Separation anxiety: A critical review of the literature. *Journal of Child Psychology and Psychiatry*, 1, 251–269.

Bowlby, J. (1961b). Processes of mourning. *International Journal of Psycho-Analysis*, 42, 317–340.

Bowlby, J. (1961c). The Adolf Meyer Lecture: Childhood mourning and its implications for psychiatry. *American Journal of Psychiatry*, 118, 481–498.

Bowlby, J. (1961d). Preface. In B. M. Foss (ed.), *Determinants of Infant Behaviour I* (pp. xiii–xv). London: Methuen & Co.

Bowlby, J. (1963a). Pathological mourning and childhood mourning. *Journal of the American Psychoanalytic Association*, 11, 500–541.

Bowlby, J. (1963b). Preface. In B. M. Foss (ed.), *Determinants of Infant Behaviour II* (pp. xi–xii). London: Methuen & Co.

Bowlby, J. (1965). Preface. In B. M. Foss (ed.), *Determinants of Infant Behaviour III* (p. xiii). London: Methuen & Co.

Bowlby, J. (1968). Effects on behaviour of disruption of an affectional bond. In: J. M. Thoday and A. S. Parker (eds), *Genetic and Environmental Influences on Behaviour*. Edinburgh: Oliver & Boyd.

Bowlby, J. (1969). Preface. In B. M. Foss (ed.), *Determinants of Infant Behaviour IV* (pp. xiii–xiv). London: Methuen & Co.

Bowlby, J. (1973). *Attachment and Loss. Vol. 2: Separation: Anxiety and Anger*. New York: Basic Books.

Bowlby, J. (1976). Human personality development in an ethological light. In G. Serban and A. Kling (eds), *Animal Models in Human Psychobiology* (pp. 27–36). New York: Plenum Press.

Bowlby, J. (1980a). *Attachment and Loss. Vol. 3: Loss: Sadness and Depression*. New York: Basic Books.

Bowlby, J. (1980b). By ethology out of psycho-analysis: An experiment in interbreeding. *Animal Behaviour*, 28, 649–665.

Bowlby, J. (1981a). Perspective: A contribution by John Bowlby. *Bulletin of the Royal College of Psychiatrists*, 5, 2–4.

Bowlby, J. (1981b). Psychoanalysis as a natural science. *International Review of Psycho-Analysis*, 8, 243–256.

Bowlby, J. (1982a). Attachment and loss: Retrospect and prospect. *American Journal of Orthopsychiatry*, 52 (4), 664–678.

Bowlby, J. (1982b). *Attachment and Loss. Vol. 1: Attachment* (2nd edn). New York: Basic Books. (Original work published 1969.)

Bowlby, J. (1990). *Charles Darwin: A New Biography*. London: Hutchinson.

Bowlby, J. (1991). Ethological light on psychoanalytic problems. In: P. Bateson (ed.), *The Development and Integration of Behaviour: Essays in Honour of Robert Hinde* (pp. 301–313). Cambridge: Cambridge University Press.

Bowlby, J., Ainsworth, M., Boston, M., and Rosenbluth, D. (1956). The effects of mother-child separation: A follow-up study. *British Journal of Medical Psychology*, 29, 211–247.

Bowlby, J., Figlio, K., and Young, R. M. (1986). An interview with John Bowlby on the origins and reception of his work. *Free Associations*, 6, 36–64.

Bowlby, J., Miller, E., and Winnicott, D. W. (1939). Evacuation of small children. Letter to the editor. *British Medical Journal*, December 16, 1202–1203.

Bowlby, J., and Robertson, J. (1952). A two-year-old goes to hospital. *Proceedings of the Royal Society of Medicine*, 46, 425–427.

Bowlby, J., Robertson, J., and Rosenbluth, D. (1952). A two-year-old goes to hospital. *The Psychoanalytic Study of the Child*, 7, 82–94.

Brandon, S., Lindsay, M., Lovell-Davis, J., and Kraemer, S. (2009). "What is wrong with emotional upset?" – 50 years on from the Platt Report. *Archives of the Diseases of Children*, 94(3), 173–177.

Brereton, E. C. (1927). *The Happy Nursery*. London: Williams & Norgate.

Bretherton, I. (1991). The roots and growing points of attachment theory. In C. M. Parkes, J. Stevenson-Hinde, and P. Marris (eds), *Attachment Across the Life Cycle* (pp. 9–32). London/New York: Tavistock/Routledge.

Bretherton, I. (1992). The origins of attachment theory: John Bowlby and Mary Ainsworth. *Developmental Psychology*, 28, 759–775.

Bretherton, I. (2003). Mary Ainsworth: Insightful observer and courageous theoretician. In G. A. Kimble and M. Wertheimer (eds), *Portraits of Pioneers in Psychology* (Vol. 5) (pp. 317–331). Hillsdale, NJ: Lawrence Erlbaum Associates.

Bretherton, I. and Main, M. (2000). Mary Dinsmore Salter Ainsworth (1913–1999). *American Psychologist*, 55(10), 1148–1149.

Burkhardt, R. W. (2005). *Patterns of Behavior. Konrad Lorenz, Niko Tinbergen, and the Founding of Ethology*. Chicago/London: University of Chicago Press.

Burlingham, D. T. and Freud, A. (1942). *Young Children in War-time: A Year's Work in a Residential War Nursery*. London: Allen & Unwin.

Burlingham, D. T., and Freud, A. (1944). *Infants Without Families: The Case For and Against Residential Nurseries*. London: Allen & Unwin.

Burt, C. L. (1925). *The Young Delinquent*. London: London University Press.

Buss, D. M. (2004). *Evolutionary Psychology: The New Science of the Mind*. Boston: Pearson.

Buss, D. M. (2005) (ed.) *The Handbook of Evolutionary Psychology*. New York: Wiley.

Cantab, M. B. (1945). A parent at hospital. Letter to the editor. *The Lancet*, June 2, 704–705.

Carling, E. (1939). Evacuation of women and children. *British Medical Journal*, October 28, 896.

Chaffin, M., Hanson, R., Saunders, B. E., *et al.* (2006). Report of the APSAC task force on attachment therapy, reactive attachment disorder, and attachment problems. *Child Maltreatment*, 11, 76–89.

Chant, S. N. F., and Salter, M. D. (1937). The measurement of attitude toward war and the galvanic skin response. *Journal of Educational Psychology*, 28, 281–289.

Cortina, M., and Marrone, M. (2004). Reclaiming Bowlby's contribution to psychoanalysis. *International Forum of Psychoanalysis*, 13, 133–146.

Crosbie, W. E. (1947). Care of children in hospital. Letter to the editor. *British Medical Journal*, February 15, 266.

David, M., Nicolas, H., and Roudinesco, J. (1952). Responses of young children to separation from their mothers: I. Observations of children aged 12–17 months recently separated from their families and living in an institution. *Courrier du Centre International de l'Enfance*, 2, 66–78.

Darwin, C. (1859). *The Origin of Species by Means of Natural Selection or the Preservation of Favoured Races in the Struggle for Life*. New York: Washington Square Press.

De Beer, G. (1958). *Embryos and Ancestors* (3rd edn). Oxford: Clarendon Press.

DeHart, G. B., Sroufe, L. A., and Cooper, R. G. (2004). *Child Development: Its Nature and Course* (5th edn). Boston, MA: McGraw-Hill.

Dennis, W. (1941). Infant development under conditions of restricted practice and of minimum social stimulation. *Genetic Psychology Monographs*, 23, Part 1, 142–191.

Dicks, H. V. (1939). *Clinical Studies in Psychopathology*. London: Edward Arnold & Co.

Dicks, H. V. (1970). *Fifty Years of the Tavistock Clinic*. London: Routledge & Kegan Paul.

Dinnage, R. (1979). John Bowlby. *New Society*, May 10, 323–325.

Donaldson, G. (1996). Between practive and theory: Melanie Klein, Anna Freud and the development of child analysis. *Journal of the History of the Behavioral Sciences*, 32(2), 160–176.

Durbin, E. F. M. and Bowlby, J. (1939). *Personal Aggressiveness and War*. London: Routledge & Kegan Paul.

Edelston, H. (1940). Visiting in children's wards. Letter to the editor. *The Lancet*, February 24, 391.

Edelston, H. (1941). Day nurseries. Letter to the editor. *The Lancet*, November 15, 620.

Edelston, H. (1943). Separation anxiety in young children: a study of hospital cases. *Genetic Psychology Monographs*, 28(1), 3–95.

Edelston, H. (1946). Children in day nurseries. Letter to the editor. *The Lancet*, October 19, 581.

Edelston, H. (1953). Visiting children in hospital. Letter to the editor. *The Lancet*, December 12, 1261.

Edelston, H. (1955). Separation experiences and mental health. Letter to the editor. *The Lancet*, September 17, 615–616.

Edelston, H. (1958). Separation of mother and child. Letter to the editor. *The Lancet*, April 12, 797.

Edelston, H. (1960). Psycho-analysis. Letter to the editor. *The New Scientist*, March 24, 744.

Editorial (1937). The dangers of being admitted to a children's ward. *The Lancet*, January 2, 39.

Editorial (1939a). A successful exodus. *British Medical Journal*, September 9, 573.

Editorial (1939b). Medical notes in Parliament: evacuation problems. *British Medical Journal*, November 11, 977.

Editorial (1940). Visiting in children's wards. *The Lancet*, January 27, 178–179.

Editorial (1942a). Loneliness in infancy. *British Medical Journal*, September 19, 345.

Editorial (1942b). War nurseries. *British Medical Journal*, November 14, 579.

Editorial (1944). War in the nursery. *British Medical Journal*, January 8, 50.

Editorial (1945). To ill to go to hospital. *The Lancet*, May 19, 631–632.

Editorial (1949). Children in hospital. *The Lancet*, May 7, 784–786.

Editorial (1951a). Mental health and the mother. *The Lancet*, May 26, 1165–1166.

Editorial (1951b). The foundation of mental health. *British Medical Journal*, June 16, 1373–1374.

Editorial (1952a). Young children in hospital. *British Medical Journal*, December 6, 1249–1250.

Editorial (1952b). The young child in hospital. *The Lancet*, December 6, 1122–1123.

Editorial (1953a). Children in hospital. *The Lancet*, March 14, 531.

Editorial (1953b). Visits to children in hospital. *The Lancet*, March 14, 539.

Editorial (1953c). Visits to children in hospital. *The Lancet*, March 28, 656.

Editorial (1953d). Visiting children in hospital. *The Lancet*, November 28, 1138.

Editorial (1958). Going to hospital with mother. *The Lancet*, 24 May, 1112–1113.

Editorial (1970). John, 17 months. *The Lancet*, January 3, 47.

Engel, G.L. (1971). Attachment behaviour, object relations, and the dynamic point of view: a critical review of Bowlby's *Attachment and loss. International Journal of Psychoanalysis*, 52, 183–196.

Erdelye, M. H. (1974). A new look at the new look: perceptual defence and vigilance. *Psychological Review*, 87, 1–25.

Evans, E. (1939). Problems of evacuation. Letter to the editor. *British Medical Journal*, October 28, 884.

Fairbairn, W. R. (1941). A revised psychopathology of the psychoses and psychoneuroses. *International Journal of Psycho-Analysis*, 22, 250–279.

Ferenczi, S. (1931). Child-analysis in the analysis of adults. *International Journal of Psycho-Analysis*, 12, 468–482.

Foley, R. A. (1996). The adaptive legacy of human evolution: a search for the environment of evolutionary adaptedness. *Evolutionary Anthropology*, 4, 194–203.

Fonagy, P. (1999). Psychoanalytic theory from the viewpoint of attachment theory and research. In J. Cassidy and P. R. Schaver (eds), *Handbook of Attachment: Theory, Research and Clinical Applications* (pp. 595–624). New York: The Guilford Press.

Fonagy, P. (2001). *Attachment Theory and Psychoanalysis*. New York: Other Press.

Fonagy, P., Gergely, and Target (2008). Psychoanalytic theory from the viewpoint of attachment theory and research. In J. Cassidy and P. R. Schaver (eds), *Handbook of Attachment: Theory, Research and Clinical Applications* (2nd edn; pp. 783–810). New York: The Guilford Press.

Foss, B.M. (1961). *Determinants of Infant Behaviour I*. London: Methuen & Co.

Foss, B.M. (1963). *Determinants of Infant Behaviour II*. London: Methuen & Co.

Foss, B.M. (1965). *Determinants of Infant Behaviour III*. London: Methuen & Co.

Foss, B.M. (1969). *Determinants of Infant Behaviour IV*. London: Methuen & Co.

Foster, M. (1945). A parent at hospital. Letter to the editor. *The Lancet*, June 2, 704.

Freud, A. (1960). Discussion of Dr. John Bowlby's paper. *Psychoanalytic Study of the Child*, 15, 53–62.

Freud, A. (1973). *The Writings of Anna Freud. Vol. 3. 1939–1945*. New York: International Universities Press.

Freud, S. (1905). *Three Essays on the Theory of Sexuality*. In *S.E.*, 7.

Freud, S. (1917). *Introductory Lectures on Psychoanalysis*. In *S.E.*, 15–16.

Freud, S. (1920). *Beyond the Pleasure Principle*. In *S.E.*, 18, 3–64.

Gerson, G. (2009). Culture and ideology in Ian Suttie's theory of mind. *History of Psychology*, 12, 19–40.

Gewirtz, J. L., and Boyd, E. F. (1977a). Does maternal responding imply reduced infant crying? Critique of the 1972 Bell and Ainsworth report. *Child Development*, 48, 1200–1207.

Gewirtz, J. L., and Boyd, E. F. (1977b). In reply to the rejoinder to our critique of the 1972 Bell and Ainsworth report. *Child Development*, 48, 1217–1218.

Goldfarb, W. (1943a). Infant rearing and problem behaviour. *American Journal of Orthopsychiatry*, 13, 249–265.

Goldfarb, W. (1943b). The effects of early institutional care on adolescent personality. *Journal of Experimental Education*, 12, 106–129.

Goldfarb, W. (1943c). The effects of early institutional care on adolescent personality (graphic Rorschach data). *Child Development*, 14, 213–223.

Goldfarb, W. (1943d). The effects of early institutional care on adolescent personality: Rorschach data. *American Journal of Orthopsychiatry*, 14, 441–447.

Goldfarb, W. (1944). Infant rearing as a factor in foster home replacement. *American Journal of Orthopsychiatry*, 14, 162–166.

Goldfarb, W. (1945a). Effects of psychological deprivation in infancy and subsequent adjustment. *American Journal of Psychiatry*, 102, 18–33.

Goldfarb, W. (1945b). Psychological privation in infancy and subsequent adjustment. *American Journal of Orthopsychiatry*, 15, 247–255.

Goldfarb, W. (1947). Variations in adolescent adjustment of institutionally-reared children. *American Journal of Orthopsychiatry*, 17, 449–457.

Goldfarb, W. (1949). Rorschach test differences between family-reared, institution-reared and schizophrenic children. *American Journal of Orthopsychiatry*, 19, 624–633.

Green, G. H. (1921). *Psychoanalysis in the Class-room*. London: University of London Press.

Greenberg, J. R., and Mitchell, S. A. (1983). *Object Relations in Psychoanalytic Theory*. Cambridge, MA: Harvard University Press.

Griffiths, P. E. (2004). Instinct in the '50s: the British reception of Konrad Lorenz's theory of instinctive behavior. *Biology and Philosophy*, 19, 609–631.

Hanley, C. (1978). A critical consideration of Bowlby's ethological theory of anxiety. *Psychoanalytic Quarterly*, 47, 364–380.

Hardy, C. (1945). A parent at hospital. Letter to the editor. *The Lancet*, July 7, 28.

Hardyment, C. (1995). *Perfect Parents*. Oxford: Oxford University Press.

Harlow, H. F. (1943). Solution by rhesus monkeys of a problem involving the Weigl principle using the mathing-from-sample method. *Journal of Comparative Psychology*, 36, 217–227.

Harlow, H. F. (1944). Studies in discrimination learning by monkeys: I. The learning of discrimination series and the reversal of discrimination series. *Journal of Genetic Psychology*, 30, 3–12.

Harlow, H. F. (1949). The formation of learning sets. *Psychological Review*, 56, 51–65.

Harlow, H. F. (1957). Experimental analysis of behavior. *American Psychologist*, 12, 485–490.

Harlow, H. F. (1958). The nature of love. *American Psychologist*, 13, 673–685.

Harlow, H. F. (1960). Primary affectional patterns in primates. *American Journal of Orthopsychiatry*, 30, 676–684.

Harlow, H. F. (1961). The development of affectional patterns in infant monkeys. In B. M. Foss (ed.), *Determinants of Infant Behaviour I* (pp. 75–97). London/New York: Methuen/Wiley.

Harlow, H. F. (1963). The maternal affectional system. In B. M. Foss (ed.), *Determinants of Infant Behavior II* (pp. 3–33). London: Methuen.

Harlow, H. F. (1977). Birth of the surrogate mother. In W. R. Klemm (ed.), *Discovery Processes in Modern Biology* (pp. 133–150). Huntington, NY: Krieger.

Harlow, H. F. (2008). The monkey as a psychological subject. *Integrative Psychological & Behavioral Science*, 42(4), 336–347.

Harlow, H. F., and Bromer, J. A. (1938). A test-apparatus for monkeys. *Psychological Record*, 2, 434–436.

Harlow, H. F., and Dagnon, J. (1943). Problem solution by monkeys following bilateral removal of the prefrontal areas: I. The discrimination and discrimination-reversal problems. *Journal of Experimental Psychology*, 32, 351–356.

Harlow, H. F., and Harlow, M. K. (1965). The affectional systems. In A.M. Schrier, H.F. Harlow, and F. Stollnitz (eds), *Behavior in Nonhuman Primates: Modern Research Trends. Vol. II* (pp. 287–334). New York: Academic Press.

Harlow, H. F., and Harlow, M. K. (1969). Effects of various mother infant relationships on rhesus monkey behaviors. In B. M. Foss (ed.), *Determinants of Infant Behavior IV* (pp. 15–36). London: Methuen.

Harlow, H. F., and Settlage, P. H. (1947). Effect of extirpation of frontal areas on learning perfromance by monkeys. *Research Publication Association for Nervous and Mental Disorders*, 27, 446–459.

Harlow, H. F., and Zimmermann, R. R. (1958). The development of affectional responses in infant monkeys. *Proceedings of the American Philosophical Society*, 102, 501–509.

Harlow, H. F., and Zimmermann, R. R. (1959a). Affectional responses in the infant monkey. *Science*, 130, 421–432.

Harlow, H. F., and Zimmermann, R. R. (1959b). *The Nature and Development of Affection* [Motion Picture]. Madison, WI: University of Wisconsin Primate Laboratory.

Hart, B. (1910). The conception of the subconscious. In H. Münsterberg, Th. Ribot, P. Janet, J. Jastrow, *et al.* (1910). *Subconscious Phenomena* (pp. 102–141). Boston: Richard G. Badger.

Hart, B. (1912). *The Psychology of Insanity*. Cambridge: Cambridge University Press.

Hartley, C. G. (1923). *Mother and Son*. London: Eveleigh Nash & Co.

Hearnshaw, L. S. (1979). *Cyril Burt: Psychologist*. London: Hodder & Stoughton.

Heinicke, C. (1956). Some effects of separating two-year-old children from their parents: A comparative study. *Human Relations*, 9, 105–176.

Heinicke, C., and Westheimer, I. (1966). *Brief Separations*. New York: International Universities Press.

Herzog, E. G. (1958a). Children in hospital. Letter to the editor. *The Lancet*, September 6, 522–523.

Herzog, E. G. (1958b). Children in hospital. Letter to the editor. *The Lancet*, October 25, 903–904.

Hinde, R. A. (1952). The behaviour of the Great Tit (Parus major) and some other related species. *Behaviour Supplemment*, 2, 1–201.

Hinde, R. A. (1956). Ethological models and the concept of drive. *British Journal of the Philosophy of Science*, 6, 321–331.

Hinde, R. A. (1957). Consequences and goals: some issues raised by Dr Kortlandt's paper on aspects and prospects of the concept of instinct. *British Journal of Animal Behaviour*, 5, 116–118.

Hinde, R. A. (1966). *Animal Behaviour: A Synthesis of Ethology and Comparative Psychology.* New York: McGraw-Hill.

Hinde, R.A. (1969). Influence of social companions and of temporary separation on mother-infant relations in rhesus monkeys. In B. M. Foss (ed.), *Determinants of Infant Behavior IV* (pp. 37–40). London: Methuen.

Hinde, R. A. (1982a). Attachment: Some conceptual and biological issues. In C. M. Parkes and J. Stevenson-Hinde (eds), *The Place of Attachment in Human Behavior* (pp. 60–76). New York: Basic Books.

Hinde, R. A. (1982b). *Ethology: Its Nature and Relations with Other Sciences.* Oxford: Oxford University Press.

Hinde, R. A. (1987). *Individuals, Relationships and Culture.* Cambridge: Cambridge University Press.

Hinde, R. A. (1991). Relationships, attachment, and culture: a tribute to John Bowlby. *Infant Mental Health Journal,* 12(3), 154–163.

Hinde, R. A. (1997). War: some psychological causes and consequences. *Interdisciplinary Science Reviews,* 22, 229–245.

Hinde, R. A. (1999). *Why Gods Persist: A Scientific Approach to Religion.* London: Routledge.

Hinde, R. A. (2002). *Why Good is Good.* London: Routledge.

Hinde, R. A. (2005). Ethology and attachment theory. In K. Grossmann, K. E. Grossmann, and E. Waters (eds), *Attachment from Infancy to Adulthood: The Major Longitudinal Studies* (pp. 1–12). New York/London: The Guilford Press.

Hinde, R.A. (2007). *Bending the Rules. Morality in the Modern World from Relationships to Politics and War.* Oxford: Oxford University Press.

Hinde, R. A. (2008). Q & A. *Current Biology,* 18(14), R581–R582.

Hinde, R. A., and McGinnis, L. (1977). Some factors influencing the effects of temporary mother-infant separation: some experiments with rhesus monkeys. *Psychological Medicine,* 7, 197–212.

Hinde, R. A., and Rotblat, J. (2003). *War No More: Eliminating Conflict in the Nuclear Age.* London: Pluto Press.

Hinde, R. A., Spencer-Booth, Y., and Bruce, M. (1966). Effects of 6-day maternal deprivation on rhesus monkey infants. *Nature,* 210, 1021–1023.

Hinde, R. A. and Thorpe, W. H. (1973). Nobel recognition for ethology. *Nature,* 245, 346.

Hinshelwood, R. D. (1991). Psychodynamic psychiatry before World War I. In G. E. Berrios and H. Freeman (eds), *150 Years of British Psychiatry, 1841–1991* (pp. 197–205). London: Gaskell.

Holmes, J. (1993). *John Bowlby & Attachment Theory.* London/New York: Routledge.

Howells, J. G. (1958). Separation of mother and child. Letter to the editor. *The Lancet,* March 29, 691.

Howells, J. G., and Layng, J. (1955). Separation experiences and mental health. *The Lancet,* August 6, 285–288.

Hrdy, S. B. (1999). *Mother Nature: A History of Mothers, Infants, and Natural Selection.* New York: Pantheon Books.

Hubbard, F. O. A., and Van IJzendoorn, M. H. (1991). Maternal unresponsiveness and infant crying across the first 9 months: a naturalistic longitudinal study. *Infant Behavior and Development*, 14, 299–312.

Hunter, V. (1991). John Bowlby: an interview. *Psychoanalytic Review*, 78(2), 159–175.

Hutton, L. (1942). Loneliness in infancy. Letter to the editor. *British Medical Journal*, November 7, 558–559.

Hynes, S. (1990). *A War Imagined: The First World War and English Culture.* London: The Bodley Head.

Irons, W. (1998). Adaptively relevant environments versus the environment of evolutionary adaptedness. *Evolutionary Anthropology*, 6, 194–204.

Isaacs, S. (1929). *The Nursery Years: The Mind of the Child from Birth to Six.* London: Routledge.

Isaacson, K. L. (2006). Mary Ainsworth and John Bowlby: the development of attachment theory. Doctoral dissertation, University of California, Davis, United States.

Jaynes, J. (1969). The historical origins of 'ethology' and 'comparative psychology'. *Animal Behaviour*, 17, 601–606.

Jones, E. (2010). Shell shock at Maghull and the Maudsley: models of psychological medicine in the UK. *Journal of the History of Medicine and Allied Sciences*, 65(3), 368–395.

Kagan, J. (2006). *An Argument for Mind.* New Haven: Yale University Press.

Karen, R. (1994). *Becoming Attached: Unfolding the Mystery of the Infant-Mother Bond and Its Impact on Later Life.* New York: Warner Books.

Keir, I. C. (1939). Evacuation. Letter to the editor. *British Medical Journal*, October 7, 745–746.

Keller, H. (2008). Attachment – past and present. But what about the future? *Integrative Psychological & Behavioral Science*, 42(4), 406–415.

Kernberg, O. (1976). *Object Relations Theory and Clinical Psychoanalysis.* New York, NY: Aronson.

Kidd, H. B. (1958). Children in hospital. Letter to the editor. *The Lancet*, September 27, 700.

Klopfer, B., Ainsworth, M. D., Klopfer, W. G., and Holt, R. R. (1954). *Developments in the Rorschach Technique* (Vol. 1). Yonkers-on-Hudson, NY: World Book.

Kortlandt, A. (1955). Aspects and prospect of the concept of instinct. *Archives Néerlandaises de Zoologie*, 11, 157–284. (Published separately by E. J. Brill, Leiden.)

Kräupl Taylor, F. (1958). Separation of mother and child. Letter to the editor. *The Lancet*, March 22, 643–644.

Kruuk, H. (2003). *Niko's Nature.* Oxford: Oxford University Press.

Kuhn, T. (1962). *The Structure of Scientific Revolutions.* Chicago: University Press.

Laland, K. N. and Brown, G. R. (2002). *Sense and Nonsense: Evolutionary Perspectives on Human Behaviour*. Oxford: Oxford University Press.

Lane, H. (1928). *Talks to Parents and Teachers*. London: George Allen & Unwin.

Lashley, K. E. (1950). In search of the engram. *Symposium of the Society of Experimental Biology*, 4, 454–482.

Lehrman, D. S. (1953). A critique of Konrad Lorenz's theory of instinctive behavior. *The Quarterly Review of Biology*, 28, 337–363.

Levy, D. (1937). Primary affect hunger. *American Journal of Psychiatry*, 94, 643–652.

Librach, I. M. (1958). Children in hospital. Letter to the editor. *The Lancet*, September 27, 700–701.

Lieberman, A. F. and Zeanah, C. H. (1999). Contributions of attachment theory to infant-parent psychotherapy and other interventions with infants and young children. In J. Cassidy and P. Shaver (eds), *Handbook of Attachment: Theory, Research and Clinical Applications* (pp. 555–574). New York: The Guilford Press.

Lightfoot, C., Cole, M., and Cole, S. R. (2009). *The Development of Children*. New York, NY: Worth.

Lindsay, M. (2009). Comments on the article "Changing attitudes towards the care of children in hospital: a new assessment of the influence of the work of Bowlby and Robertson in the UK, 1940–1970" by Frank C.P. van der Horst and Rene van der Veer (*Attachment and Human Development*, 11(2), March 2009, 119–142). *Attachment & Human Development*, 11(6), 563–567.

Lomax, E. M. R., Kagan, J., and Rosenkrantz, B. G. (1978). *Science and Patterns of Child Care*. San Francisco: W.H. Freeman and Company.

Lorber, J. (1947). Care of children in hospital. Letter to the editor. *British Medical Journal*, February 15, 266.

Lorenz, K. Z. (1935). Der Kumpan in der Umwelt des Vogels. *Journal für Ornithologie*, 83, 137–213 and 289–412.

Lorenz, K. Z. (1937). The companion in the bird's world. *The Auk*, 54, 245–273.

Lorenz, K. Z. (1952). *King Solomon's Ring*. New York: Crowell.

Lorenz, K. Z. (1981). *The Foundations of Ethology*. New York: Springer-Verlag.

Lowrey, L. G. (1940). Personality distortion and early institutional care. *American Journal of Orthopsychiatry*, 10, 576–585.

Mac Keith, R. C. (1953). Children in hospital: preparation for operation. *Lancet*, October 24, 843–845.

Macdonald, A. H. (1942). Loneliness in infants. Letter to the editor. *British Medical Journal*, October 3, 409.

Maclennan, B. W. (1949). Non-medical care of chronologically ill children in hospital. *The Lancet*, July 30, 209–210.

MacMunn, N. (1921). *The Child's Path to Freedom*. London: G. Bell & Sons.

Marris, P. (1958). *Widows and Their Families*. London: Routledge & Kegan Paul.

Mason, E. (1967). Films on children's hospitalization and maternal deprivation: an annotated bibliography. *Community Mental Health Journal*, 3(4), 420–423.

Mayhew, B. (2006). Between love and aggression: the politics of John Bowlby. *History of the Human Sciences*, 19(4), 19–35.

McDougall, W. (1927). *Character and the Conduct of Life*. London: Methuen.

Meadow, S. R. (1964). No, thanks; I'd rather stay at home. *British Medical Journal*, September 26, 813–814.

Miller, H. C. (1927). *The New Psychology and the Teacher*. New York: Albert & Charles Boni.

Monro Davies, H. G. (1949). Visits to children in hospital. *The Spectator*, March 18, 362.

Moss, E. M. and Harlow, H. F. (1948). Problem solution by monkeys following extensive unilateral decortication and prefrontal lobotomy of the contra lateral side. *Journal of Psychology*, 25, 223–226.

Myers, C. S. (1915). A contribution to the study of shell shock. Being an account of three cases of loss of memory, vision, smell, and taste, admitted into the Duchess of Westminster's War Hospital, Le Tourqet. *The Lancet*, February 13, 316–320.

Myers, C. S. (1916a). A contribution to the study of shell shock. Being an account of certain cases treated by hypnosis. *The Lancet*, January 8, 65–69.

Myers, C. S. (1916b). A contribution to the study of shell shock. Being an account of certain disorders of cutaneous sensibility. *The Lancet*, March 18, 608–613.

Myers, C. S. (1916c). A contribution to the study of shell shock. Being an account of certain disorders of speech, with spacial reference to their causation and their relation to malingering. *The Lancet*, September 9, 461–468.

Neville, J. G. (1953). Visits to children in hospital. Letter to the editor. *The Lancet*, April 11, 743.

Newcombe, N. and Lerner, J. C. (1982). Britain between the wars: the historical context of Bowlby's theory of attachment. *Psychiatry*, 45, 1–12.

Nicholls, D. G. (1945). A parent at hospital. Letter to the editor. *The Lancet*, June 16, 771.

Nicholson, C. (1945). A parent at hospital. Letter to the editor. *The Lancet*, June 2, 704.

O'Conner, T. G. and Zeanah, C. H. (2003). Attachment disorders: assessment strategies and treatment approaches. *Attachment & Human Development*, 5, 223–244.

Parkes, C. M. (1995). Lectures and memoirs: Edward John Mostyn Bowlby 1907–1990. *Proceedings of the British Academy*, 87, 247–261.

Penfold, J. (1953). Visiting children in hospital. Letter to the editor. *The Lancet*, December 5, 1210–1211.

Pickerill, C. M. (1955a). Nursing by the mother. Letter to the editor. *The Lancet*, October 1, 726.

Pickerill, C. M. (1955b). Nursing by the mother. Letter to the editor. *The Lancet*, October 29, 926–927.

Pickerill, H. P. and Pickerill, C. M. (1945). Elimination of cross-infection: an experiment. *British Medical Journal*, February 3, 159–160.

Pickerill, C. M. and Pickerill, H. P. (1946). Keeping mother and baby together. Letter to the editor. *British Medical Journal*, September 7, 337.

Pickerill, H. P. and Pickerill, C. M. (1947). Keeping mother and baby together. Letter to the editor. *British Medical Journal*, June 7, 826.

Pickerill, C. M. and Pickerill, H. P. (1954a). Elimination of cross-infection in children: nursing by the mother. *The Lancet*, February 27, 425–429.

Pickerill, C. M. and Pickerill, H. P. (1954b). Nursing by the mother. Letter to the editor. *The Lancet*, April 10, 784–785.

Pickerill, C. M. and Pickerill, H. P. (1954c). Nursing by the mother. Letter to the editor. *The Lancet*, May 29, 1130–1131.

Pickerill, C. M. and Pickerill, H. P. (1954d). Nursing by the mother and cross-infection. Letter to the editor. *The Lancet*, September 18, 599–600.

Pickerill, H. P. and Pickerill, C. M. (1954e). Visiting children in hospital. Letter to the editor. *The Lancet*, January 9, 102.

Pines, M. (1991). The development of the psychodynamic movement. In G. E. Berrios and H. Freeman (eds), *150 Years of British Psychiatry, 1841–1991* (pp. 206–231). London: Gaskell.

Pinneau, S. R. (1955a). The infantile disorders of hospitalism and anaclitic depression. *Psychological Bulletin*, 52(5), 429–452.

Pinneau, S. R. (1955b). Reply to Dr. Spitz. *Psychological Bulletin*, 52(5), 459–462.

Prance, C. H. G. (1939). Evacuation. Letter to the editor. *British Medical Journal*, October 7, 746.

Rapp, D. (1988). The reception of Freud by the British press: general interest and literary magazines, 1920–1925. *Journal of the History of the Behavioral Sciences*, 24, 191–201.

Revel, D. (1928). *Cheiron's Cave: The School of the Future*. London: William Heinemann.

Ribble, M. (1943). *The Rights of Infants: Early Psychological Needs and Their Satisfaction*. New York: Columbia University Press.

Rickman, J. (1939). Evacuation and the child's mind. Letter to the editor. *The Lancet*, December 2, 1192.

Rivers, W. H. R. (1918). The repression of war experience. *The Lancet*, February 2, 173–177.

Rivers, W. H. R. (1920). *Instincts and the Unconscious*. Cambridge: Cambridge University Press.

Riviere, J. (1927). Symposium on child analysis. *International Journal of Psycho-Analysis*, 8, 370–377.

Robertson, J. (1952). *A Two-Year-Old Goes to Hospital* [Film]. London: Tavistock Child Development Research Unit.

Robertson, J. (1953). Some responses of young children to the loss of maternal care. *Nursing Times*, April, 382–386.

Robertson, J. (1956). A mother's observations on the tonsillectomy of her four-year-old daughter. *The Psychoanalytic Study of the Child*, 11, 410–433.

Robertson, J. (1958a). Children in hospital. Letter to the editor. *The Lancet*, November 8, 1958.

Robertson, J. (1958b). Children in hospital. Letter to the editor. *The Lancet*, November 29, 1958.

Robertson, J. (1958c). *Going to Hospital with Mother* [Film]. London: Tavistock Child Development Research Unit.

Robertson, J. and Bowlby, J. (1952). Responses of young children to separation from their mothers II: observations of the sequences of response of children aged 18 to 24 months during the course of separation. *Courrier du Centre International de l'Enfance*, 2, 131–142.

Robertson, J. and Bowlby, J. (1953). *A Two-Year-Old Goes to Hospital*: a scientific film. *Proceedings of the Royal Society of Medicine, 46*, 425–427.

Robertson, J. and McGilly, K. (2009). Comments on "Changing attitudes towards the care of children in hospital: a new assessment of the influence of the work of Bowlby and Robertson in the UK, 1940–1970" by Frank C. P. van der Horst and Rene van der Veer (*Attachment & Human Development*, 11(2), March 2009, 119–142). *Attachment & Human Development*, 11(6), 557–561.

Robertson, J. and Robertson, J. (1971). Young children in brief separation. *Psychoanalytic Study of the Child*, 26, 264–315.

Robertson, J., and Robertson, J. (1989). *Separation and the Very Young*. London: Free Association Books.

Rochlin, G. (1971). Bowlby J, *Attachment and Loss. I: Attachment* [Book Review]. *Psychoanalytic Quarterly*, 50, 504–506.

Roëll, D. R. (2000). *The World of Instinct. Niko Tinbergen and the Rise of Ethology in the Netherlands (1920–1950)*. Assen, The Netherlands: Van Gorcum.

Roiphe, H. (1976). Bowlby J, *Attachment and Loss. II: Separation, Anxiety and Anger* [Book Review]. *Psychoanalytic Quarterly*, 65, 307–309.

Rosenbluth, D., Bowlby, J., and Roudinesco, J. (1950). Séparation d'avec la mère en tant qu'experiénce traumatisante subie par l'enfant: quelques notes sur la manière de recueillir une anamnèse pertinente. *Courrier: revue medico-sociale de l'enfance*, 1, 9–15.

Roudinesco, J., David, M., and Nicolas, J. (1952). Responses of young children to separation from their mother. I. Observation of children aged 12 to 17 months recently separated from their families and living in an institution. *Courrier du Centre International de l'Enfance*, 2, 66–78.

Rowell, T. E., Hinde, R. A., and Spencer-Booth, Y. (1964). "Aunt"-infant interaction in captive rhesus monkeys. *Animal Behaviour*, 12(2–3), 219–226.

Rudnytsky, P. L. (1997). The personal origins of attachment theory. An interview with Mary Salter Ainsworth. *The Psychoanalytic Study of the Child*, 52, 386–405.

Rusby, J. S. M. and Tasker, F. (2008). Childhood temporary separation: long-term effects of the British evacuation of children during World War 2 on older adults' attachment styles. *Attachment & Human Development*, 10(2), 207–221.

Rusby, J. S. M. and Tasker, F. (2009). Long-term effects of the British evacuation of children during World War 2 on their adult mental health. *Aging & Mental Health*, 13(3), 391–404.

Russell, P. (1945a). A parent at hospital. Letter to the editor. *The Lancet*, May 19, 642.

Russell, P. (1945b). A parent at hospital. Letter to the editor. *The Lancet*, June 16, 770–771.

Rutter, M. (1972a). *Maternal Deprivation Reassessed*. Harmondsworth: Penguin.

Rutter, M. (1972b). Maternal deprivation reconsidered. *Journal of Psychosomatic Research*, 16, 241–250.

Rutter, M. (1979). Maternal deprivation, 1972–1978: new findings, new concepts, new approaches. *Child Development*, 50 (2), 283–305.

Sable, P. (2004). Attachment, ethology and adult psychotherapy. *Attachment & Human Development*, 6, 3–19.

Salaman, N. (1942). Loneliness in infancy. Letter to the editor. *British Medical Journal*, December 12, 708.

Salter, M. D. (1940). *An Evaluation of Adjustment Based on the Concept of Security* (University of Toronto Studies, Child Development Series, No. 18). Toronto, Canada: University of Toronto Press.

Schoo, R. (1954). Nursing by the mother. Letter to the editor. *The Lancet*, May 29, 1131.

Schur, M. (1960). Discussion of Dr. John Bowlby's paper. *Psychoanalytic Study of the Child*, 15, 63–84.

Seay, B., Hansen, E., and Harlow, H. F. (1962). Mother-infant separation in monkeys. *Journal of Child Psychology and Psychiatry*, 3, 123–132.

Seay, B. and Harlow, H. F. (1965). Maternal separation in the rhesus monkey. *Journal of Nervous and Mental Disease*, 140, 434–441.

Senn, M. J. E. (1977a). Unpublished transcript of an interview with Dr. John Bowlby in London.

Senn, M. J. E. (1977b). Unpublished transcript of an interview with James Robertson in London.

Seton, E. T. (1899). *Wild Animals I Have Known*. New York: Charles Scribners Sons.

Simpson, J. A. (1999). Attachment theory in modern evolutionary perspective. In J. Cassidy and P. R. Schaver (eds), *Handbook of Attachment: Theory, Research and Clinical Applications* (pp. 115–140). New York: The Guilford Press.

Simpson, J.A. and Belsky, J. (2008). Attachment theory within a modern evolutionary framework. In J. Cassidy and P. R. Schaver (eds), *Handbook of Attachment: Theory, Research and Clinical Applications* (2nd edn, pp. 131–157). New York: The Guilford Press.

Singer, P. A. D. (1975). *Animal Liberation: A New Ethics for Our Treatment of Animals*. New York: New York Review/Random House.

Skeels, H. M. (1936). Mental development of children in foster homes, *Journal of Genetic Psychology*, 49, 91–106.

Skeels, H. M. and Dye, H. B. (1939/2002). A study of the effects of differential stimulation on mentally retarded children. In J. Blacher and B. L. Baker, *The Best of AAMR. Families and Mental Retardation: A Collection of Notable AAMR Journal Articles Across the 20th Century* (pp. 19–33). Washington, DC: AAMR. (Original article published in 1939.)

Slade, A. (1999). Attachment theory and research: implications for the theory and practive of individual psychotherapy with adults. In J. Cassidy and P. R. Schaver (eds), *Handbook of Attachment: Theory, Research and Clinical Applications* (2nd edn, pp. 575–594). New York: The Guilford Press.

Slade, A. (2008). The implications of attachment theory and research for adult psychotherapy: research and clinical perspectives. In J. Cassidy and P. R. Schaver (eds), *Handbook of Attachment: Theory, Research and Clinical Applications* (pp. 762–782). New York: The Guilford Press.

Smuts, A. (1977a). Interview with Dr. Fred Stone on 1st August, 1977. Unpublished (Archives Tavistock Joint Library).

Smuts, A. (1977b). Interview with Dr. John Bowlby on 6th June and 23rd July, 1977; and additional written material sent by Dr. Bowlby in September and October, 1979. Unpublished (Archives Tavistock Joint Library).

Sommerhoff, G. (1950). *Analytical Biology*. London: Oxford University Press.

Southborough, Lord (1922). *Report of the War Office Committee of Enquiry into 'Shell-Shock'*. London: HMSO.

Southgate, J., Ainsworth, M., and Southern, D. (1990). Remembrances of John Bowlby who died on September 2nd 1990. *Journal of the Institute for Self-Analysis*, 4(1), 4–15.

Spence, J. C. (1946). *The Purpose of the Family: A Guide to the Care of Children*. London: NCH Epworth Press.

Spence, J. C. (1947). The care of children in hospital. *British Medical Journal, January 25*, 125–130.

Spencer-Booth, Y., Hinde, R. A., and Bruce, M. (1965). Social companions and mother-infant relationship in rhesus monkeys. *Nature*, 208, 301.

Spencer-Booth, Y. and Hinde, R. A. (1966). Effects of separating rhesus monkeys infant from their mothers for 6 days. *Journal of Child Psychology and Psychiatry*, 7(3–4), 179–197.

Spitz, R. A. (1945). Hospitalism. *The Psychoanalytic Study of the Child*, 1, 53–74.

Spitz, R. A. (1946). Anaclitic depression. *The Psychoanalytic Study of the Child*, 2, 313–342.

Spitz, R. A. (1947). *Grief: A Peril in Infancy* [Film]. New York: New York University Film Library.

Spitz, R. A. (1951). The psychogenic diseases in infancy: an attempt at their etiologic classification. *The Psychoanalytic Study of the Child*, 6, 255–275.

Spitz, R. A. (1955). Reply to Dr. Pinneau. *Psychological Bulletin*, 52(5), 453–459.

Spitz, R. A. (1960). Discussion of Dr. John Bowlby's paper. *The Psychoanalytic Study of the Child*, 15, 85–94.

Spitz, R. A. and Wolf, K. M. (1946). Anaclitic depression: an inquiry into the genesis of psychatric conditions in early childhood, II. *The Psychoanalytic Study of the Child*, 2, 313–342.

Spitz, R. A. and Wolf, K. M (1949). Autoerotism: some empirical findings and hypotheses on three of its manifestations in the first year of life. *The Psychoanalytic Study of the Child*, 3–4, 85–120.

Stephen, E. and Whatley, E. (1958a). Children in hospital. Letter to the editor. *The Lancet*, September 20, 641–642.

Stephen, E. and Whatley, E. (1958b). Children in hospital. Letter to the editor. *The Lancet*, November 22, 1123.

Suomi, S. J. (1995). Influence of attachment theory on ethological studies of biobehavioral development in nonhuman primates. In S. Goldberg, R. Muir, and J. Kerr (eds), *Attachment Theory: Social, Developmental, and Clinical Perspectives* (pp. 185–201). Hillsdale, NJ: The Analytic Press.

Suomi, S. J. and LeRoy, H. A. (1982). In memoriam: Harry F. Harlow (1905–1981). *American Journal of Primatology*, 2, 319–342.

Suomi, S. J., Van der Horst, F. C. P., and Van der Veer, R. (2008). Rigorous experiments on monkey love: an account of Harry Harlow's role in the history of attachment theory. *Integrative Psychological & Behavioral Science*, 42(4), 354–369.

Suttie, I. D. (1935/1988). *The Origins of Love and Hate*. London: Free Associations Books. (Original work published in 1935).

Tanner, J. M. and Inhelder, B. (1971). *Discussions on Child Development*. New York: International Universities Press.

Thom, D. A. (1927). *Everyday Problems of the Everyday Child*. New York-London: D. Appleton and Company.

Thursfield, H. (1939). Evacuation. Letter to the editor. *British Medical Journal*, October 7, 746.

Timberlake, W. (1993). Animal behaviour: a continuing synthesis. *Annual Review of Psychology*, 44, 675–708.

Tinbergen, N. (1951). *The Study of Instinct*. Oxford: Oxford University Press.

Tinbergen, N. (1963). On aims and methods of ethology. *Zeitschrift für Tierpsychologie*, 20, 410–433.

Tinbergen, N. (1974). Nikolaas Tinbergen. In: *Les Prix Nobel en 1973* (pp. 197–200). Stockholm: Imprimerie Royale P.A. Norstedt & Söner.

Tinbergen, N. (1991). Some personal remarks. In P. Bateson (ed.), *The Development and Integration of Behaviour: Essays in Honour of Robert Hinde* (pp. 463–464). Cambridge: Cambridge University Press.

Tinbergen, N. and Tinbergen, E. A. (1983). *'Autistic Children': New Hope for a Cure*. London: George Allen & Unwin.

Trist, E. L. and Murray, H. (1990). Historical overview: the foundation and development of the Tavistock Institute. In: E. L. Trist and H. Murray (eds), *The Social Engagement of Social Science: A Tavistock Anthology. Vol. 1: The*

Socio-psychological Perspective. Philadelphia: University of Pennsylvania Press.

Van der Horst, F. C. P. (2008). John Bowlby and ethology: a study of cross-fertilization. Leiden University, The Netherlands: Doctoral dissertation.

Van der Horst, F. C. P., and Van der Veer, R. (2009a). Changing attitudes towards the care of children in hospital: a new assessment of the influence of the work of Bowlby and Robertson in Britain, 1940–1970. *Attachment & Human Development*, 11(2), 119–142.

Van der Horst, F. C. P. and Van der Veer, R. (2009b). Separation and divergence: the untold story of James Robertson's and John Bowlby's theoretical dispute on mother-child separation. *Journal of the History of the Behavioral Sciences*, 45(3), 236–252.

Van der Horst, F. C. P. and Van der Veer, R. (2009c). Why we disagree to disagree: a reply to commentaries by Robertson & McGilly and Lindsay. *Attachment & Human Development*, 11(6), 569–572.

Van der Horst, F. C. P. and Van der Veer, R. (2010). The ontogeny of an idea: John Bowlby and contemporaries on mother-child separation. *History of Psychology*, 13(1), 25–45.

Van der Horst, F. C. P., Van der Veer, R., and Van IJzendoorn, M. H. (2007). John Bowlby and ethology: an annotated interview with Robert Hinde. *Attachment & Human Development*, 9(4), 321–335.

Van der Veer, R. and Valsiner, J. (1991). *Understanding Vygotsky. A Quest for Synthesis*. Oxford: Blackwell.

Van Dijken, S. (1998). *John Bowlby: His Early Life*. London: Free Association Books.

Van Dijken, S., Van der Veer, R., Van IJzendoorn, M. H., and Kuipers, H. J. (1998). Bowlby before Bowlby: the sources of an intellectual departure in psychoanalysis and psychology. *Journal of the History of the Behavioural Sciences*, 34, 247–269.

Van IJzendoorn, M. H. and Sagi, A. (2008). Cross-cultural patterns of attachment: Universal and contextual dimensions. In J. Cassidy and P. R. Shaver (eds), *Handbook of Attachment: Theory, Research, and Clinical Applications* (2nd edn, pp. 880–905). New York: The Guilford Press.

Van Wagenen, G. (1950). The monkeys. In E. J. Farris (ed.), *The Care and Breeding of Laboratory Animals* (pp. 1–42). New York: Wiley.

Vicedo, M. (2009a). Mothers, machines, and morals: Harry Harlow's work on primate love from lab to legend. *Journal of the History of the Behavioral Sciences*, 45(3), 193–218.

Vicedo, M. (2009b). The father of ethology and the foster mother of ducks: Konrad Lorenz as expert on motherhood. *Isis*, 100, 263–291.

Warme, G. E., Bowlby, J., Crowcroft, A., and Rae-Grant, Q. (1980). Current issues in child psychiatry: a dialogue with John Bowlby. *Canadian Journal of Psychiatry*, 25(5), 367–376.

Wicks, B. (1988). *No Time to Wave Goodbye: True Stories of Britain's 3 500 000 Evacuees*. London: Bloomsbury.

Winnicott, D. W. (1942). Loneliness in infants. Letter to the editor. *British Medical Journal*, October 17, 465.

Winnicott, D. W. (1989). *Psycho-analytic Explorations*. Cambridge, MA: Harvard University Press.

Wolf, K. M. (1945). Evacuation of children in wartime: a survey of the literature, with bibliography. *The Psychoanalytic Study of the Child*, 1, 389–404.

Wooldridge, A. (1994). *Measuring the Mind: Education and Psychology in England c.1860–c.1990*. Cambridge: Cambridge University Press.

Zazzo, R. (1979). *Le colloque sur l'attachement*. Paris: Delachaux et Niestlé.

Zepf, S. (2006). Attachment theory and psychoanalysis: some remarks from an epistemological and from a Freudian point of view. *International Journal of Psycho-Analysis*, 87, 1529–1548.

Zuckerman, S. (1932). *The Social Life of Monkeys and Apes*. London: Kegan Paul, Trench, Trubner & Co.

Name Index

John Bowlby – From Psychoanalysis to Ethology: Unraveling the Roots of Attachment Theory, First Edition. Frank C. P. van der Horst.

Subject Index

John Bowlby – From Psychoanalysis to Ethology: Unraveling the Roots of Attachment Theory, First Edition. Frank C. P. van der Horst.